SISTERS SINGING

BLESSINGS, PRAYERS, ART, SONGS, POETRY AND SACRED STORIES BY WOMEN

EDITED BY
CAROLYN BRIGIT FLYNN

FOREWORD BY
DEENA METZGER

WILD GIRL PUBLISHING
SANTA CRUZ, CALIFORNIA

Wild Girl Publishing
POBox 1301
Santa Cruz, California 95061
www.wildgirlpublishing.com

© 2009 by Carolyn Brigit Flynn
All rights reserved.
Printed in the United States of America

Permission credits can be found on page 398 and constitute
an extension of the copyright page.

Cover art by Durga Bernhard, © Durga Bernhard /durgabernhard.com
Cover production by Courtnay Perry
Book layout and design by Jane Nyberg
Music transcription and chords for some songs by Jerry Paul

Library of Congress Cataloging-in-Publication Data

Sisters singing : blessings, prayers, art, songs, poetry and sacred stories by
    women/ edited by Carolyn Brigit Flynn; foreword by Deena Metzger.
    p.   cm.
  Includes index.

    ISBN-13: 978-0-972-814-62-1
    ISBN-10: 0-9728146-2-0
    1. Spirituality. 2. Women—Religious life. 3. Women—Prayers and
    devotions. 4. Poetry—Women authors. 5. Sacred Songs.   I. Flynn,
    Carolyn Brigit, 1958 - .
  BL 560 .S57 2008
  291.433

First publication 2009
1 3 5 7 9 10 8 6 4 2

SFI CERTIFIED SOURCING
FIBER USED IN THIS PRODUCT LINE
MEETS THE SOURCING REQUIREMENTS
OF THE SFI PROGRAM
WWW.SFIPROGRAM.ORG

This book is printed on paper produced from wood grown in sustainable forests.

3/09

SISTERS SINGING

DATE DUE

*This collection is dedicated
to the generations to come—
May we keep our covenant with the future.*

*And to the spirits of Sisters Singing—
All blessings upon you, our Grandmothers.*

Mystery's Shoes

If you are not sure how to travel,
step into Mystery's shoes
and walk the labyrinth,
round the spiral path of stones
to the sacred center.

Or go shoeless as the monk,
who knows rice will fall into his bowl,
or the child at the edge of the wide sea.
Go as your own bare self,
and feel the silky dust beneath each step.
In truth, nothing separates the foot from the path.

Gail Brenner

Contents

Songs of My Sisters

In the Oak Grove

In Praise of Water

In the Name of Raven

Prayers for My World

Foreword

Women praying. Let us pause before these words. Women praying.

We pause before these words because for centuries women have been systematically excluded from the priesthood or restricted in their religious lives. As if we don't know how to pray. As if women don't understand the sacred.

Women praying. The truth is that women have always been praying. A woman's life—her body and her soul—is often, more than anything, prayer. Women have known the sacred in everything they do and see and touch.

For all the centuries that women have been denied public prayer and public access to the Divine, they continued to walk the holy ways even when it meant a sometimes secret, clandestine relationship with the sacred. The blessing of prayer is that nothing can stop the silent, unspoken, sacred joy of reaching to the Divine from the heart. Everywhere, freely uttered or cruelly repressed, women are praying and these prayers enhance the world. The great song that sustains the universe may well be that of women in all places singing grief and gratitude and exultation.

This is not so much a book of prayers but a book of women praying. Prayer is, first of all, the fully embodied activity of praise. This book is a document of praise. Prayer is invocation. This book calls Spirit down into the world. Prayer is blessing, a request to the Divine to penetrate the world. Prayer is the gift of beauty to Beauty through which the world recovers its original form, the altar it can become once more. These writings seek the restoration of the sacred universe. Prayer is an offering, an offering of the self to the Divine. These women writers offer themselves: Here we are. Speak through us. Use us. Come through us. Let us serve you.

One does not need religion to know the Divine. Rather often it interferes with the deep knowing of the heart. These writers, these women, see the Divine everywhere. Look at the Earth, they say, She is the Sacred Mother. Their words reveal Her radiance. The sacred tree. The sacred animal. The sacred body. Vision. It has always been this way. Women know the Divine in the world, in family, in their children, in community, in themselves, in the body, in their work. In what they love. In lamentation and grief. In their anguish for the ruin of our world. Among the dead and in their determined hope for the future. The Sacred is in Life and the Mystery is revealed here.

Women have had to carry this knowledge against all odds. And now is the time that it can be spoken. And so we speak it and we sing it. We mourn and we rejoice. Death and Life. Praise.

When you read these texts, you will know they are written with the luminous Holy Letters that the Divine has extended to us over the centuries. You will feel the Letters as they inscribe themselves on your heart and soul. And so you, too, will know the Sacred. It is Here. Among us. Emerging. Now.

Blessings.

Deena Metzger

Introduction: When Sisters Sing

A world comes born when a book is made. It is a community, a kinship, a collaboration among souls who come together to create a thing of beauty that will wing its way into the world. With a luminous collection such as *Sisters Singing*, the community is rich, varied, sweet, and profound.

The sacred writing, art and music in this volume are part of a global web of prayers, peacemaking and creativity devoted to singing the world back to wholeness. Yes, a world lives inside these pages: a world of hope, of alignment with beauty, of devotion to allowing our deepest soul to speak, and a commitment to a livable future for our descendants and all earth creatures.

Because I have had the privilege of working closely with these sacred offerings, I know the luminescence and beauty that awaits the reader new to this book. *Lucky you*, I want to say. It will all be new. Walk through bare-footed, loose-clothed, or naked. Open your heart to the sacred stories, the poetry, the art and songs, like fresh grasses and elemental flowers in an open field. May there be nothing between you and the sisters as they sing.

In an anthology such as this there are many visions, but only one weaver. The weaver takes the sacred threads, the various visions and voices, and binds them together. She places two pieces of poetry side by side, or art by a unique story, because they belong next to each other. She allows them to help each other, to provide support and sustenance, to become woven into a whole song, a new wisdom blanket. And she sits back, as I have recently done, breathless, for beauty has come born.

A few years ago I learned a term from the world of carpentry that delighted me. A piece of wood attached alongside an existing beam for extra support is called a *sister joist*. And the verb describing the particular and specific action of providing essential, side-by-side support is known as *sistering*. Thus we see from an ancient handcraft of brothers a truth so old, so necessary, so obvious, that it comes unbidden outside the world of women. To *sister* is to provide an extra bit of vital support, to stand beside, right next to, to support invisibly—to hold someone up.

And of course, in truth, we all know what a sister is.

Most of us have one, a true one, if we are lucky. Some of us are gifted with sisters through blood and family lines. But beyond that, we find that our sisters simply emerge along the journey of our lives. Here, at this moment, this woman came forth at just the right time. She brought me tea, or good whiskey. She let me put my head in her lap. She held me to her breast, and let me cry. She listened. She did not need me to be more, or different, less broken-hearted, more wise. She knew I needed simple reinforcement, help where I felt weak. She provided that help. She held me steady. She *sistered* me.

In many ways, to *sister the world* is to provide just this same sort of sustenance and invisible reinforcement for the earth herself, and for the entire world community of humans, animals, forests, deserts, rivers, oceans, and plants. To sister the world is to be part of the web which those who pray each day weave around the planet. These people, these pray-ers of the world, are woven within the living spirit of the earth. They know what is at stake. Imagine the world with no prayers in it. No quiet blessings before dawn, no whispered prayers in a morning garden, no heart praise walking a beloved path, no silent meditation at the zendo or in someone's living room, no prayer bells, no sacred songs, no drums and rattles at community circles, no chants, no rosaries, no mantras.

It feels lonely and cold—for humanity and for the planet. It feels, in fact, like we would feel if we had no sister joist, no support, no energetic web holding us together. Prayer is endemic to the human core, as much a part of being human as walking upright.

Yet in truth it is remarkably easy to lose our connection to prayer. Our hearts often feel broken by a world caught in war, and by bleak concern for the future of the earth. We sometimes feel detached from all that is holy to us. We know we once touched it—but then it was gone. And in many ways, how could this *not* be? We are called into the physical world: reaping, loving, building, creating. We are doing our work, caring for others, going to jobs and meetings, tending our families. But there is something in us hungry. It is ancient, musty, deep at our core. It is a need as old as humanity. We have it in us to pray, to touch the divine, to feel the stars.

Thus *Sisters Singing*. Here is a collection of writing from our sisters who have entered the world of spirit and returned with a song. *Here, here*—she wrote it down, she sang it out, she caught something ephemeral in her hands for a brief moment, and offers it to us. This book and the

writings, songs and art which live within provide that essential *sistering*…
a deep support, steady sustenance to hold us up, a sense of hope, and the
wellspring that emerges when we touch what is authentic within. It is a
book which transcends religious boundaries and speaks to the interior,
intimate aspect of sacred experience—the lived, embodied interaction
with the essential mystery at the heart of all life.

Every single human, every animal, every growing bush, every plant
and stone has its own way of spirituality and holiness. It would be impossible to categorize women's varied and intimate ways of prayer and connection to spirit in one way. Yet it can be said the common, daily, often
invisible acts of sacred *sistering* are deeply intrinsic to the female soul. In
our time, wherever we grew up on the planet, we have come of age in a
world where the voices and soul experiences of women have not been
fully included in religious traditions and holy texts. In some cases wom-
en's authentic sacred experiences have been systematically and harshly
repressed. We all suffer from the loss of that wisdom, the lack of what it
might teach and where it might lead. This book of women's sacred writing, art and song is an offering to help restore a holy balance. It is a book
for us all, men and women, as we repair our world and move toward creating a living, viable future.

The grandmothers of the many traditions and ways of prayer in this
book are its guiding spirit. I can see her now: old Great-Great-Grand-
mother, holding this book in her hands like a sacred rattle, prayer beads, a
rosary or a drum. Chuckling, dancing, humming softly in a green open
field, she sprinkles holy waters over us, sacred seeds. She feels the hum
within the book.

Open *Sisters Singing* to any page, and use it as a talisman or a divination. It will give you a message from the beyond. Or make your way to a
certain section and enter the world of silent meditation, or nature, or
mothering, or prayers for the world. Or read, as I have done, from cover
to cover. Here you will find the secret melody, the hum that makes its way
through the book. It vibrates, it whirls; there is a song within the whole.
Pick up the book, and you know: the sisters are already singing.

Carolyn Brigit Flynn

WHITE LOTUS

The lotus is one of the world's most celebrated and sacred flowers. Its elegant blossoms come to life in watery ponds, lagoons, marshes and flooded fields. In spiritual life, the mud from which the lotus emerges can be seen as life's difficulties and disenchantments, from which we sometimes blossom in moments of inner shining and oneness. These writings speak of leaving the mundane world and touching the sacred through formal ritual, meditation, ceremony, or journey to a holy well or shrine. Though the forms vary widely, each piece carries our human urge to touch the sacred, to meet the spirits, to allow our hearts to whisper to the divine.

Circle of Women

I imagine
a circle of wise women,
smoke rising.
The silhouette of ridges.
View from mountaintop.

Manzanita curls up
to lizard.
Ocean breath
finds its way
on the tail feather of a hawk.

There are shells
and traces of
sand among fern.
Once ancient waves rose,
crests high as this knoll.
Once grizzly roamed
in search of berries.

My tribe has come here
to tell tales as old
as bedrock.

From their spirit wells
they dip and spin
a story that will piece
the world back together.

Lea Haratani

Meditation

I close my eyes to see myself
there in the darkness
where my heart begins her breathing.
I am breath.
The give and take of planets and trees.
The rise and fall of tides.
The painted skies of dawn and sunset.
The chrysalis opening.
The cocoon giving forth to wing.
I sit in the darkness and speak my name.
I call myself back.
Name myself
as though I am the mother.
Hold my breath in the quiet of my arms.
Cradle and comfort.
Body of sorrow.
Body of joy.
Body of earth and bone,
like the clay between fingers,
molding itself into a hand.

Johanna Courtleigh

When I Am Silent

When I am silent
it is possible to see
particles of dust collide
without making a sound,
each speck of carbon
from the bone of some
fallen bird.

When I am silent
it is possible to hear
how song lines flatten
the edge of time, my own
heartbeat below the bridge,
where a stream with its
memory of cloud
flows into a deeper river.

When I am silent
it is possible to take
the smallest hand and walk
the garden wall where memory
of fuschia and blackberry is
untangled from the tears
of a blue-eyed girl who
steps through the gate lonely.

When I am silent
it is possible to smell
the colors violet and azure
here in the midst of black.
Now, radiant with hope, I
lift my hands to incense rising,
bow my head low
to be blessed by ancestors
who whisper and wait.

Ziggy Rendler-Bregman

Meditation Journey

for Rodger Kamenetz

First one puts it on like a tiara
or a jewel in the navel;
then one enters it like a tent, a tallis,
or a Goddess temple, an Om
that trembles on the pathway
of the breath, a music that lifts
like prayer, from the golden script.
Or it disappears like the dust
of an emerald. Or rages like the face
of your own demon self. Perhaps a raving avatar
from the Red Hot Klezmers. Or the long silence
of an Orpheus journey, the seduction
of Aphrodite or the moon boat
of Artemis. The heartbeat
at the center of the universe
          listening to you
                    listening.

Pesha Joyce Gertler

White Lotus of Peace

White lotus resides in the heart
Content in glorious perfection.

Light from a thousand glowing petals
Peers through darkness
As sun peeks through cloud and disappears.

Her potency
Lies unclaimed,
Resting in elegance.

Her fragrance too subtle to smell.
Her form too brilliant to behold.
Her petals too delicate for touch.
Her nectar too sweet for taste.
Her soothing song too quiet to hear.

Waiting
For kindness and compassion
To release her wisdom.

Then gentle flower
Becomes brilliant flame
Melting layers of fear.

Only a pure heart gives life
To the lotus
Who blooms into radiant majesty.

A restless mind cowers
As the effulgent lotus
Reveals divine essence.

Merged with the heart
Into light and love
Her majestic form is a glowing guide
To peace.

Ratna Jennifer Sturz

Dragonfly on Lotus Blossom

Photograph

Karen Koshgarian

Pema Osel Ling Meditation Retreat

I start preparing for the retreat weeks in advance by trying for a generosity of spirit. I am surrounded by this spirit. Somehow instinct has led me to good people in my life. But deep down I doubt I have this spirit within me. I feel a little like a parasite, a barnacle who gets by on the nutrients and energies of those around me. I have grave doubts about the retreat. I doubt I am good enough to sit gracefully among meditators or serious students of anything.

I start practicing, though. Kind gestures, a nod in someone's direction, stillness. I collect these deeds like mementos and start carrying them around with me, a collection of goodness I hope makes me worthy. Early Friday, the morning of the retreat, I have a treasure trove. My bowl is full. I feel confident. I am ready. And then while reading a small book, *Everyday Sacred*, I learn that what I need is not fullness, but emptiness. If I arrive at Pema Osel Ling with a mind full of too many things, there will be no room for more knowledge to come in.

And I come back again to spirit. Can one acquire a generous spirit? Along the way, could that happen? Or is it inborn? Is it passed down soul to soul? Now, I know about the work of writing. I can chatter with the best of them. The word, the clutter of words. I could fill notebooks. I could fill heads. But the spirit thing is something else. Does it come from stillness? What have I overlooked in my rush down the path?

I roll down the car window on Highway 1, overburdened. I let the fall air tug apart my collection of good deeds, my overflowing bowl spread across the landscape on either side of me, scattered. Thus I arrive in a state of reception. Ready to allow for the possibilities. And this new emptiness, rather than leaving me adrift, frees me. I enter with a lightness of being and an eagerness of spirit that someday, somehow I might be free enough to allow generosity to flow in, like something natural, like something given, one soul to another.

Day One

When I first arrive, the teacher says, "Go down to the meadow and see the Buddha." So I go, aware of my breath coming in and out, my feet on the dirt road, the swish of my arms against my body. I round the bend into the sun. I think, I'll follow the sun. I'll go this way to the Buddha. I come to the meadow but there is no Buddha. Only a harbor full of masts waving colorful Tibetan prayer flags. No boat. No sea. Only shore. As far as the eye can see, only shore. And I wonder, what does it mean not to find the Buddha? I go back up the hill, where the teacher directs the traffic of new arrivals. "I didn't find the Buddha," I say. Had I known it would be some of the last words I'd speak for days, I might have elaborated.

Around the dinner table that night I think, This is swell. I'm Nancy Drew, ready to solve a mystery with a bunch of girl chums, talking and laughing, a real camp scene. A drape falls over this scene an hour later with the words, "We are now in silence." The retreat will be in silence all four days. I am cast off, free sailing into an abyss, and my descent cannot be stopped by the thorny branches of words I use to make sense of my world.

Day Two

A day ahead of sitting and they don't mean hanging out. I am angry I didn't know about whole-day silences. Angry at my roommates for not letting me sleep. Angry at my fatigue. Then, like a leaf blown in the wind, this anger turns and becomes the grief that it really is. Like cream rising to the top, sweet delicious grief that I allow in and wrap around my diminishing self.

I struggle all day, consider leaving. I can't spend another night without sleep. I could escape in the middle of the night, or very early in the morning. I begin to take hope. I feel like the nun getting ready to leap over the wall. I'll write a note: "I'm breaking out. Pass it on." All day I picture rounding the corner by the Corralitos Meat Market, snapping on the radio and letting loose with rock and roll all the way back home.

But I try. I do try. I walk, looking at the ground, trying to keep my mind focused on my breath. I see blades of grass. I see a perfect mushroom. Then my heart is the only thing I see. Pounding so loudly in my silent ears, the sound covers the ground like a stain, like an umbrella larger and more perfect than the mushroom. The shadow of silence.

In the meditation house we are all clearing our throats. Trying to clear out the unspoken words. Trying to strangle the voices as they sift down through our beings. Not unnoticed, not without pain.

Day Three

I wake after a whole night's sleep, filled with hope. The silence seems natural as we all move around one another like creatures in the very deepest part of the ocean.

At breakfast I see my friend take her food outside to eat. I think this seems like a good idea. I join her, respectfully sitting at a table nearby. As soon as I lift spoon to mouth I feel my presence in her scene. A clutter among the trees. A disturbance in her stillness. I eat quickly and retreat to a white plastic chair, probably bought from Orchard Hardware. But it is sacred. I sit overlooking the Santa Cruz mountains. A layer of clouds is building. Far away a hawk circles. I am overwhelmed by the immensity of the landscape. Of the immensity of my spirit at that moment. High up in the highest tree a blue jay grates like nails on a chalkboard, reminding me there is a world out there that needs my attention.

I am interrupted by the teacher. "Buddha," she says softly, and motions with her head. I nod and the two of us start down the hill, where Friday I went looking. We enter a huge tent, and there he sits. I gasp. The sheer size takes away my breath. The breath I've been cultivating for three days, gone. We stand in silence. I wonder why I didn't see the Buddha on Friday. I think, maybe I wasn't ready to see the Buddha. And I wonder what will it be like to head home into town. Maybe, I think, a little like a monk going to Disneyland. And I wonder, too, will I turn on rock and roll as I round the market in Corralitos? I don't know. It depends on who has the upper hand at that moment, the Blue Jay or the Buddha.

Day Four

Those nagging little children. Just thoughts rising to the top of the pond. Sitting in darkness, a roomful of silent women, invisible except for our collective energy keeping us afloat. 'Well' on the in-breath. 'Joy' on the out. Then hearing nothing but the ache in the shoulders, the neck. Pain fading with my breath. The screech of an itch along my cheekbone. Back to my breath.

Sit

Walk

Dharma Talks

Blue to black. Are we rising or descending? Where is this place I am in? I am alternately swallowed by silence and joyful to be here. Deep in the pocket. This palm of redwoods. Deep within the dripping earth. Down to the core. Am I in the core? Have I reached it? Or do I still need the rock and roll? Do I need the thrashing sound to cover the limp pale beating of my heart? Do I need cover? Dive! For cover. Dive for the truth! Dive! Dive! Into the deep. Into the wreck.

Sit

Walk

Listen

The leaf on the small oak hangs patiently next to the giant redwood. Waiting for the next raindrop to finally reach it. Being last in line isn't so bad. You've had the luxury of time. You've had the breath of stillness. The sound of the refrigerator clicking on. The churning of water for tea. Rain falling from the eaves. My breath in and out. Voices, car engines, the scrape of chairs.

Leaving, I walk down through the rain and am stopped by a person asking for directions. It takes a moment for me to respond. My voice sounds harsh against the soft underbelly of the forest.

Sit

Walk

Breathe

The Latin root for perfect is the word "complete." I have completed this retreat. I have come close to my perfection for this day.

Walk

Breathe

Listen

Cooper Gallegos

Buddha

Wood Block Print

Gaza Bowen

Following in the Footsteps

He gets off work at eleven, picks us up
at midnight. We squeeze into his car,
three Americans eager to follow our teacher
along the sleeping coast of Japan,
three winding hours to *Tsubaki Jinja*,
the shrine of *Sarudahiko no kami*,
who guided the deities of heaven
in their descent to the earth
at the beginning of time.

No priests up yet. We doze
in the tiny Toyota, uncomfortable
in the winter's chill, until dawn reveals
the lines in our teacher's face, weary
from swing shift at the factory.

Into the prayer hall we follow him,
where his own teacher, the founder of Aikido,
once made an offering of his art
to *Sarudahiko no kami*. They say
sparks flew from his spinning staff
like lightning in the night sky.
A deep silence resounds in this hall.
The wooden floor gleams, inlaid
with sacred symbols: triangle, circle, square.

The priest begins the purification ceremony.
Sound rises from the earth
to the High Plain of Heaven:
Taka ama hara ni, mototsumi oyasume okami...
To the rhythm of the chant, he adds
the solemn thump of a drum,
a lilting flute, free as a jazz player's jam.
He kneels on the *tatami* in priestly robes,
a stiff black hat, thousand-year-old fashions
from the imperial court of Heian.

Our teacher wears khakis and
a thin jacket with a company logo.
Wooden staff in hand, he leads us
in the steep ascent of the sacred peak
behind *Tsubaki Jinja.* Suddenly he accelerates
faster than my eye can comprehend,
floating effortlessly up the mountain
like *En no Gyoja,* the *yamabushi* ascetic
who, they say, flew magically
over these same slopes
thirteen centuries before.

He disappears around a bend.
I will not fall behind. Legs pump hard,
push rapidly up the trail after him,
legs strong from pushing off the mat
in the Aikido *dojo* every day, long hours
of hardship and joy. I give it my all,
but I'm losing ground, I can't sustain this…

Then his voice reaches down to me:
Maka Hannya—the Heart Sutra's opening phrase.
I sing it back to him, repeating the sounds:
Maka Hannya—and he proceeds,
Hara Mita—
Hara Mita—I link with him, drop into a rhythm
of foot and voice and nothing else;
Shin Gyo—pulling me up the mountainside,
Shin Gyo—I follow in his footsteps,
phrase by ringing phrase, until we emerge
steaming with sweat and sound
into the clearing at the top of the peak.

Silence opens wide. The Pacific
stretches before us, the waking patchwork of
rice paddies and village houses, the dark tops
of sacred *sugi* trees surrounding the shrine.

Following our teacher, and his teacher before him,
we raise our staffs to the empty sky, and bow.
In unison, we begin to move, to spin,
to gather the light.

Linda Holiday

Fire Dance

Bhutan, November 2000

The young boy
Maybe seven grabbed my hand
In the dark
Held it tight
Tighter than I have ever been held
He led me through a small gate
We were crushed and
I worried for him
His size
I wondered why me
He wanted something from me
Not what I had expected
But to tell me to
Go slow
Be careful and watch for my life
His body shook and I knew
He feared for his
I moved slowly
He pulled me past the others
Another way
He ran dragging my feet
Over craters and voices
After a lifetime
He left me dangling like
Wilted irises
People swimming around me
Pushing yelling in firelight
He evaporated in darkness
To run through the burning wall
Into the Dance
Our hands never met again
The smell of smoke
Hangs like a skirt
Made of questions I cannot ask

Linda Barton

Prayer in the Andes

Etching

Michelle Francis Doyka

Cosmosis

What story doesn't tell it?
What story doesn't create it
in the telling?

One day, when conditions were right,
when mineral and gas,
warmth and moisture
were all exactly right, a seed cracked
open and became
root and stem.

Touching ever the darkness,
seeking ever the light,
giving its all, until at last
it created a seed.
It is said that Brahman cracked
open and everything poured out

from the passion fire of self-sacrifice.
The Void begat the All
out of Love.
Brahman cracked open
and spread an infinite banquet—
though some would still nibble
at the crusty edges
of the starry universe.

Christine McQuiston

Flametender

Kildare, Ireland, circa 100 C.E.

Awakening in the dawn, I begin singing prayers to Goddess Brigid as soon as I open my eyes. Rising, I gather a thick cape about my sleepy nakedness and slip silently out of my house. Making my way through the quiet village by foot to Brigid's well, I pause at the entrance to sound another prayer, this one more throaty. Hand over heart, I cross the simple wooden bridge as I take in the powerful beauty of the well, the dense stand of birch trees along the northern edge, a profusion of yellow and purple wildflowers overrun with honeybees, and at the center, the sparkling water flowing from the well, through a stream, into a glistening pool.

Moving forward, my bare feet enter green grasses wet with morning dew, red-winged blackbirds pecking among the blades. Taking a large, round black stone from a bag near the entrance, I approach the low rock wall of the well, singing softly in answer to the water's crystalline song. Placing the smooth, dark orb on the shelf of well wall facing north, I follow the trail of gurgling water to the west where it pools deeply, ringed by rock and fern and reed, beneath the bending oaks.

Near the water's edge I pick up the wad of cleansing herb cradled in a scooped-out rock. Removing my cape, I strip away the drowse of sleep and step into the cool water. It is clear and welcoming, and with prayer for clarity and freshness, I sink into its depths, feeling the life flow of Brigid all around me. Slowly, meticulously, I bathe my human form, blessing each part as it is washed, the pungent herb slippery in my hands. Holding a deep breath I plunge beneath the surface, rolling my body around and around until I spiral to the surface once again. In silence I climb the slight slope of the pool and rise to stand, clear water lapping at my thighs. With renewed purpose, I leave the pool to stand in the morning light.

Turning with the four directions, I feel the breath of Brigid in the early air, a slight breeze drying my body as I sing praises to the powers of air, fire, water and earth. With larger and larger strides I walk a circular path within the holy circle surrounding Brigid's well, my praying voice exciting the birds into songs of their own. The air caresses me and kisses me and my skin dries gently, the tickle of those kisses refreshing.

As the praisesong fades in the sweet air, I make my way back to the well. On the far side is a holy arch, a natural curve of thorn and vine and tendril, beneath which a pattern of flat stones marks the holy source of the well itself. Here I bend and drink deeply three times, a swallow each for Brigid's three aspects of inspiring, healing, and smith-crafting.

Crossing the threshold for the last time, I open another storage bag, and pulling out fresh clothes, I begin to dress. I cover my clean body with robes of green and brown woven from the reeds that line the pools and streams of Brigid's well. I drape my shoulders with shawls of dark blue, made from strands of dyed wool, thick and furry. My head I wrap in red, the sheen and glint of an ancestor's braid still lively in the light.

After dousing myself from bare foot to headwrap with sage smoke and lavender, I pull on my special sturdy reed-and-felt fire boots, glossed over with waxy shine. Standing tall, I put on the rings of woven grasses, the bracelets of twined reeds, the necklace of chiseled stone. Saying final prayers of thanks and praise, I leave the well, exiting through the low branches of the pine trees that shelter the southern side.

The path to the temple is hard packed by pilgrims' feet, lined with ferns and vines, hedges and stones. The early air is crisp and clean, letting you see across the open plains and up the hill to where the fire temple beckons me. I stand a moment, taking in the sight of my destination. It is a round structure on a round hill, rising out of the sky.

On foot I breathe deeply, controlling my eagerness with measured steps. I keep my head up and look at the sky, the plains of the village and the fields beyond spreading out as I ascend the sacred hill. The quiet deepens as I leave behind the ordinary, and everything takes on new clarity under the growing light of day. The temple is not centered atop the hill, but is situated a little to one side, facing south. I bend my neck back a little to take in the full height of the temple, and as always its perfect roundness causes my heart to beat faster.

The temple is made of sacred stones, each gathered from a holy place kept secret, and carried in hand by ancient women. The stones, gray and brown and black and blond, fit together like fingers on a hand. None of the stones themselves are massive, yet the structure they create together is large. The roof is thatched and peaked, edges of the strong brush creating cooling eaves all around.

Three times three I circle the round stone temple, sounding a chant of greeting on the first round. On the third round I praise the muse, she who inspires and provokes. On the fifth round I celebrate the midwife, she who creates and births. On the seventh round I honor the smith, she who crafts and completes. My voice rings out in the still air and even the birds are silent in this mysterious moment, as I release aspects of being human and open to the possibilities of becoming divine.

The flametender within the temple answers my first call with a trilling song. On my fourth turn she sings a song of openness and receiving, her voice light and welcoming. On the sixth turn she grunts a chant of laboring and birthing, the rawness of her cries sending the crows flying. On the eighth turn her voice lowers to a drone as she intones a hum of hard work and focus. On the ninth rotation both she and I join together in a new song, one never heard before, as the two of us pour our souls into our voices, creating a prayer of pure, spiritual joy.

Still singing, we meet at the temple doorway facing east. It is a round opening in a round building. We both stand a moment facing each other as our song melts to silence. The threshold shimmers with mystery, and as I smell and hear the fire burning within, my breath quickens. Turning to face the world, I say one last prayer to the open air, as the departing flametender faces the interior, saying one last prayer to the fire.

In perfectly timed movements we each turn into the temple doorway and step together through the glowing threshold. Facing each other in passing, our backs and buttocks rub against sacred stones as our breasts and bellies brush against holy flesh.

The departing flametender steps into the everyday world as I move into the brightness of the eternal flame. My heart is beating faster, faster, faster as I enter the holy circle of the sacred fire. Brigid's brilliance draws me in and in and in until I am enveloped, I am swallowed, I am extinguished and Brigid is birthed yet again.

Mary Blaettler

Editor's note: The goddess Brigid is a beloved female deity in the Celtic tradition. Her sacred wells are found throughout Ireland, including in Kildare, where Celtic priestesses took turns tending a flame burning in her name for several hundred years. After Christianity came to Ireland, the goddess Brigid was named a Christian saint. Catholic nuns continued to take turns tending her sacred flame until the 16th century. Brigid's flame was officially relit in Kildare in 1993.

Triple Spirals

Digital Collage

Jane Nyberg

Avalon Priestess

Glastonbury, the ancient Isle of Avalon, England

I am oldest of old
I am newest of form
I am the spring beneath the hill
I am the waters of the well
I am the sword of the male
I am the yoni of the woman
I am the blood-red birth
I am the duality of death
I am the lion's mouth
I am the tree's roots
I am the climber of the hill
I am the descent beneath it
I am the persecutor
I am the slaughtered
I am the vessel for the memories
I am the wail of the mourning
I am the vase for the healing
I am memory re-membered
I am the hope of my lineage
I am the one who once were many
I am the carrier of the flame
I am the past and I am future
and my quest is now.

Jodine Turner

My True Name

When I was growing up, I believed that my parents had given me the wrong name. I didn't know what my real name was; I only knew that the name my parents called me did not fit the free spirit inside. Harriet Muriel was much too old-fashioned a name for me. I wanted to sing and dance and laugh and do wild and crazy things. Instead, I was an obedient little girl who spent her days quietly sitting in the corner with her hands in her lap or reading a book. A still small voice kept urging me to shed my given name and free the wild person inside of me, but it took more than fifty years before I listened to that calling.

In Judaism it is traditional to give a newborn baby a Hebrew name at birth. Usually the child is named after a beloved relative who has died, and it is believed that the dead relative's soul lives on in the body of the newborn. The Hebrew name my parents gave me was Chaya Mira, after my mother's youngest brother Hymie, who died when he was thirteen. Chaya means "to life" and Mira is the diminutive of Miriam, the sister of the prophet Moses.

Miriam was always my hero. She was a prophetess, a seer, and a leader of women. In the biblical story, after the Jews were freed from slavery, the Egyptian Pharaoh's army pursued them to the Red Sea. Miriam, holding her timbrel high in the air, led the women singing and dancing as they entered into the icy waters. When the sea parted all of the Jews were saved, safe and sound on the other shore, but the Pharaoh and his army were swallowed by the sea that engulfed them. Since I was a little girl I have dreamed of taking up my timbrel and dancing with the women, leading them to freedom.

As my sixtieth birthday approached, I found myself called to explore the deeper roots of my Jewish heritage. I wanted to embark upon a spiritual journey to learn Hebrew and to chant Torah. I decided to create a ceremony that would culminate in my taking a new spiritual name. Because I love the biblical Miriam so much, I decided that my new name would be Miriam. I didn't know what my last name would be, but I have always admired the meaning of Chaya, "to life." So I settled upon a lovely version of my original Hebrew name.

I said my new name over and over. *Miriam Chaya. Miriam. Chaya. Miriam Chaya.*

Most people who receive a Hebrew name use it only during holy ceremonies at the synagogue when they are called to say the blessings before reading Torah. But I decided to use my new name on a daily basis. This was a bold decision, a commitment to the new person I was becoming, and I felt its impact deep in my core.

As the time for my name change approached, I began to feel like a bride preparing for a spiritual wedding. The night before my ceremony, I decided to go to the *mikvah*, a Jewish ritual bath that is used by women to purify themselves before their wedding. The rules for cleanliness are very strict. I wanted to cleanse myself before taking my new name. I wanted to purify my body so that I could offer myself in a marriage between my worldly self and my spiritual self. I wanted Shekinah, the feminine face of God, to be present when I took my true name.

I had butterflies in my stomach as I knocked on the door of the ivy-covered cottage in Berkeley. My heart was beating fast when a beautiful young woman in a long flowing dress and sandals opened the door. She greeted me warmly.

"Welcome to the mikvah. We've been expecting you. Please follow me."

She took a key off the hook as I followed her into the lush garden filled with red and white azaleas. It was twilight. The sun had just set, but a glimmer of light lingered on the trees. A slight breeze blew the branches and cast a mystical shadow on the simple wooden structure.

"This is the bathhouse," she said, as she led me up four wooden steps, unlocked the door and walked into a darkened room. Silently she lit a candle and pointed to my shoes. I slipped them off and placed them on a low shelf. She took my hand and led me into the bathroom with a small sink, toilet, and bathtub with a clear plastic shower curtain. On the towel rack was a white thick bath towel. On the back of the door were two hooks to hang my clothes.

"Be sure to empty your bladder before entering the mikvah. There is kosher soap for you to wash your body, both inside and out. You will find a generic shampoo with no fragrance in the medicine chest. Be sure to rinse your hair thoroughly. You will also find manicure scissors to cut your fingernails and toenails. Please remove any extraneous hairs as well. When you are completely ready, knock on the door and the mikvah attendant will examine you thoroughly before allowing you to enter the holy water. Good luck."

She turned to leave, but I grabbed her hand and squeezed it once, then looked deep into her eyes. "Don't worry. You will be just fine," she said. She hugged me and left the room.

Alone at last, I looked into the mirror and saw my wrinkled face and graying hair. "What are you doing here, Harriet? You are not a bride. You are not even an orthodox woman. You are an old woman of sixty years, well past menopause. Why are you here?" Ignoring the doubting questions, I took off my clothes and hung them on the hook on the back of the door. "I am here for a holy purpose," I told the questioning eyes. "Do not judge me!"

I turned on the hot water in the shower and jumped in, soaping up my body and shampooing my hair. The hot water was comforting and I felt my tense body begin to relax as I meticulously followed the cleansing directions. When I finished, I grabbed the thick bath towel and vigorously rubbed my back, my breasts, my legs, and my hair. I paid special attention to my feet, making sure that no trace of dirt remained. When I was satisfied, I wrapped the bath towel around my body. Holding it closed in front of me, I knocked on the door and waited for the mikvah attendant.

Slowly the door opened and a young woman in a white terrycloth robe greeted me with a warm smile. She gestured to a chair, inviting me to drop my towel. Stark naked, I was embarrassed and shy to stand before this stranger whose job was to examine my body for any remnants of dirt or any other foreign substances before allowing me to enter the sacred waters. I was shivering and frightened as she carefully checked my body to make sure that nothing had escaped my rigorous cleansing. Suddenly it dawned on me, "What if I don't pass the test? What if she does not allow me to enter these sacred waters? Does that mean that I am destined to be Harriet Muriel for the rest of my life?"

The mikvah lady cleared her throat and woke me from my reverie. I opened my eyes to see her standing in front of me with cotton swabs in her hand, ready to poke and probe, to examine each crevice and orifice of my body, to search for a trace of dirt that might be lodged in the hair I had shampooed briskly and dried with a rough towel. I put my hands behind my back, afraid that my fingernails and toenails, cut to the quick and meticulously cleaned of any trace of nail polish or dirt, would betray me.

She began by gently separating the strands of hair on my head with a sharp comb to make sure that I had thoroughly rinsed out any remnants of soap. Satisfied that my hair was clean, she looked at my freshly scrubbed face, making sure there was no trace of cleansing oils or cream. Now she turned to my fingers and toes, which she carefully examined for any hangnails or raw cuticles. When she finished her examination, she gently patted my hands as she turned them over.

"Perfect! Now it is time to go into the mikvah."

The small room was dimly lit with candles. A square tub surrounded by four freshly scrubbed white walls dominated the room. She sat on the top step and gestured for me to join her. I sat next to her and put one toe in the water, smiling when I found that it was pleasantly warm. I put both of my feet into the water and wiggled my toes, listening carefully to her every word as she explained, "In order for you to have a kosher mikvah, you need to dip your body into the holy waters three times. Each time you dip, your entire body has to be completely immersed in the water and be free floating. No part of your body or your head can touch the side or the bottom of the pool in order for me to pronounce each dip kosher."

Cautiously

   I walked down

      the three steps

  to the pool and

     lowered myself

       into the living waters.

My body was shaking. I knew that I was going through a transformation, leaving my birth name behind me and embracing my spiritual name. I thought I was totally prepared to say goodbye to Harriet Muriel and hello to Miriam Chaya; but when I tried to immerse my whole body into the holy water, something held me back. A leg, a hand, or even my head kept popping out of the water. Something, or someone, seemed to be calling me. I heard a voice whispering in my ear. Suddenly it dawned on me that Harriet Muriel was calling me.

"Do not abandon me. We have known each other for sixty years. I am your history. I need you and you need me. Together we can be stronger. Please let me come with you."

As I listened to her pleading voice, I knew what I needed to do. I reached out my arms and embraced the little girl who was me as a child. I held my imaginary Harriet in my arms and felt our bodies relax as we dipped together into the holy water.

"Kosher," the mikvah lady pronounced in a loud and clear voice.

Holding the young woman Harriet, we dipped a second time. "Kosher," I heard as my head emerged from the water. Now, for the third and last time, the adult Harriet and I dipped deeply into the waters. I felt her strength catapult us into the air, leaping upward in triumph.

"Kosher," I heard for the third and last time, as Harriet Muriel and Miriam Chaya became one.

Miriam Chaya

Invocation

Honor the air present in every breath,
witness the flame sacred in the heart.
Feel the pulse of waters within,
stand firm in the earth that supports.
For with these things,
we are the spirit of the world.
May we do the holy work.
May we be the holy hands.

Lora Dziemiela

ODE TO THE

MOTHER

*The Great Mother is one of humanity's oldest divine figures.
For many millennia an all-abundant female form—the per-
petual source of life—was the holy ground of our ancestors'
souls. These writings speak to the love of the Great Mother,
and evoke the goddesses who are vital to many religious traditions. They sing of mothering and birth, nurturing at the
breast, and the joy and difficulty of raising children. Here
you will find prayers and homage for our mothers, our children, and for the wondrous cycle that brings forth the endless
rounds of human life.*

Ode to the Mother

O Mother of the worlds,
the overworlds and the underworlds,
may I behold you everywhere,
in the eyes of my lover,
in the song of birds.
Your indescribable beauty
laid out before me
in canyon and woods
and in the sweeping skies.

Just now with the morning sun
gently breaking
through gray rainy clouds,
my heart ached with the sweetness
of remembering
the luminous transparency
of your ageless face.

Andrea van de Loo

Great Mother Prayer

O Durga
O Sophia
O Kali Ma, O Kali Ma

O Mary
O Morgana
O Earth Mother, O Earth Mother

O Kuan Yin
O Pele
O Green Tara, O Green Tara

O Lilith
O Saraswati
O Ganga Devi, heavenly ambrosia

O Baubo
O Brigid
O Mohini Murti, Divine Enchantress

O Spider Woman
O Skeleton Woman
O Dakini Woman, O Dakini Woman

O Cybele
O Sehkmet
O Oracle at Delphi

O Isis
O Innana
O White Buffalo Calf Woman

O Above
O Below
O Within, O Within

O Earth and Water
O Air and Fire
O Spirit, O Spirit

Sonya Lea

Black Madonna

Gouache Painting

Durga Bernhard

Prayer to Earth Mother

When I was fifteen I walked to church every Sunday in San Angel's cobblestone neighborhood in Mexico City. After mass, I walked home slowly with Custodia or Luz past the old beggar women with their hands outstretched,

Una limosna, señorita, por el amor de Dios,

the barefooted younger women with babies in their rebozos selling candles for votives, their big sad eyes imploring help, the small children with crusts in their eyes and tangled hair hustling chewing gum. I walked past lovers pressed against the walls of colonial houses, the smell of urine and the little statue of la Virgen de Guadalupe in a niche in a wall with fresh flowers laid at her feet.

Once I went to la Basilica de la Virgen de Guadalupe in downtown Mexico City. I watched women make their way up to the altar on their knees. Some came from kilometers away, on their knees, holding rosaries:

> *Madre Santísima*, have pity on us, born as we are in this tortured land.
>
> Look at our desperate conditions, dear Mother of God, how am I going to feed my children? Where is the next tortilla coming from?
>
> *Madre Santísima, ten piedad de nosotros.*
>
> What about medicine for my poor old mother who I had to leave at home on a *petate* on the floor too weak to get up anymore?
>
> Mother of God, help me, what am I going to do?
>
> Please don't let my old man come around drunk once again.
>
> *Madre Santísima, ten piedad de nosotros.*
>
> Don't let him beat me.
>
> *Madre Santísima*, look at me, I am on my knees, look at the blood. I come before you, supplicant.
>
> Have pity on us, Mother of God.

I heard these prayers over and over, but they only took root in me years later when I went to a Taizé service in the United States.

All around, floor candles flickered. I knelt by the bare wooden cross and bent my forehead to it.

Women came and knelt around me, their foreheads to the cross, singing, "Jesus remember me, when you come into your kingdom, Jesus remember me, when you come into your kingdom."

"Jesus take my suffering," I prayed, forehead on the cross, and gave my suffering over till I was soothed.

Now, I turn to Earth Mother and ask: if I kneel upon you and open my arms, put my forehead to your hills and grasses, will you receive my suffering?

> Earth Mother
> receive in your great bounty
> all the blood that has poured over me,
> the sorrow that has mired me down.
> Let me be free,
> so flowers and trees may sprout from me to the heavens,
> so birds may come and perch on my wings
> and sing their eternal song of gratitude.
>
> Dear Earth Mother,
> may your bounty feed the downtrodden,
> may you comfort each knee and forehead pressed into your
>   layers,
> may la Virgen de Guadalupe's roses flourish
> and the trees that become crosses be strong,
> may your robes encompass stars, moon and ocean, day and night
> and hold me in its folds, Earth Mother.

Gaël Rozière

What the Moon Knows

Nothing dies forever.
Not if you wait long enough.
Not with time on your side.
The moon knows.
She has watched stone towers dominate
fields where May dancers once bloomed
watched wind and war and
sunset after sunset   open
space
just enough   here   and here
for flowers to resurrect themselves
a breath of hope in concrete.

Nothing lives forever.
Not even stone.
Count the cycle of   sunrise moonrise sunrise   long enough
and the Temple of Artemis, outside Selçuk
wonder of the ancient world,
which ate the many breasted mother like a
split and juicy pineapple,
is no more than slabs of marble
on a shallow pond,
and the double church of Mary
which rose to supplant her down the road
is but the frame of a once-stone church.

Yet look how the spiral changes,
stays the same.
The moon in all her faces
smiles
on mother god,
virgin goddess,
virgin mother.
Female. All female
on this ancient holy land.

We make so much of becoming a man—
the study, the Torah, the tallis.
But women…
nature names women.
The moon calls us into being.
Where is our moon song?

Nothing dies forever.
Temples nailed shut,
women burned,
mysteries abandoned
or driven underground.
The moon can wait.
Some winters last longer than others.

She dreamt of flying.
Not like birds,
not wings outstretched,
but skywalking.
Up untouched stairs
down near-glass streets
sometimes   only sometimes   tree-ward.
Skywalking.
Heart light   standing flight.
Eight clicks of the planet
twenty   forty
as dreams teach their silent lessons.
One day, dreams, like flowers,
slip between the cracks at dawn.
One body leaves the ground in joy,
remembers.

And the flowers,
year after year,
generations down the road,
send signals on the wind,
pollen and whispers,
inexplicable, unlikely,

calling the dormant female seedling,
the ready hip, the restless arch,
the half remembered dream.
Beloved, it's Midsummer.
It's Moontime.
It's Beltane.
Come dance!

Deborah Edler Brown

The Powers of Life–An Elemental Chant

We are alive!
    as the sound of Her sacred name.
We are alive!
    as the soil of Her blessed form.
We are alive!
    as the dance of Her waters flow.
We are alive!
    as the breath of Her restless winds.
We are alive!
    as the spirit of the awesome One.
We are alive!

Sandra Pastorius

Note: With many voices, this chant can be sung call and response.

Prayer for My Mother

at 83 years old

Spirit of the trees
move like soft wind
over my mother's face tonight.

Spirit of the ocean
the goddess of warm water
bathe my mother's back with
the ebb and flow of peace.

Spirit of the birdsong
Spirit of the angel's voice
allow whole and pure high notes
and deep and low notes
to resonate sweet in the marrow of her bones.

Spirit of the spider
spin ease into her hands
let her handmade quilts
become their beautiful expressions
of her love for us all.

Spirit of the sacred earth
Spirit of the leaves and flowers
let your greens and reds and yellows
come to her eyes every day.
Encourage her tenderness,
let her tend to you
as you tend to her,
Spirit to spirit
soul to soul
breath to breath.

Let my mother make lemon pies
from the south-facing Meyer tree in her yard.
Let her roses grow endlessly,
their fragrances full.

May my mother be blessed
with all that is
holy and all that is good.

Jean Mahoney

Letter from Home

Sewn, Embellished Paper

Diane Roberts Ritch

Transcendence

for Naomi

This small creature,
with her familiar-smelling flesh
(flesh that is not metaphor,
that is comparable to nothing,
not the down beneath a duckling's wing
not the petal of a newly opened rose
not the melting sweetness of whipped cream)—

This small creature,
with her five strong fingers
grasping at my one,
tugs at me like the moon
calling forth a spring tide
of blood and love and bliss.

She is my prayer,
and she is its answer.
She stops time,
and she reminds me I will die.
We laugh together,
and somewhere
underneath the laughter
I grieve to know
that she will suffer
and I cannot protect her.

I invite her to watch
the ladybug
flaunting red wings
on a bamboo stalk.
I invite her to count
nine ducklings
trailing their mother

on the rippling lake.
She invites me to imagine
the unimaginable world
she will inhabit
without me.

Laura Wine Paster

A Midwife's Invocation

I call on Artemis, huntress, protector of animals and birthing.
　　Help me to trust birth.

I call on Diana, keeper of the moon, and the cycles of women's lives.
　　Help me listen to women.

I call on Hecate, wise crone who stands at the crossroads.
　　Make me a guardian of the passage.

Great goddesses, fill this vessel with your wisdom.
　　Guide my hands. May they be gentle and strong.
　　Guide my heart. May I be open to giving and accepting love.
　　Guide my words. May they be kind and true.
　　Guide my thoughts. May they be compassionate and free of judgment.
　　Guide my spirit. May I be connected with the higher beings.

I put my roots deep into Mother Earth.
　　I draw her energy into my belly for gestation and creation.
　　I draw her energy into my solar plexus to fire my will.
　　I draw her energy into my heart for opening to love.
　　I draw her energy into my throat to awaken my authentic voice.
　　I draw her energy into my third eye to enliven my inner knowing.
　　I draw her energy into my crown for connection with spirit.

I call on all the women ancestors who have given birth before us.
　　Come gather round. Support this woman.
　　Guide her to access her power, confront her fear, and find strength.

I call upon my sister and brother midwives from past, present and future.
　　Encircle and embrace me with your loving intentions
　　for the sacred work we do.

As we ready ourselves to accept new life into our hands,
　　let us be reminded of our place in the dance of creation.

Let us be protectors of courage.
Let us be observers of beauty.
Let us be guardians of the passage.
Let us be witnesses to the unfolding.

Cathy Moore

The Push

PUSH, PUSH, BREATHE, PUSH

Primordial primitive wave

BREATHE, BREATHE, PUSH, BREATHE

Placenta shimmering ocean

PUSH, BREATHE, PUSH, BREATHE

Emerging spirit afire

BREATHE, PUSH, BREATHE, PUSH

Transparent golden dance

Judith Tamar Stone

Prayer for New Grandchild

New silky velvety being
We await you
Tiny alien, navigating star years
Spinning into the whirligig
Taking the waters
Slippery missile running the rapids
Shooting the waterfall
Little comet blinking, sucking, falling
Into our arms

Judy Schatan Phillips

Ohialehua

Photograph

Holly Metz

Musings of a Prolactin Junkie

I am lying awake enjoying the early morning quiet as the clock flips to 5:42, the moment of Chelsea's birth. She is fourteen today. I look at my husband Andrew in his easy sleep, climb out of bed and ascend the stairs of the small cabin to peek at Chelsea and Kate, her younger sister, asleep in the loft bed. They are sleeping peacefully, covers kicked off, revealing long limbs like willow branches in the dawn.

I slip out on a hike to visit the waterfall above our camp. Alongside the trail there are lush mounds of lupine with spires of purple flowers and spent pea pods, and wild sunflowers, vibrant yellow atop feathery leaves. A breeze rises gently and the aspen begin to shimmer in the morning light. With each gentle gust of wind the sound of flowing water appears, as if a faucet has been turned on and then softly off, and all settles into stillness except the crunch of dirt and rock underfoot, and my breath growing deeper as the switchbacks rise steadily.

In this reverie I am back at Chelsea's birth—the moment after a long labor, when she was born. Andrew says that as her head emerged she had her eyes wide open, looking around the room. Then her body slipped out—whoosh, and she was here, glorious and heaven sent. She is a curious girl with a delightful sense of humor, and her dad likes to remind her that she was born checking things out.

Approaching the waterfall, the sound is symphonic. It's not a tall waterfall, more a place where the creek courses down the hillside, dropping and spilling between rounded boulders of granite tumbled in disarray. The rocks are mossy and wet, and the earth surrounding these rivulets is fertile with rich soil, tender grasses, vibrant ferns and small wildflowers. I climb up the hillside, find a rock to sit on, and slip my feet into the cascading water. It is cold and moving fast, eager to get where it is going.

Bathed in cool light and gentle mist, the energy is lush, vibrant, healing. One cannot hold a negative thought here. All is peace. The stream has beckoned me to it, and I am reminded that the same magnetism that pulls us towards a flowing stream attracts us to new life. People are universally drawn to new babies, to nuzzle them close, to gaze into their wise eyes and experience the calm, peaceful feeling of holding a new babe in arms.

Last year I was sitting with my eighty-year-old friend Lenore when she said, "I was caught in traffic this morning, feeling frustrated. Then I looked around me at all of the people sitting in their cars and I realized that every one of these people was once a little tiny baby, and they're *all* precious." We sat for long moments in quiet, taking in her lovely revelation. Yes, we can take every human being—travel back to their beginning, see them as a fragile, precious newborn with a tiny nose and a wrinkled brow—and see the goodness in them, unshaped yet by the life to come.

I was at a breastfeeding conference a few years ago and learned that just holding a newborn baby on your chest, skin to skin, raises your level of prolactin. Prolactin is the hormone responsible for ensuring a good milk supply and, along with oxytocin, contributes to the feelings of relaxation and well being that mothers often feel when holding and nursing their babies. The good news is that mothers who aren't able to breastfeed, and fathers and others caring for new babies can also experience this nourishing feeling of well being. No wonder so many parents express how wonderful it is to have their newborn baby sleep on their chests.

Hearing about these hormones of bonding at the conference, I felt a deep sense of belonging and a kinship with the other women in the room. I'd found a place to hang my hat: I am a prolactin junkie. Looking around the room at the La Leche League leaders, lactation consultants and nurses—all women who cared deeply about mothers and babies—the realization was clear. These were women who wanted to stay connected with birth and new families long after their own children venture into the world of soccer teams and sleepovers, dating and dancing. This was a room full of prolactin junkies.

Sitting by the running creek, I am reminded of summer days when Chelsea was a young girl and loved to putter in the garden. Many mornings I would sit on our porch steps nursing baby Katelyn, and chatting with Chelsea while she collected tiny snails and caterpillars. I would gaze down at Kate suckling, her dimpled hand resting on my breast. With her belly full of warm milk she would slide off, cozy on my soft lap, and doze peacefully, her sleep interspersed with little bursts of sucking, tiny lips pursing up and down, dreaming about her favorite activity. I miss those days.

Nature intended for us to keep our babies close. When a new baby is held in arms it's easy to see the sequence of communication that tells us she is hungry. She may begin by gently stirring and turning her head side to side, then suck her lips and bring her hands up to her mouth to suck on her knuckles, then actively root—the dramatic signal when she turns her head to the side with a wide open mouth, searching for the nipple—all this well before she needs to cry to tell us she is hungry.

And when a hungry baby does cry, one can't help notice the image: face red, brow furrowed, hands clenched into little fists held near her mouth. When I see an image of a person fighting, face tense with fear and anger, fists held high near the jaw, I cannot escape the likeness of a hungry baby, taut with unmet need: "Feed me, nourish me, hold me."

After a baby has been fed, her face relaxes, her arms stretch down by her side, hands uncurl, fingers gently open…a meditating Buddha.

Looking up into the aspen and conifers, I'm reminded of how much babies love to gaze up into trees. I remember setting both Chelsea and Kate as newborns on blankets and lying beside them as they contentedly watched the contrast of light dancing through the foliage of chestnut and maple trees. As older babies and toddlers they were calmed and nourished when carried in the backpack, hiking in the woods. It was such a sensory experience, bouncing along, feeling the breeze, listening to the leaves rustle in the wind—all the while enveloped by lush greenery.

Earlier this summer I was sitting under an expansive madrone tree. After long moments of gazing into its vibrant green mosaic, I closed my eyes and was startled to see the counter image on the inside of my eyelids: the leaves deep red, the branches grayish-white curving vessels, artery feeding arteriole, ending in capillary. I was gazing into a beautiful placenta.

This ancient madrone left me wondering if all those tree-gazing babies are comforted by the most deeply familiar sight, reminded of the time in their amniotic bath, gazing into their tree of life. And when these tiny, yet-to-be-born babies get sleepy and close their eyes, do they see green and dream of trees?

I slide my feet out of the cold water and wrap them in my sweatshirt. Sitting here and breathing this nourishing energy fully, I remember Molly's baby, Jack.

Molly called to say that her baby had arrived, a little boy, at noon, twelve oh eight to be exact, and could I come tomorrow? I arrived the next morning and let myself in, puttered in the kitchen briefly, putting away groceries and setting an amaryllis in water, then tiptoed upstairs.

"Hello," Molly called in a soft voice, "we're in here." I stepped in to see Molly lying in bed in a jumble of soft blankets, her new babe beside her, wrapped in red fleece. After greetings and a hug we spent long minutes gazing at his sweet face, his full cheeks like his sister Ellen's, his perfectly formed mouth and tiny nostrils. As she began to tell me her story and to orient me to her wants and needs, I massaged her feet. Molly asked me to open the blinds so she could see out into her garden on the foggy day.

Changing Jack's diaper, I wiped his bottom with several warm wet cloths. Meconium was everywhere. Up in my arms, his bare bottom wrapped in a cloth diaper that looked as big as a beach towel, we headed into the bathroom for more wipes. I carefully stepped around the bed and as we passed near the window he grimaced, squeezing more tightly his already closed eyes, reminding us of his extraordinary transition. "Thank you," Molly said as she sipped her tea.

"Thank *you*," I responded.

Driving home on a prolactin high, I relived the tender details of the morning and the beautiful energy of this new babe, born into a warm and welcoming family. I felt the corners of my mouth lift and a smile unfold as I involuntarily breathed these images deep into my belly, deep into my bones. After years of actively striving to achieve this state—yoga class, mindfulness meditation—here it was. Effortlessly breathing deeply into this calm center, this feeling of peace could not be suppressed.

Nourished by the vibrant energy of the flowing stream, I slide my tennis shoes on and say a prayer of gratitude—for our family, for these beautiful woods, for this summer retreat where the children are so free—for this rich life.

I head back down the trail with a monarch butterfly as my companion, home to make birthday pancakes.

Maggie Milazzo Muir

A Parent's Pledge

I welcome you my child to the realm of earth, wind, fire and air.

I felt the exact moment your spirit shot through your father's heart and into my being. My ripening body plump as a pomegranate, I awakened to the power of pulsating life.

My wish for you is that you sink down into your womb-sprung body. Drink deeply of your senses. Listen to your blood knowing. Listen to the wisdom of breath flowing through your heart. Embrace the sensate wisdom of your gut.

Your precious body, capable of wriggling with pain or pleasure, is your best and most truthful friend. Embrace and pay attention to its exquisite language. It will cradle your spirit, as I cradled you to my chest the moment you emerged from my womb. Give your body healthy food, water, good exercise and rest, challenges it can meet, and lots of love and pleasure.

As for mistakes, make them and bump up against the edges of yourself. Learn who you are: your needs, your desires, your gifts. Let life hold you in its blood-spattering sunsets and vistas of flaming fall colors. Let the rivers echo your song and the clouds paint the sky with your dreams. Hold onto everything and nothing at once, and never let anyone but you decide your path.

Your wholeness is your birthright. As your parent, I pledge to allow space for your growing and unfolding, and to tend to my own.

Welcome, my Child, to the joys of life celebrated in the lap of Gaia!

Ahraiyanna Della Tone

Mother and Child

Acrylic

Barbara Thomas

A Prayer for One Who Comes
to Choose This Life

May she know the welcome
of open arms and hearts
May she know she is loved
by many and by one
May she know the circle of friendship that gives
and receives love in all its forms
May she know and be known
in the heart of another
May she know the heart
that is this earth
reach for the stars and
call it home
And in the end
may she find everything
in her heart
and her heart
in every thing

Danelia Wild

A Mother's Right

He said, "Mom, don't worry about it."
"I am your mother, of course I worry."
"*Mom*, don't worry! I've got it handled."

The mother notices a word form,
crawl across her tongue.
She wants to say it, surrender a soft *OK*.
How easy to let the simple sound
slip between her lips.
Yet utterance of those two syllables
could, would, change everything.

She sucks back the word,
lips snap shut.
The letters reverberate in her head
OK, OK, OK
rattle around in her skull,
slide down to her heart.

A mother holds
her children in her body,
a safety zone in blurred time
where feet step over rusty nails,
falls are soft landings,
broken hearts remain whole.

In the world of man-made time
bare feet puncture,
arms twist and snap,
ended love stings.
Still, it is a mother's right
to protect as best she can
and if she were to let go
with an *OK*
would the order of life tilt off its axis,
send humankind spinning into orbit?

Maybe it's just me, a mother,
but I travel in front,
witness hard edges,
soften them
as a psychic bends a spoon.
My children walk into their own lives,
step on rusty nails and I bleed.

Carolyn Davis Rudolph

Heart Wood

for my son

here at La Push, waves pound
rocks and wood, wear them down
to their strongest shape

we sit at a driftwood fire
pound on logs with sticks
syncopated rhythms
long silent between us
now freed

I have loved you all your life
but can't seem to let you know it
words too explicit
voice too loud
timing's off

I give it up, let go, pound
sympathetic rhythms
while you count out heartbeats
on soft rounded wood

who needs words
when we have an ocean?

June BlueSpruce

That One Moment

When you fall
unexpectedly to your knees
in front of the plush blue couch
lips mouthing *thank you, thank you*

when all the years
you thought she would never grow up,
feared some quirk of fate
would spirit her away
like it did her older brother

when all that disappears for awhile

as you remember her, walking
away from you toward the dormitory
quick spunky step, high heels clicking
cascade of glossy black hair
swinging back and forth
and just before the glass doors
swallow her, she turns
gives you a *shit, I can do this* grin

which is the picture you hold

that one moment when gratitude
becomes your body, angel
of flesh without wings, and you kneel
with centuries of what prayer
might really be, and

you lift your hands, almost
bring them together
palm to palm, fingers pointing
upwards.

Kate Aver Avraham

SONG OF A

LUSCIOUS WENCH

The innate wisdom of the body is one of the great gifts of human life. We are born knowing how to smile, to kiss, to reach and soothe someone with our hands, how to make love. These wench-songs and sacred art celebrate the numinous knowing of the body, and praise the spirit that is imbued in skin, muscle, blood and bone. They honor eros and intimate partnership as holy energies which are themselves a spiritual practice. These works pay homage to the third body of love and tenderness that exists between lovers. Here, our body is the pathway, it is the dance, it is the prayer itself.

Body of Joy

My body is
a living breathing instrument
of the divine.
My body is the music
of angel choruses and choirs,
chants by Krishna Das,
the cords and strings of Liebert's guitar.
My body is
la luna negra ...
pure grace unfolding,
a billion whirling dervish cells dancing,
the universe of stars in motion.
My body is
rhythmic swells and sways
tender to the touch,
playful rainbows,
cherubim who love too much.
My body is the bliss
of pure consciousness,
ecstatic love holding laughter,
moonbeams, sunshine, dolphin smiles.
And my face is a poem.

Louisa Calio

Song of a Luscious Wench

Of a woman in her divine glory
of jubilation in the cells,
of sweet juices flowing
like waterfalls,
meadow creeks,
glistening, shining,
rushing, moving.

And then again still,
reflecting
earth and sky.

In this body of mine
so little earth,
so much light.
Just particles floating
in space,
in the breath of
the Great Mother God.

No need for anything
but the sacred fire
of my own sweet breath
moving through me
on streams of quiet bliss.

Andrea van de Loo

With Our Bodies Pray

Praise be for a thicket of waxwings on a spring morning,
for a dozen young chickadees splashing in raindrops
caught in the leaves of a butterfly bush.
Praise be for the rust and black towhee hopping on flagstones,
for bunches of grosbeaks, for nesting blue herons.
Praise be for his hand, stroking my hair, warm in the sunlight,
his fingers undoing buttons on my shirt.
Praise be for moist air caresses,
for the thumping of wing beats, for ducks overhead.
Praise be for the splash of a seal chasing salmon,
praise for the warmth of his arm against mine.
Praise be for his strong arms and shoulders,
for the curve of his chest, our legs intertwined.
Praise be for face against shoulder,
for gentle embraces, inhaling his scent.
We pray with our bodies
every day we say yes—
to the juncos, the sword fern, the smell of wet soil—
say yes to the passion that lifts us and breaks us.
Every day, we say yes and we pray.

Emily Lardner

A Thousand Senses

What if every single thing is a prayer? Anything that makes life live—what if it is all a prayer?

I make no effort to look for it—every tiny thing is irresistibly imbued. My senses are fired with delight. I have five senses, I need thousands more. Every thing gives and receives pleasure. In my adoration of a flower, the fragrances sweeten my glands and the color livens my eyes.

Because I know that love has no form and I know that my function in the world is to love, I ponder what my body would look like if all I did was love. Would it look like this? What if this is what love looks like in a body? If I choose to love every single day, will I begin to look different? Would the form of each of us begin to soften around the edges? Would our skin edges dissolve and our bodies blend together in a swirl of texture?

What if the lines around my eyes released showers of effervescent sparkles when I smiled? What if I heard music through my fingernails and danced with my eyelashes? What if I smelled with the soles of my feet and could see with the ends of my flying hair? What if all these things were really happening every moment, and I just forgot to notice? What if I don't know how to notice? What if I perceived the universe like a jellyfish or an ant? What if their perceptions reverberated around me and I received those signals and couldn't name them?

What if every single anything that coursed through me attested that life is ALIVE! What if under my skin were more colors than had ever been named and they were all communicating with each other with every single movement, from a whip of my head, the slow flutter of my eyelid, to the explosive lifting of my arms in a dance of praise?

Marci Graham

Learning How to Breathe Underwater

Acrylic, Gold Leaf and Glitter

Carol Gaab

Kadistu, Holy Woman

Raven-haired Kadistu, full lipped, and spicy wet.
Circle my body in your radiance.
Circle my body in your radiance.

Dark eyes to journey deep, separate one, full one,
Savor her gentleness when the world grows cold.
Savor her gentleness when the world grows cold.

Abandon your fears in her embrace,
And find the embodiment of heaven and earth.

Petalled labyrinth to secret pathways of the heart,
Queen of Love, whose kiss is life.
Queen of Love, whose kiss is life.

Breathing, releasing, the sigh of the universe,
Smiling, she's opening, and births a new star.
Smiling, she's opening, and births a new star.

Shudder of awe awakens each cell.
Pulse of time where time knows no end.

Rocking the sea, a tidal wave of salt spray.
Pouring herself into each quake.
Pouring herself into each quake.

I love, she loves, tasting of Mysteries,
The dawn's silky dew.

Ruth Barrett

At Midlife

It doesn't interest me
forging through wilderness,
crossing raging rivers,
scaling mountain peaks
or suffering hunger and thirst
from a vision quest
not my own.

What I want to know
is the source of fire in my loins,
the pound of mustang hoofs galloping
in the canyon of my heart,
the illumination of the burning bush
in the desert of my longing.

Have I taken birth
for just this moment of desire
for a higher lovemaking
to sweep me upward?

inspired by "The Holy Longing",
Johann Wolfgang von Goethe

Sarojani Rohan

Where God Lived

I wanted to know where God lived   if you could find her in the rose garden at the end of the millennium   if she lived in the throat of a young woman who wouldn't shut up about quitting her job   if she lived in the beads of sweat in the hollow clavicle of two people making love   I wondered if God lived two doors down from the botanica across from the shoe repair shop or behind the Dos Hermanas bakery or between the Bombay Sari store and Mission Liquors or over the railroad tracks next to the community garden that grew gaunt anemic sunflowers and pumpkins with powdery mildew   I inquired after God in the dilapidated house where the heavy metal heads lived and played their music too loud at all hours of the night but the last time they saw God was at a Black Sabbath show   So I asked their neighbors who had a meth lab in the basement and two rib-thin German shepherds in the backyard which was a constant sea of mud and shit and the dogs never stopped barking but they hadn't seen God since Altamont when she popped out of a cracked skull   I looked for God in the Christmas decorations adorning Main Street or the rain-slick alleys that led to the frontage road and the highway beyond that and the egrets taking flight in the marshes   I looked for God in the canals and walnut groves outside Yuba City in the sky turning from pink to blue   I found God in a lover's face when I snapped a photo of her smiling   that one bright golden light a big bang   the start of the universe glinting from her teeth   from her earth-colored eyes

Patti Sirens

Awakening

Predawn morning, electric.

Our bodies intertwined, immaculate,
my thigh burrowed between the white fire of your legs.

Turning to my side, half asleep,
I move closer into the warmth of your skin.

Your velvet fingertips trace the small of my back,
upward along the arc of my neck—

a ravishing tremor.

In silence you lean in, gently taste the inside of my thigh.
Consumed, eager, I awaken.

As it is with lovers, we need no words.

Speak to me with your touch,
hold my heart in your palm,
enter me with your silky dance.

Let your tongue of sweet nectar wrap itself in mine.

Buoyant and ripe, wanting, primal—
mouths open, moist lips playful, teasing.

I fall more deeply into you.
Our touch grows firm, you cradle my head in your hand.

Tenderly tugging locks of my hair, you thrust your hips over
my rupturing cavern.

I quiver, incandescent,
as our hearts merge.

Soul to soul, breath to breath, eye to eye,
together we welcome the dawn.

Caroline Koch (Stronck)

Primordial Love Poem

I want to adore your body
just as it is.
I want to adore every scar,
every fold and crevice.
I want to know every hair,
where all your moles are,
every corn on your foot,
and especially
the places that make you insecure
so I can adore them most of all.

I want to notice every part of you,
like the undulating ocean of your eyes
and love especially the right one
when it gets tired
and a little bit red.

I want to know every place
it feels good to touch,
how much or how little,
how soft, how hard,
how fast, how slow.
And once I learn these things
with my eyes
then my nose
then my ears
then my fingers,
I want to teach my mouth
the tasting of you—
every inch of you.

I want to experience
you all in all,
through all five senses.
No, not five,
but six.

I want to experience you
through my sixth sense
and come to know
your soul.

Diane Wolverton

Mmmmm…

Watercolor and Pastel on Paper

Robin Rector Krupp

Sacred Things

Your smile: a frequent visitor to your face
Your frown: invited by disturbing thoughts
    or unsolved problems
They remind me of a well-laid fire
Dancing in our hearth
Each flame alive and always changing,
Formed and re-formed by the fuel that feeds it
Changing faster even than our children grow
Or seasons change
Smile becoming frown
A raising of the eyebrows
The mindless moments
When you contemplate your nails
Or watch a speck of dust float through the air

Your footfall: padding softly toward me
On your way to bed
The way your body moves:
When mood and music catch you up
    and spin you round
    and send you
    finger-snapping lindy
    through the house
They remind me that all things possess a rhythm
And that underneath our complex melody
Lies a simple, sturdy 4/4 beat—
A syncopation here, a missed beat there—
But nonetheless a rhythm we can
    sing to
    dance to

Standing with you
Underneath the branches of an ancient oak,
    or *khupah*,
    or the street lamp on the corner

I thee wed,
Today and every day
Let us tend our hearth
    and keep our private dance hall
    warm and brightly lit

Riva Danzig

EVERYDAY
OFFERINGS

Perhaps in the end it is the sacred moments in everyday life—making soup, a daily walk, sitting up early one morning before dawn—that most move us and change us. These inner spiritual moments hold profound self-discovery, and a deep appreciation for the gift of our lives. This writing and art celebrates the sacred in the everyday: feeling the seasons, writing in the early morning, tea with a friend, the grace of cooking, growing older. In these offerings we see our ordinary, daily lives suddenly illuminated—filled with moments of simple beauty, awash in light

That Time of Year

Wanting to write a poem
I rinse brown rice,
slice ginger, sprinkle thyme,
roast the aromatic roots,
boil the rice in fragrant stock.

When the windows sweat with steam,
I write a poem in the frost
signed with a melting thumbprint.

In the shadow of starlit verse
hearts of onion curl open and crisp,
hissing their pleasure when dropped in the soup:
communion clear and simple.

Sarah Knorr

Peanut Butter and Jelly

Pastel on Paper

Robin Rector Krupp

Prayer for What Must Be Done Next

Oh morning song that is not heard
until light of day glimmers dawn
always the melody rising while
the wings of a dove come to
settle at the door of your heart.

Opening to the sound of your name
carried on the first breeze of day
come home now to rest in the silence
of this good morning where
nothing will be asked of you
nothing to make, to say, or to do.

This is the prayer
for what must be done next,
to listen for the song
of your own heart,
awakening.

Ziggy Rendler-Bregman

Before Dawn

It is way too early to be awake.

I arise and make tea. Stand by the window.

Out in the dark I see there's been snow. Enough to turn the landscape white, the black driveway a stark contrast, even in this midnight light.

This chaotic planet feels more and less like where I belong. Challenging and blessing with every exhausted breath.

I think of the woman I heard on NPR last night, who lost sixty of her family in one fell swoop. An earthquake in Iran, and she, sole survivor, now challenged to keep her body here, to go on living and find some semblance of love to pay homage to.

It is a testimony to the human spirit that so many more of us have not chosen to just abandon ship and make our way quickly, desperately home.

Within these frail psyches a pulse of hope loves life and watches in awe as the snow falls its grace, awaiting the signs of blossoming spring with a faith that sends out an SOS, an incantation to God, calling itself prayer.

We search the scrubby twig for its first tiny nub, promising bud, bloom, leaf, fruit. We tolerate the cold, enthralled with the white peaks and barren valleys that make this season winter.

Determined spring grasses push their way through the cracks in the frozen sidewalk. The trapped fox gnaws off a paw to flee through the snow. The salmon finds her weary way upstream again and again. Sperm battle their way in through the thick egg membrane.

I have always known this love. Even as a little girl, watching squirrels dance the high wire above the frozen landscape as I put out crumbs and reached to stroke their wild swishy tails. Or slurping honeysuckle from long sticky stamens, standing by the fence in the thick heat of summer. Waiting for the thunder clash after a rickety stab of lightning. Or holding a pale round robin's egg carefully in my palm, its blue an early morning summer sky. Alive in the dance of the body, each cell so perfect and casual in its knowing of itself as Holy.

Time will pass and the snow will melt. The steam from the cup will drift off and become the air. Day will overtake night, without much notice really. Bears will stretch and awaken and rise. Geese will head north, without conversation or consideration. And the woman in Iran will eventually find her breath again.

The earth will carry on without or in spite of us. The planets will turn, as they have always done. And we will act out our parts, chaotic and random, in this perfect, mysterious, well-choreographed dance.

I am alive in this pre-morning dawn. And despite weariness, the dark, and the challenging grace of snow, I stand in reverence. And when I remember, I bow. I bow.

Johanna Courtleigh

Everyday Offerings

For years I have maintained an inner conversation about the nature of this worldly life. There have been complaints directed to whoever is in charge. May I speak to your manager, please? There has been begging. Pleading. Negotiations. *If only, then I promise I'll...* and *What were you thinking?* and *You've got to be kidding me.* I've been annoyed at what I consider the smugness of whoever set this in motion with the attitude, "Don't look at me. I've done the best I can. Now you're on your own." I ask again, What could possibly be the purpose of all this suffering? The endless torrents that persist and bring us to our knees. Were we meant to crawl on all fours?

There were times when I wondered with whom, exactly, I was engaged in this relentless dialogue. The realization didn't surface until I was well into my adult years of husband, children, station wagon, and mortgage...that I might be talking to God. But how could it be possible for me to engage in conversations with God when I had previously decided that God did not exist? In fact, with the world's seemingly endless suffering, how could there be an in-charge, all-powerful God looking down at us? For many years I could not, would not, even speak the word.

Yet the moment of realization is vivid. I was by myself on a winter afternoon walk, Sadie, our golden retriever, my only companion. It was a trail I came to most days after dropping the kids off at school—essential to endure the tedium of motherhood. This was my daily meditation, and my survival depended on this walk and this trail. On that day the wind blew cold and damp against my exposed face, stinging with bitterness. I listened to the ache and moan of the trees. An oyster sky threatened to unload a storm. I wondered if I would be forced to retreat and give up my ritual walk. My internal voice yelled out at the damned wind. I leaned the weight of my body into this force. I worked myself into a fury. Words overflowed and spewed out of my mouth. I shouted at this cursed wind as it whipped around me. I competed with it to be heard. I met its force with my complaint against it.

In a brief moment, I was suddenly outside of myself and handed the blessing of observation. I witnessed a funny little creature as she carried on, flailing against her windmill. I recalled that this could be her tendency. I burst out laughing at the sight of her. Hilarity took me over. I snorted at the wind thrashing around me.

Suddenly I loved this wind. I loved my body as it moved through the crisp chill. A thought burst, rained down on me—I was drenched with the idea of it. *That* God, the one claimed to live in the sky, note-taker, watcher God, was not my God. I had this other God. My God lived with me on earth. My God was this gale whipping around me, this crisp winter air, the slate clouds above. My God was present in the shy deer frozen to my right, camouflaged by tall pampas grass. The God I knew was vivid red strawberries, ripe in season; the bounty at the farmers' market; the laughter of my boys as it drifted from the other room; the sweet jack-o'-lantern smile of my husband. Yes, this was the God I knew. The God that created orgasms, and the knowledge that they are not only good, but divine.

Nightly I washed dishes, after yet another dinner prepared to satisfy the appetites of my children. Off they went, released to their own ways with claims of homework and other excuses. I didn't mind. This was my time, in the silence of my kitchen, my temple, hands submerged in hot soapy water. I knew this was prayer. It was my personal prayer, a prayer for all of it. The prayer that satisfied all those relentless questions that have no answers. The prayer that is my daily sacrament to the God I know.

Carolyn Davis Rudolph

Any Tiny Thing

In my longing for a beloved,
do I forget to notice cascades of yellow roses
entwined in the orange tree outside my door?
Walking arm in arm with my intimate friend,
do I cast my eyes on each passing man
and for a fleeting instant wonder...this one?
As the waves in furious frothing make their runs to shore
and the sea otter tumbles underwater somersaults
and dolphins crest the swell
and pipers dash into the foam,
do I breathe in the absolute privilege
of everyday magnificence?
Do I forget to feel the gentle sea breeze
sculpt my face with its foggy fingers?
Forget to notice the seventeen
colors of sand encrusted on my toenails
as I brush my feet dry?

I have no time to lose.
I have no time to turn away.
I have no time for blind longing
for that which may never ride over the golden horizon.
Turning my back on even the tiniest delight will
surely put me into poverty.
I cannot risk missing any tiny thing.
Longing for what might be, what could have been,
what may never be has robbed me,
shattered fragile things,
left me on hands and knees
sifting through shards for the illusion
that there is more than this:
the vibration in my throat long after the chant
the fire of expression days after the words
the dance in me after the music's last strum
the song my breath actually sings in my heart.

Marci Graham

Tiferet

He tells me about the women's shoes, how they are covered with sequins and high heeled, strapped across the ankle. I picture them moving across the floor, the beautiful women poured into their dresses, with their partners' hands pressed into their back in just that place across from the heart where wings would grow. He tells me he thinks that dancing the tango could become an addiction. My dear friend and ex-husband, once a passionate zen practitioner, has drunk of this liquor and has become a passionate practitioner of the tango. He drives through the streets of L.A. listening to tango music of the thirties played on the bandoneón, imagines dancing with the perfect partner in close connection, body to body like a hand in a glove. The turn and swivel of the pelvis, a seamless motion, two bodies moving as one.

I'm sitting in my pajamas. The morning light pours in through the window and I know that I am not seen as a potential tango partner. I feel a pang of disappointment. I would love to glide on that dance floor, one with the music. I go out into the bright day, down to the glorious ocean, to that reckless water, to the light, and I feel the loneliness and also the beauty.

Just the other night, I remember watching a violinist on the stage, her dress satiny and an amazing color of roses. The fabric clinging to her body shows her muscles and her breathing. She looks like a goddess on a Greek urn. She is young and this is no small thing, to play before the gathered audience and the black-clad musicians. She is almost impatient, it seems, tapping her bow. She is Diana, Artemis, we her unwitting prey.

She lifts the bow to her instrument as if she would loose an arrow and strokes the strings. They vibrate with sound and I am suddenly transfixed, shot through my heart. I have entered the soul of my people. The sound is that place, the meeting ground. It is the holy apple orchard. It is the dwelling place of Shekhinah. It is all the pain and sadness of my tribe. It is all the unbearable sadness and also the joy. We are carried by this simple action of her arm, the muscles' tension and release, the body's facility and ease. The music has captured her and is playing through her willing body and inside our own bodies, a resonant vibration, and we are weeping and at the same time in a kind of ecstasy.

I am alone here and I want to make love, to embrace, to join with the beloved, to celebrate, to offer my body, to give thanks. I watch the audience and the performers, watch the young man who played the double bass in the intermission as he weaves his way between adoring mother and adoring sister and his new girlfriend. The webs of connection are visible, tender, complex. When the music begins again he can let it all go and enter the moment.

I ask myself, what is the place of beauty for me? Is it the arched windows of my house, the way the light moves across the floor, the vivid colors? This is only a part, like the sequined shoe of the tango dancer. The dance itself is something else. I know that for me it is the voice on the end of the phone trying to tell me the story and it is my ability to listen, to hear between the words, that vast silence.

Sitting at Sara's table at night, a candle burns. The traffic rushes past outside. We have eaten food from her island, food from a culture that no longer exists, that perished in the ovens of Poland with those who died. Leeks and spinach *bourekkas* and her special rice with piñon nuts. She is telling me about her life, about the time she fell into an abyss, when all seemed lost, all was taken away. She tells me about the men in her life who treated her badly, but mostly she speaks about what sustained her and continues to do so. The operas, the music, the poetry. How she and her husband would sit weeping together as they heard *La Traviata*, *La Boheme*. She is sharing these jewels of her life with me. I am in awe. We are laughing as we speak, even of the sadness. Time has vanished.

As I hear her words, I am at the feet of my mother and my grandmother and my great-grandmother. I am drinking in the connection with life. The connection with this mystery, with the traditions of my people: the ragged cloth, the worn bag carried from place to place that holds the *tallit* and the *tefillin*, blue velvet like a desert night embroidered with gold. I am here in this dark place that holds the trees at night glistening with fruit.

Inside I am a dancer. I wear a costume of black lace. I wear the strap shoes with the heel of the flamenco dancer, a shawl with red flowers. I move to the sounds of hands clapping and the voice of a singer who cries like the wind. I am in the heart of the meeting, in the words not spoken but clearly heard. I am in the touch of the hand in that place opposite my heart where there would be wings.

Alison Bermond

Daybreak

Dawn is coming, she heard them whisper. Look out, Dawn's on the way! They scattered down hole-ways, took cover under boulders, shielded themselves from Dawn's clomping footsteps, the immense shaking, her scalding rays.

She's just over the hill, can't you tell?

Since when has Dawn gone bad?

Oh, ever since that group of women went mad for her, three hills over. Now they wander loose with their hair matted and staring eyes. It's said they can curse you with a look.

So why blame it on Dawn?

Well, if they'd stayed with us, down among the passages where water drips time, they'd have been okay. But they longed for the light, they craved it like a drug, and when Dawn got hold of them they were never the same.

Do you know what happened?

Well, at first it wasn't so bad. They'd venture Upworld for rituals a few times a year, always returning to us here at Homesafe. Then the stories began circulating—women astride the sky, women loving in the light, even that the word 'day' originally meant 'between sunrise and sunset.' And then there was that business with the paintings.

The ones from the traveling exhibit? I heard about those.

Everywhere they were shown, discontent and discord followed. Women began uncovering parts of their bodies, following an ancient cult of sunworshippers. Just a bunch of pale larvae, if you ask me, not attractive at all.

And Dawn? Where does she come in?

The way I heard it, the painting that started the furor was of Dawn lying on the hills just east of here. So many folks woke with a thirst for Upworld after seeing it that viewing was restricted to those with Level Three scans, the most psych-stable. Even then, the overtly sensual nature of Dawn was profoundly disturbing.

Who did the Dawn painting?

It was one of those madwomen. She claims it was her first true sight of Dawn, the first time she stayed Upworld for an entire cycle. She showed it to her circle and they all began upworlding whenever they could, and painting more pictures to bring it back. They didn't even care if they were caught. They'd just stare right through you with those sun-blasted eyes. It became bad luck to speak with them and even worse luck to catch them. Why, if they had their way, we'd all be lying about in the sun's rays! To hear them tell it, there's little danger Upworld any more. Well, you can't prove it by them, seems to me they're all sunblind or maybe lightning-struck, and more than a little crazy.

Why are you up here then, with Dawn so near?

Hey, my place is still down under in Homesafe—I'm just thinking that a quick sight of Dawn could show me what all the fuss is about.

So you've seen the paintings. What did you think?

Well miss, at first they're hard to see, the loud colors coming at you, saturated with light, glowing and stark. Not even pretty, some of them. But they can bend your mind open, and that's what's dangerous. You look too long, you start thinking you can go where you want, do whatever you want, be an Upworlder if you dare. No security! No stability, no sheltering stone, no heartbeat of earth surrounding you! Like you have a right to all the light and color in the world. It's a shame. Me, I stay with the small doses. I know where my safety and sanity lie.

Well, I'm going out to meet Dawn.

Now why would you gamble with your good self like that?

Well, I lost my mother to the nightblindness and my father to heart-sickness—I won't expire as they did, slowly and painfully.

Is it suicide you're after, then?

Not at all, kind sir, just a glimpse of Dawn.

Melody Culver

Beets of Life

Remember the one about being thankful for our food because something gave up its life so we can live by eating it? I wasn't impressed at all when I heard it the first time or the hundredth time. So, my thinking went, I am supposed to thank this bunch of beets because I was able to afford them to make soup? I may be thankful about the being able to afford them part, but not because they were going into my system, becoming part of me and part of the chain that continues, or the circle where everything appears, disappears and comes back again.

A few days ago something happened and I finally got it. I got the part about life that is given up on our behalf, although it sure wasn't a decision on the part of the particular bunch of beets that enlightened me. I bought them at my Sunday farmers' market two weeks ago. I cooked the leaves, since they were organic. I saved the three or four roots because I didn't have time that day. Or the next or the next, and so it became a week-old bunch of beets in my refrigerator, and then a ten-day-old bunch of beets on that cold shelf.

Their day came because I hate to let food spoil, and I took them out. Would you believe it? Right where I cut off the greens, there they were: tender, curled, green life pushing through, coming from the depths of the deep purple-red bulbs! I was astounded. I still am. It made me wonder, in a split second of confusion, if the center of my beets was green, inhabited by tiny little unfurled creatures, full of life, ready to hit the road when no one was looking.

I really got it—it was their life I would sacrifice and consume that day so that I could live. The thought upset me in its clarity. I became a bit resistant to the sacrifice. I did it anyway, and thanked them sincerely.

Carmen Rita Menéndez

Chinese Vegetables

Gouache and Watercolor Painting

Karen Koshgarian

Prayer for Writing

I am a practical person, so I begin my prayer
by asking to write smaller and faster and more often.
I ask for impossible things—an ordered mind,
a neat internal Rolodex of scrumptious words,
an impressive array of metaphors,
like wild brown trout jumping freely into my mental creel.
I ask for better metaphors than that.

I light candles to the goddess and the muse, to Hestia and Erata,
for the freedom and tenacity to follow
each pregnant thought through its twisting, turning
and backtracking. I pray to give it birth on the page.

I save my secret prayers for something larger.
These are the quiet behests in the dark,
the ones spoken aloud only in solitude.
These prayers are for passion. For wild internal dogs
let loose to prowl my psyche in search of blood truths;
canines chomping on my bones,
their long noses turning up the mold and residue of my life
to find desire still shining.

I want to want. I want to dance it out on a page.
I want to hear unbridled craving drumming inside my frame.
I want to know the truth of me, the totally impractical
and shining truth that is mine, the fantastic mystical
bright orange, hot pink truth. I want letters of introduction
to that wild being hiding in the recesses.

This is my prayer, now whispered.
I pray for permission to be loud, verbose, wise.
I pray to pray with all my heart.

Gretchen Sentry

A Prayer for Winter

As the air burns our lungs
let us remember
the stillness of tombs
and be gladdened in cold
As leaves come brittle and brown
may we rejoice
in the promise of rest
the ease of sleep and renewal
May cats curl at our feet
and yawn
May the bitter taste of smoke
and damp
fill our nostrils
with remembrance
of springs past
and summers to come
May our blankets hold us
in secret
our skins preparing
to burst

Rose Lobel

A Writer's Prayer

A writer's prayer
begins on the fringe of mist
twisting around the body of a tree
and winding its way into the sky.
A writer's prayer
rests on the opening of a day
when the door opens
and the first thought
goes to wondering how the light will hit the tree
or if there will be mist clinging to the lavender.
A writer's body
is a body of wind
stirring up dirt and leaves,
falling into words
put together, carved and etched.
The ache of the world
can be held by the arch of a hand holding a pen.
The writer's body
is steeped slowly throughout the day
changing colors like tea water
moving from clear to brown, red, or a mustard yellow.
The body of a writer
is a political action
with each swing of a letter
each truth written
the world is broken open,
a vein of truth exposed.
A writer's prayer is for herself.
That she will hold to slowness
that she will hold to the beauty of a candle
that with the dirt and grit of living under her nails,
she will write her body into language.

Sarah Jones

Spring at Seventy

There is a sweetness to spring carried on ribbons of cool air. Wild blossoms open up in the forest and the orchards, with scents that are meant to seduce, draw in the bee, the hummingbirds, the heart. The air carries sweetness and prayers. On each breeze a memory, a plea, a wish.

I am becoming more a creature of habit. I rise with the light each morning. I breathe in the sweetness. I have before me an abundance of day. Each day growing, giving me more time to be myself, as opposed to that other self who travels at night, through darkness.

This year the light gives me more satisfaction. It is a calmer light. We are past the season of great flashes, past the season of cool gray light and haze. This light is creamy, soft, and gets into more corners. Even my shaded places are brighter. This light is quiet and steady, friendlier. What was hard is softened. What was impenetrable looks more inviting in this spring light. What once had jagged and rough outlines has been patted into a smoother shape, almost smooth enough to roll.

Yesterday my son asked me if I was happy. He asked deeply. He is trying to know what happiness is, what it looks like. It has always been a stranger to him.

I was surprised by the question. I blinked, as if the question itself was too bright. I answered, "Yes," and was unsettled by the truth of it. There are still a few rough places, things about my life that need tweaking. A few worn spots need reweaving, but this spring the light brings sweetness. Happy? It would be a waste of time not to be happy, and time is so precious now.

Each day there are a few more moments of light. It is as if they are spoon-fed to me. A few sips in the morning, a bit more time to contemplate, to luxuriate, to let new and old thoughts flow through me. I might even write them down. There is a little more light each evening. Time to plant, dig in the garden, watch swallows dine from evening air currents.

I am pleased the light creeps up on me like that. I could not bear to have it jump out of winter shadows, whole and blinding. I like having the time to acclimate, put my toes in, wade around, smell the pears and plums being created, smell the sweetness of crab apples being born.

This is the season of acceptance. This is a time of forgiving. Time to move dark things on their way. Newness is wanting to come into the light, so much sweetness about to blossom.

Gretchen Sentry

The Crowning

My small body is bowed
coifed with red shawl
I am the woman waiting at the well
who listens to croaking wood frogs
feels the serpent rising
thirsts for black winged women—
Vulture, Owl, and Raven

Shapeshifters
Sing new flesh onto old bone
Craft sharpened beaks
Carve all-seeing sight
Out of the still nights of imagining

As both Mother and Daughter
I call up turquoise waters
Swell seed and star
Paint purple green mountains

With my antlers I touch the earth and stars
my hooves paw the ground.
My graceful body quivers
with the synergy of spiraling light.
I wind a wreath of arbutus leaves round my head
Fragrant pink flowers perfume the air as I leap
over blue green waters

Birthing this third one—
the body of crone
whose head is crowning in my dreams

Sara Wright

Spiral Woman

Clay

Kathleen Marie Pouls

The Crone I Will Become

Her hair grows long and full and gray, and she moves with ease between the realms of solitude and community and the bower she shares with her beloved. She no longer visits the hiding places where she once took refuge. Instead, she lifts her hand in prayer, calling out the ten thousand beautiful names of God. She sits in meditation before her altar and enters the indwelling stillness that is her home. She dances with her sisters in moonlight, at home also among the redwoods and madrones.

She falls asleep to the lullaby of her own heartbeat, or perhaps sleeps entwined with her beloved, breathing out as he breathes in, her chest falling as his rises and they do not break the mammalian longing for skin on skin, even in sleep.

She stretches into yoga poses she once could not imagine, dances the hula on the beach, holds a baby in her arms. Yet so much has fallen away, walls, routines, the habits of personality, that it does not surprise her to spend less time in her body. Even the need for words evaporates for great stretches of time; she meditates without a mantra, watches steam rise from a cup of tea without writing a poem about it.

She sways in the wind like a willow; she stands in her essence, quiet and stately as the redwood standing sentinel at her door.

Mary Camille Thomas

THE COMING

OF GRACE

Our lives can sometimes feel like passages through harsh landscapes that shake us to our core. Yet these difficult passages bring us to our most profound transformations. In the midst of heartache and greatest need, we find that grace descends. And at the end of it all, we often discover that we have become someone new, stronger and more alive. These works touch the tender moments of heartache, illness and inner strangeness that we all experience at times. They illuminate the path of healing—when awe, self-love and grace touch our very being, leave us breathless, make us whole.

The Coming of Grace

If you come closer.
If you stand here, just, quiet in the gray of evening.
If you let the salt sea mist weave a cloak around you,
and meet your skin as if it were a wave,
as if it were a lover, enfolding.

If you come to the place where the ocean meets the sky.
Take a small boat, all the way out to where the universe began.
If you are quiet enough, then you will hear the singing.

In the heart of the land, stone.
In the belly of the ocean, fire.
The light of dawn takes her time to awaken you
on a sleepy shore a dozen continents from here
dreaming a memory of the first speaking of your true name.

Place the stone, carefully, in your mouth.
Put the fire in the palm of your hand.
Speak what you remember, but do not tell everything.
The heavens are open, and someone is always listening.
Even God, sometimes, is allowed to have his secrets.

Take your boat and tie it to the sunrise.
Place the flame in a crystal vase and put it on the table.
Bury the stone in the garden with the flowers.
Take off your cloak.
Have a long drink of the sea.

Even if you are lonely, you have been chosen to be here.
Even if you are afraid, someone is always beside you.
Behind the clouds are worlds too brilliant to imagine.
Behind your eyes is more than you could begin to know.

Bow to the sun.
Give her your hair to weave a rainbow in.
Though the day is long, and you walk a far distance to the sea,

its undulating rhythm will call in the night,
and let you down, finally, into sleep.

Ask for everything and do not worry.
Ask for nothing and be at peace.
Even God closes his eyes sometimes.
Even the sea is sometimes still.

At any moment, somewhere in the world, it is night.
You will walk on water when it is time.
Even this, too, will prove to have its season.

Johanna Courtleigh

In Impossible Darkness

Do you know how
the caterpillar
turns?
Do you remember
what happens
inside a cocoon?
You liquefy.
There in the thick black
of your self-spun womb,
void as the moon before waxing,
you melt
(as Christ did
for three days
in the tomb)
conceiving
in impossible darkness
the sheer
inevitability
of wings.

Kim Rosen

Faith

Faith blows invisible, like wind
rippling through a line of prayer flags.
Today not a breeze stirs, only
the memory of air on my skin.

> In the doldrums I cast a spell
> to raise the wind; I wait
> and watch for signs.

Sometimes faith surrounds me
like a blanket, soft, warm,
holds me like a lover
shaping his body to mine.

> In the chill I reach blindly
> into the bag of yarns,
> knit a companion of prayer.

Some days faith pours into me
like richness I never earned.
Diamonds of sunlight leap off the ocean;
I shine from inside out.

> In the darkness I imagine
> the coming of day. I remember
> the earth turns and turns.

Linda Holiday

This Life

Like you
I go on living
As though this life
Is not utterly horrific
And utterly exquisite.
As though this life
Does not bring you to your knees
Again and again
Does not give you wings to soar
Over the canyons with ecstasy.

I, for once,
Want to run to the village square
Tear my clothes in fury
Shake my fists to the heavens
And roar with rage
Foaming at the mouth.
I want to fall on my knees in gratitude
Let the rain of Grace fall upon me
Turn my tear-washed face
Towards the sky
And sing the devastating beauty of
This life.

Maria Papacostaki

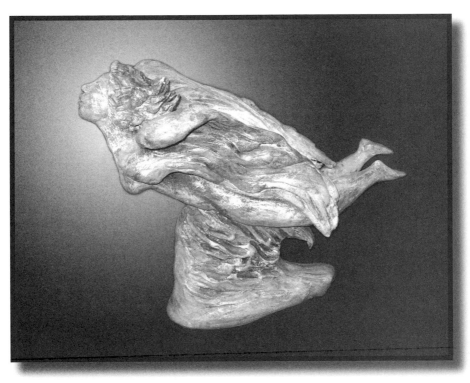

Flying Recognized

Clay, Patina

Kathleen Marie Pouls

Prayer

That he might find his flint
lost years ago;
slipped from his pocket
when he climbed into the limbs
of the great oak
to meet his first love.

He did not miss it then.

Her light was enough.
And he could not have known
that he couldn't warm himself
at the fire of another forever,
or that standing in her light
he would cast so large a shadow.

It was the sorrowing season that brought him to his knees.

Even the oak bowed low
beneath the weight of that winter.
Some of its limbs broken
and his own heart,
fenced behind its icicled cage of ribs,
twisted like a bow drill between his frozen fingers.
Twisting, twisting and still no spark.

This is my prayer then:
that he bend his face to the frosted ground,
his falling tears
the first spring thaw,
unearthing what he'd thought he'd lost
from its mudded sleep.

This is my prayer:
That he might find his flint.
Strike it against steel.
Burst into Holy flame.

J. Esme Jel'enedra

Your Task

You may choose a charmed blade
with carved and jeweled shaft,
address it in sacred tongue
as sister.

Or you may seize a simple knife
from your consecrated kitchen
knowing that the blade chose you
and serves you.

Your work remains the same: you must cut
away, and cut away, until everything
that is not you is gone.

Your pain is real, and vital.
You will bleed.
The truth will stay.

Cara Lamb

My Own Strange Song

In Praise of the Divine

It is immense this lassitude I will not recognize—
the word itself an enemy upon the shores I walk
late nights beneath a sallow, hangnail moon
near you, always near you. Dark stranger to me,
wild rose in an open field of crab grass, sun burnt dry.
A finer woman than I would tear her fingers raw
to uproot the choking greens cinching this wild flower's waist.

Midnight blue blown down the mountainside—
soft the sea between us lapping our backsides.

Cacophony. I've always loved the word.
A deafening jumble of noise. No voice rising
to the top. No whine singled out. No whip
or whir winnowed free. Blessed be
the metal barrel full of unrelenting sound I run from.

I have hungered for you long past my frozen limbs
and tried to stop the flow of gall,
bitter vinegar full of herbs I've wintered in. My skin
is now a ragged tatter, my heart a bursting plum.

Round, round past the bitter moon, I cry—
harrowed woman, a nest of blackbirds
in my hair. Who, if not you, will plow me
under until I turn up rich, moist and brown?

I am prone to extremes of joy and madness.
Nights, I cull nits from my hair and feed them
to lice who laid them, or pull you to myself
to rest in you the pounding drumbeat in my bones.

Arctic rasp. Long I have pulled this sled
across a sea of frozen white—no strength to hold
my body tight against desire this tundra spawns.

There are no salmon returning, rising or dying
in me. No pink muscle throwing herself homeward,
not a single ripple in the sea of cold. No blunt crack
of the ice breaking anywhere. Wherefore, I return
to the sea I am from to languor there,
hangnail moon rising, hair full of blackbirds shrieking.

Sharon Rodgers Simone

Yatagarasu / Faith

Reduction Lino Print

Gaza Bowen

Unsprung Root

The underbelly of night
swallows light
in swift and shuddering sweeps

The wing of the crow
slashes through the darkness
a sharpened beak
sinks into fresh death
still quivering with surrender

And then stillness
spreads like a puddle
from the fathomed depths
the dark of dark
the irreducible
the unentangled point
from which direction invents itself

Stillness
and then vibration
silence
and then sound

Resonating—
rippling through the marrow
a deeper rhythm
thrummed from the unsprung root

Karen Sallovitz

Lessons from the Edge

Getting cancer took me to the edge of my life, to a place where I fell to the death of the self I had known before. The identity in which I had known myself, counted on, lived from, instantly disappeared. My compass was broken. Feeling lost in space, and at the same time caged. Broken dreams, will, and heart. Scary enough to want to wrap myself up where nothing could touch me. A nightmare I could not wake up from, and yet I was asked to walk among the living. Time languished, oozing slowly over every moment, then just as easily left me dizzy as it sped by. Always night. Each day wondering if I would eventually wake up. Everything I wanted to avoid encircled me like unwelcome houseguests that wouldn't leave. All the sharp-nailed victims digging into my flesh, wanting my attention. The devil who tried to kill me and steal my soul. The have-to's and the should's clamoring for my time and energy. And the loss, eternal loss.

I thought I might drown in my own tears. Little did I know those tears would actually carry my poor tired body and spirit through this most difficult of times. Some new and old parts of myself would gently move in with me, making less space for the encroachers. New rooms were being built even while the old rooms were being deconstructed. So much going on right under my nose. The empty cell blossomed into a warm womb in which I could welcome back my orphaned children one by one, giving them the best lap they ever had.

In the midst of my deep aloneness, a Divine Feminine presence made herself known on my first day of radiation. As everyone scurried out of the room to save themselves from being contaminated, she came and held my head with her loving hands. She never failed to show up, five days a week for seven weeks, always there. Her presence has informed my new life. I kiss the ground she is part of. Not in my wildest dreams would I have imagined feeling this gratitude—for what took my life has actually given me life.

For me, living at the edge means navigating the fine line between outer and inner worlds. Initially having both feet in my inner world, and then slowly, very slowly, learning to have a foot in each. Then slowly, very slowly, learning to move back and forth between and together, trying not to forget where my true home lies. Remembering that I am made mostly of water. Remembering my animal nature. Remembering to see through my spiritual lenses. Remembering what it feels like to be left for dead, with vultures making their rounds. Remembering the preciousness of my life and whatever time I have left. Remembering I am not alone. Even when I feel totally forsaken, my Divine Feminine is always with me. Remembering that achieving greatness is really about loving myself and others. Climbing the highest mountain takes less courage than the path of learning to love.

After much rest and recovery, I endeavor to live at the edge of my life as much as I can, though I frequently have to take a deep breath and renew this intention. It helps when I remember that though the edge is sometimes deep, dark, and scary, it is also exciting, juicy, and alive! Traversing this ledge takes much courage, steadfastness and loving patience. It is life at its deepest and most thrilling, and for me, the only kind worth living.

Carol Gaab

Sankofa Love Song

Here's the kind of faith my mother has: she wears a crisp winter-white blouse to her chemotherapy treatments, unfastening three buttons and holding it open for the rust-red iodine wash and IV connection to the port just above her heart.

When I was a child, Mother went to Richmond to nurse and companion our Aunt Alice near the end of her journey with cancer. Alice died in her arms as Mother sang a sweet old hymn. On the long drive home, Mother pulled her car off the highway to cry all the tears she had held back. That night, she gently explained that while we had hoped for Alice's healing on earth, she had received a more perfect healing in heaven.

Five years ago, after complications following her mastectomy, Mom awoke in the hospital, uncertain whether she would live to see daybreak. The thought came: "A breath here or in heaven would be just as sweet." She lives with that certainty every day.

After a break from treatment, she showed me how her eyebrows have grown back. When she removes her knitted hat, she has almost an inch of soft, downy hair. She no longer runs her hand over her naked pate as if to console it, no longer exclaims upon looking in the mirror, "My poor little head!" But it is, she insists, still too soon to go hatless.

Reviewing the new CT scan findings with her oncologist, Mother learns of an increase in the size and number of inoperable lesions. There is no way to guess whether chemotherapy might buy enough good time to offset the side effects.

Mom asks the doc point-blank what he predicts for her life expectancy. He replies directly, "Mrs. Oliver, you have already outlived your expected life span." Mother's hands are raised like a champion's, pumping the air overhead with clear delight at having outlived her doctor's best guess.

A week later I ask if she's made a decision about the chemotherapy. "Not yet, but I will by next week." She is not troubled either way, she says, and I can tell from her voice that she means it. She mentions that she has switched to the 9 a.m. aerobics class, which is more rigorous than her customary 10 a.m. one. "I don't like going so early, but the workout feels really good."

Cancer can claim but it cannot extinguish.

In the predawn dark I awaken, and immediately begin to visualize the cancer being sifted from Mother's being. This time, I am startled to see that I am the filter removing the cancer cells. Our bodies pass through one another. Every cancer cell is culled out and rises to my skin to form a harmless white powder that just blows away. This is a novel variation on the visual prayer I send up day and night.

It reminds me of the small lies we are taught as children, like the notion that there is such a thing as a solid object. Instead, we are all galaxies of whirling subatomic specks. In theory, two bodies could pass through one another, their molecules politely bowing as they slide in the spaces between electrons, protons and the rest. Coming as close to blending as two beings might come, then moving back to their separate trajectories. The dance of mother and child, gestation and birth, love and letting go.

We would hold her feet to this planet if we could, but she has other plans. Watching Mother let go with such grace, I remember playing on overhead bars—how you must release one rung to swing forward to the next, and how during that arc, you can fly.

There is an Egyptian myth about the weighing of one's heart. Only if the heart is as light as a feather may one proceed to the afterlife. My mother's heart, for all it contains, will be ether-light against the dead weight of the feather.

In one of her essays, Mom wrote "I can still see it in my memory window." I polish that window often, even as I look for the dawning day in the window of things yet to come.

My granddad used to sit on his gravestone every so often to have an easy chat with my grandmother, buried just beside the spot reserved for him. Mom rests in her mother's rose velvet rocker when she wants an extra measure of peace. In an age when people change and places are lost, the remembrance of love is the surest source of home.

When Mom got cancer I turned everything into a mantra of hope. My computer password was her name followed by "forever." But after several recurrences, I traded hope for faith, replacing "forever" with "home."

It leaves her more room to fly.

Sarah Knorr

At the Hospital

1.
Your blood
in bag, basin, and jar—
raspberry red
glows in the blanched clinic.
I look around for my customary resentment
but it has left by the door.
Instead, I covet your beautiful blood.
I want it contained in receptacles.
I want it staunched.

Just as the galaxy will not relinquish
one single star or planet,
just so do I cherish every drop
of your vermillion life;
life so potent—
you can bleed such blood
cry such tears
bear such pain.

2.
Once there was a time
when your life flowed like an accidental river
into my ocean.
My ocean foamed and crashed on your shores
thoughtless.
Our waters commingled,
created an estuary.
I did not ask for my waves
to be dissipated in this delta.
You did not ask for your sweet waters
to grow salt.

Perhaps there were other destinations
for our separate waters
one so rough, the other calm.

But the estuary insisted
conscquence of gravity
and Coriolis effect.

Now the estuary has its own integrity.
It sustains a universe
distinct from any other,
mysterious as any other;
it never drains completely
nor blooms poisonous.

3.
This time when I drove you
to the hospital
I did not panic.
I felt your pain
was manageable.
As I absorbed it, it dissipated.
It would not go on forever.
It would resolve.
Your courage, my patience
capable together of healing
this too.

An odd development:
that your physical debility
should feel like my own.
That I should see myself in you
after all these years.

Suddenly, your illness,
your every dilemma
hold me fascinated
as if there were nothing else
I'd rather fix mine eye upon.

Elizabeth Tozier

The Loom

A Dream

I see myself standing on the earth, eyes closed, arms raised slightly from my sides, palms open and facing forward. Behind me I perceive something flowing out—an energetic band that extends like a river, supple and strong, farther than I can see beyond the horizon.

In front of me, myriad threads move towards and enter my body. Behind me, the blanket of my being, woven now into a pattern, a story, stretches out, alive and moving.

My body is a loom: energies enter, touch, intertwine, and the fabric of life emerges.

I am studiously attentive to the converging threads, the loom of my body, the patterned blanket streaming into infinity. What astonishes me is the perfection of it all. This woven story carries no tangled threads, no knots, no holes—only a seamless weaving.

What is equally surprising is that I am not the weaver. I do not create the pattern. I offer myself and help bring forth the pattern simply by being.

I am sleeping, and awake, aware. I understand there is nothing but love and beauty here—only love and beauty.

Valerie Wolf
Grandmother White Bear

Self Portrait as a Tree

Tempera on Paper

Cathy Williams

Ceremony

I want to marry myself
an excited voice whispers
as I speed down the long farm road,
past fields of blue sky,
breathing in spaciousness,
a gentle wind moving through my bones.
Lightheaded and giddy
I laugh to myself.

Dare I say this out loud?
Breaking all the rules
passed down through the generations
who told me who I should be,
what I should want,
how I should live?

I want to marry myself!
This time hearing my own voice.
Tasting the words
as they vibrate through my tongue and body,
echoing the safe chamber of my car.

Do I even know what this means?
Some part of me does.
As usual she is several steps ahead.
Rooted in instinct
I let the words be spoken
again and again,
knowing they will lead me.

Trust, she says,
you belong only to yourself.
A virgin for the first time,
the veil gently flows across my face.

Carol Gaab

Keep Walking

It is a good road.
Its mean passages and dark turns
Are but a fleck in the great sky.
At night ten thousand galaxies
Send us their light.
Who knows who is praying for us
Beyond the bent window?
The ancient pebbles
Bleeding in our shoes
Are the stuff that keeps
The road held tight.
It is a good road.
Beauty too abundant to behold.
Tell the shattered girl
Whose skin is bruised
Her life beams beyond her.
Everything
Is larger than we thought.

Carolyn Brigit Flynn

To Call Myself

To call myself beloved
I would not be taller
or younger, or more beautiful.
White hair would still creep
like sticks gathered for
a wood rat's nest.

I would not be smarter or wiser,
more eloquent or quick witted.
I would have the same slow cadence,
answers arriving long after
the question suspended in air
was carried away by the wind.

My head might be held a little higher
my steps slightly firmer on the earth.
Nothing from the outside would change,
except perhaps the way I looked towards dawn
gentling myself to rise.

Lea Haratani

Blue

Acrylic on Canvas Paper

Hannah Peabody

A Poem

What if I was innocent
and everything I touched became
more lovely?

What if I chose colors to please me
and when I went walking
every green and glorious thing
was a dear part of my
own self?

What if I could only make more
beauty here,
and the blue and the gray sky
that hawks fly through
was my wide open freedom?

And the warmth of the sun?
All mine.
And if I am seen it will be the firelight
and the birdsong
that I am.

Nancy Grace

Inculcation

Mother, sister, daughter,
partner, lover, friend,
crone, widow, orphan,
pigeon, spider, stranger—
Lay down your burden.
There is a reservoir
waiting to be filled
with your tears.

The girl made of salt
longs to return to the sea.
Dissolve yourself.

I will adorn the sarcophagus of our pasts with lilac,
rosemary, candied skulls, a mosaic of photographs.
Ornate shall be this memory
so that it may never lose its splendor,
so that it may radiate through Earth's vibration.
I will make fresh again the face of death,
the pulsing of veins, the changing verbiage of days, the wreckage.

Come, beloved, be loved,
for already the rain
is rising from the ground.
The sky thirsts for your anguish,
and longs to gather you
in frocks of cirrus clouds
and release you over the desert,
which has prepared itself for your coming:
Aridity is only the symptom of a long wait.
The time is ripe for the flood.

Take these inculcations into your womb.
Speak them when you rise up
and when you lie down,
in the place where you momentarily make your home

and in the heart where your soul resides.
Remove the bindings from your eyes.
Let these words become a signpost
that you may cultivate a forest of living waters,
sprouting from your every pore.
May you sweat your prayers,
nourish your fingertips and your hip bones,
and pour the sustenance of these gritty moments
daily over your body.
Shower your spirit with this one phrase of truths and histories:
I am alive.
I am born. Again. And again.
I jump off the edge. Every moment.
I am alive.

Rae Abileah

Note: An inculcation is a teaching or prayer repeated regularly in order to impress it upon one's mind. This poem, which is for the divine feminine in each of us, is an alternate version of the V'Ahavta, *the Jewish prayer that commands one to speak the words of love of God "when you sit at home, and when you walk along the way, and when you lie down and when you rise up..."*

I Am Nothing
Without My Dead

This beautiful line from a poem by Deena Metzger speaks to the essential, mysterious connection between the living and the dead. The older indigenous traditions of the earth hold the ancestors at the center of spiritual life, and teach that the living must hold their dead in a daily, conscious way. These writings and art hold stories of dying, grief, mourning and relinquishing beloved ones. They tell the stories of the ancestors, and acknowledge both the joy and the heartache of touching their legacies. In these works we remember that we live in a web, a linked chain of death and birth, ancestor and newborn, the always-connected spiral of human life.

The Cup Runneth Over

for Sandra, in her last days

I hold the cup to your lips
tip it slightly—
only a few drops of water trickle in
so you can swallow
without drowning

We repeat this ritual
sip after sip
as minutes turn to hours—
me, offering the cup
at the parched edge of your lips
you, seeking the drops
like a fledgling
fallen from the nest
looking up, immeasurable gratitude
in your clear, blue eyes

and I wonder
can anything, ever again
be as holy as this.

Kate Aver Avraham

Last Moments

Weeping on my deck,
four hundred miles north,
I cup my father's last moments in my hands
as prayer, a hope
that in the final seconds, alone,
struggling for breath
he lifted up—surprised—
floated like milkweed   oat grass   dandelion spores
past the clogged trachea tube,

looked down and laughed!
Free, finally, from the IV
        the dripping meds
        and brown sludge
        the dried husk of his body
no longer tethered to the catheter tubes
bulging against his neck.

Look! He shouted
turned a cartwheel in the stale hospital air
danced across the blood-splattered tiles of the ceiling, giddy
at finally cutting the rope
he'd given into my keeping.
But now, he smiled
What have I been so afraid of?

And thinned
became thistle down   oak leaves   redwood pollen
breezing over the plants in my garden,
a redtail catching thermals
spreading glad wings as he circled my house
one fierce cry before
I couldn't see him anymore.

Marcy Alancraig

Sliding Down the Great Mother's Breast

We birthed her. Like a team of midwives, we guided her through the maze of her becoming. We wiped her forehead, smoothed her hair, and held a damp rag to her parched lips. We lifted her to her feet when she said, "Up! Up!" Her son held her in his arms, swaying to music only the two of them could hear.

We sat, sang, massaged, chanted, and prayed. In turn, we'd say, *Go to the Mother. Push out through your crown. Let go, let go.* I reminded her of a dream she'd had in which she was told she knew how to die, that it was as easy as sliding down the milk ducts of the Great Mother's breast.

At last the moment came. A quiet breath, a long silence, a deep sigh. She was gone.

We six women left the room so her son and partner could be alone with her.

"What do we do now?" one asked.

I suggested we could wash her body.

"I don't know how," another said. "I've never done it before."

"I haven't either," I said, "but our bodies must remember—women have done this for thousands of years."

I ran water in a basin. Someone added an essential oil and someone else found washcloths. We washed her body and anointed it with lotion while we sang and chanted. I selected a green dress patterned with roses, perfect for burial in the arms of Mother Earth. I combed her hair. Someone placed flowers in her hands.

Later, as I left the hospice, I saw movement beneath a small dogwood tree, its boughs heavy with red-tipped flowers. A newly emerged moth, large and velvety brown, with circles like eyes on its still-damp wings, fluttered on the pine mulch readying itself for flight. I watched for a long time, hoping to ensure its safety.

I knew that I couldn't. I was gone before it flew away.

Peggy Tabor Millin

Goddess

Clay

Susan Rothenberg

Lillian

Next on my list of residents to visit in the nursing home was a woman named Lillian. I'd arrived early to make my rounds. The activities director had made a list of those persons she thought would especially benefit from my healing songs. Lillian was in room 312 in bed C in the subacute ward, but when I entered her room, beds A and B were vacant. Bed C was by the window with the curtain drawn, hiding the view of the world outdoors. The room was dim.

Although nothing especially had been said about Lillian beforehand, I could tell she was dying. A veritable bag of bones, she sat bent down in her wheelchair beside her bed. A nasty looking mess of freshly vomited food lay in a puddle on the bedding, spilling beside her lunch tray. I quickly looked away and back to the sick old woman before me. "Would you like for me to sing a special song for you?" I inquired. She nodded a wisp of approval, eyes cast down, hopelessly attached to a face and neck unable to rise to the occasion.

I'll be loving you, always … I began, crooning gently, *with a love that's true, always.* Lillian clucked an approval, mouthing the word "always" each time we came around to it.

Days may not be fair, always … but that's when I'll be there, always … I swayed rhythmically back and forth as I sang to Lillian, doing my best to cover her in soothing sounds, giving her a "sound bath." I was standing quite close beside her chair, but since I was standing up I towered above her, and our eyes were not meeting.

I hunkered down in front of her now, catching her eyes for the final refrain, *Not for just an hour, not for just a day, not for just a year, but always.*

We stared curiously at one another, eyeballs to eyeballs. Lillian's were huge, rather vacant, dark with secret stories she had no way to tell me. Against the severe hollows of her cheeks, her eyes seemed rather ghastly to behold.

I started another song, one that just popped up from somewhere inside of me. *Let me call you sweetheart,* I sang hopefully, searching for Lillian inside those bug eyes, *I'm in love with you …*

I adjusted my gaze to take in her whole face and head. Thick white hairs launched recklessly out of her chin and tufts of gray hair broke out all over the top of her head. This was a woman who had aged hard, with rough, raggedy edges. Fascinated, I sang on through my observations, *Let me hear you whisper that you love me, too.*

Lillian craned her head, turning her eyes, bulging sockets and all, and seemed to find me there, crouched before her with my guitar on my knees, singing this love song to her, to us, to both of us.

Keep the love light burning, in your eyes so blue …

Shivers ran along my spine, as always happens when I am taking in something bigger than myself. Here I was, singing a love song to an archetypal hag. But "hag" comes from the Greek word for "sacred grove," for "holy."

Let me call you sweetheart … I shivered again, as I understood somewhere deep inside of me—in a place only the music knew—that with Lillian's silent help, I was singing for myself as well. We both had become Crone: ancient song, timeless text. In one breath the Scorned and Forgotten One arose between us, and in the next, the Wise Woman. What a strange and wondrous duet, this song of honoring, of remembering, of singing over the bones, re-fleshing us each back to life; even as She, singing from within me, also sat before me in the guise of Lillian, wasting away, dying.

My song continued to come and I could do nothing but serve its purposes until, as mysteriously as it had begun, I arrived at its end, and to the end of my time with Lillian. *I'm in love with you …* My voice trailed off into silence. I patted Lillian's hand, thanked her and left to make my rounds. "I'll be back in two weeks," I told her, not knowing if she understood, or heard me, yet certain our souls had touched each other in a way I would always carry with me.

Two weeks later on Monday morning, I came to make my rounds. Reporting to the activity director's office, I asked if she had any particular instructions for my visit that day. There was difficult news: Lillian had died a few days before. We observed a moment of silence, words too cumbersome and awkward to try.

In memoriam, Lillian's astonishing, frightful, beautiful face, her high, frail cheekbones and those enormous eyes are forever impressed upon me. Through them I was able to witness the visage of the Crone, to see my own ancient face. We sang of Life, and we sang of Death, and knew that Love was all we had. And was all we needed.

Let me call you sweetheart, I'm in love with You.

Marcia Singer

The Funeral

After Allen Ginsberg

Like crows,
in our mourning clothes
we followed slowly
behind my mother's coffin
in the midsummer heat

None of us cried
it was too hot for that
and the night before
we had kept wake

In a cemetery overlooking
the Salonika Bay and
the TV antennas
we buried my mother in
the dry earth
The wreaths had already wilted
smelling sickly sweet
Not one shading tree for
us to stand under
The priest in his black
robes mumbled prayers with
the speed of sunlight
as if they did not matter to my mother

Then he poured wine
and spread boiled wheat
and pomegranate seeds
over the new grave
according to our customs

The pigeons, having seen
this many times before
flew down on the grave
not thinking of the dead

or the living
to feast on the seeds
Lord Lord Lord coo coo coo
Lord Lord Lord coo coo coo
   Lord

Maria Papacostaki

Ohio

As it turned out, I was the one to volunteer to scatter the ashes. It was a beautiful day in Ohio. The sun was shining, and most of the trees' leaves were on the ground.

We went to the park where my mother loved to picnic. We walked down a well-traveled trail. Several of us were dressed in black and we were an odd sight walking on a path in the woods. We had walked quite a way when by consensus, as a group, without a word, we all stopped to admire a huge old oak. Across the way, off the path, was another, and it clung like a queen waving from her balcony over a beautiful arroyo. We seemed to wander over there, of one mind, peering over the cliff to admire the view that oak tree had.

This seemed to be the right place and moment and I made a sinuous line of ash with what felt to me like a dance gesture so that the line lay along the edge of the cliff, inside the area delineated by the tree. At the end the line curved back, like my mother waving goodbye from her porch until you rounded the corner of her street.

My brother-in-law, who has never asked me for anything, asked me "Can we cover the ashes?" I asked him, "Would you feel better?" "Yes," he said, and we covered the ashes with leaves. Brown, dried oak leaves and a few others with brilliant color. Chaney means oak grove, coming from *chen* in French, oak.

And so we left her there under an oak tree with winter coming. And she was there for me that day in the woods when I felt wild with sadness, she said it was okay, it was all okay. It was okay to leave her there. Leave her there alone in the woods to become part of the land she loved so much. Her Ohio, her central Ohio.

And my father alone in the lake, the great lake that he loved, Lake Erie. My mother on the land. My father in the water. The land and the water of my family for so many generations. Ohio.

Libby Chaney

One Hundred Year Old Apple Tree

Photograph, Big Prairie, Michigan

Terese Armstrong

Life After Death

January: another year begins, nearly four years after Earl was swept away by flood waters. So much of my focus has been on survival, on stilling the pain. "It is not the pain that matters," Stephen Levine noted, "but how we choose to relate to it."

I am now choosing life after death.

Part of moving ahead involves saying goodbye. At least for now. My sister Betsy offers to accompany me on a pilgrimage to Flemington, New Jersey, where Earl's remains are buried in the Higgins family cemetery. Betsy's sons, Devin, an old soul at age six, and Ryan, an eleven-month old bundle of energy and happiness, are in the back seat of the van. As we ride through the serene winter countryside, Betsy gently tries to prepare my nephews for their first visit to a graveyard. "Do you know what a cemetery is?" she asks.

"It's where dead people live," Devin responds quickly. I smile. Wise child!

The cemetery is on a hill overlooking the town where Earl's father grew up. As we wind up the narrow lane to the gravesite, I flash back to my only other visit here, when we finally laid Earl to rest. Earl's father, a lay minister for the deaf, officiated over the simple graveside service, his graceful hands signing a heartfelt prayer even as tears streamed down his cheeks. I nearly collapsed with weeping and exhaustion, following my lonely and intense nine-month-long ordeal waiting for the recovery and identification of Earl's remains. Earl's mother quickly grabbed my arm to support me. She is the strongest woman I have ever known, to have lost two of her triplet sons within a period of five years and yet have the capacity to uphold me.

Nearing the Higgins family plot, Betsy pulls over and lets me out, indicating that she will join me once she has parked the van a little way up the hill and bundled up the children. In truth, she is allowing me a moment alone, to absorb the impact of seeing Earl's grave again. All is stillness and peace in the soft, gray light of the wintry afternoon. I take a deep breath and study the gravestone resting flat against the earth.

As my heart begins to swell with sorrow, suddenly little Ryan comes running down the hill toward me, a grin a mile wide on his face. With arms outstretched, as if we haven't seen one another in years, he races over to me, plants his feet smack in the middle of Earl's gravestone, and hugs me. Tears fill my eyes. This child symbolizes life embracing me, welcoming me, inviting me to play again.

"The kid's got no respect," Betsy laughs as she and Devin join us at Earl's grave. She gently sets her hand on my shoulder and gives me a reassuring hug.

"I miss Earl," says older, wiser Devin, who remembers days of hunting Easter eggs, making ice cream, boating on the lake at the cabin in the mountains, and playing ball with Earl and me.

"Me, too," I whisper, "me, too." I lay two yellow roses and a small herbal wreath made of rosemary, thyme, sage, and lavender on the grave, and whisper goodbye to Earl. The sweet herbal aroma fills the chill air and conjures up images of the Shakespeare herb garden that Earl and I planted together in Colorado.

As delicate flakes of snow begin to fall, I think about the great unknown and wonder what future life I will build. I could say a "happy" one, but I am not sure what that means any more. Perhaps it is enough to build a life that is loving, not demanding, flexible, not rigid, tolerant, not self-righteous…a life that does not fear the depths and rejoices in the heights…a life that faces itself squarely and chants, "This I am…this I have been…this I am becoming!"

"Let's go get some hot chocolate!" Betsy says, shivering, her breath making ghosts in the cold air. Devin and Ryan laugh and stumble over one another, clambering up the hill towards the parked van. As we leave the cemetery, I silently reflect on the quest that has brought me to this singular point in time.

The grace I have been allowed through the life I shared with Earl and the devastation of his death is in realizing that there is an open, flexible, compassionate way of relating to everything we experience, including natural disasters and sudden death. It is not so much a process of learning how to "get over" a profound loss, but rather how to allow it to be there, lightly, gently, like a fine thread woven forever into the tapestry of who we are.

Nancy J. Rigg

If You Died

If you died I'd get floral sheets and fluffy pastel towels
and always know which drawer the scotch tape was in
and the scissors. I'd put all the silverware

in the dishwasher sharp points down.
And throw out all the coffee mugs
that didn't match or weren't cute

and get rid of the garbanzo beans and the pickles
in the refrigerator. There would be neat stacks
in the garage—water and canned goods

and flashlights and batteries and extra toilet paper.
I'd never leave the seat up.
If you died I'd still light candles on the table

when I ate dinner. For a while.
Then I probably wouldn't eat
and then only eat out with friends

and then only eat home alone
from plastic containers
and cartons with the same fork over and over again

and look at your empty chair
and push the pepper grinder to your silent side of the table.
I'd only have half as much laundry, and never light a fire.

Once in a while I'd reach in your closet
and take one of your shirts and
rub it on my face

and down my chest
and breathe in the scent and cry.
And I'd sleep with that shirt on my pillow all night.

And put it on in the morning, wrinkled,
and stay home for days,
maybe even a week

with unopened mail and unanswered calls
wondering why I ever wanted to be without you.
But you're alive and with your genetics

you will probably be 102 like your father
or 101 like your mother.
So now I have the luxury.

I can't wait to hear you leave,
the car engine in the distance.
I can't wait for my own time.

Only just now I realized that we breathe
the same molecules.
And when you die I will be gasping for air.

Cheryl Gettleman

What the Meadow Gave Seventeen Years Later

Quintet for Nathan

1.
I lie, belly down, in the dry autumn meadow
golden grasses cushion my flesh, my sweating
desire to remember.

I rest my cheek against the mounding earth
the way a baby would splay across its mother's chest
when the nipple is empty.

I am like this a long time, or maybe
it is only a moment that seems
like the prone forever we dream of.

2.
Though nothing I dream of
can bring you back
to lie beside me in this umber field.

Not a hundred dreams of raven
flying until she returns from
the blue-black canyon of death.

Not a thousand wishes blown
from the seed fluff of cottonweed
split open by copper slants of sun.

Not the tawny-furred coyote
mythic head bent skyward, howling
for one lost pup.

Nothing will ever bring you back.

3.
And yet, this meadow grit
that presses against my skin

also mends

this ground that stores the seasons
in its womb of dark dirt

warms me

and when I smell the musk
of earth's grasp on roots

I can finally remember you beyond the dying,

4.
can finally see
your amber-brown eyes again,
the way you rolled your fingers into fists
then flapped your thin arms
up and down in rhythm to a song,
the perfect V at the nape of your neck
when you leaned over the table to color,
the cleft in your slightly jutting chin...

5.
...which I can hardly distinguish now
from a crevice in the granite cliff above me

and the amber eyes of autumn leaves
that blink when they flutter down

and your hands, fir branches, waving
in the deep blue wind blowing

across this meadow

where I lie, belly down
holding the warm, dry ground

of you.

Kate Aver Avraham

The Homecoming

1

When my son David called last February with the news that my brother's ashes had been found in my parents' attic thirty-two years after his suicide, I was shattered. It was early morning and I was barely awake when my son asked me if I wanted him to bring the ashes to Maine. "Of course," I screamed into the phone in a mindless explosion of grief. I was desperately trying to take it all in, my parents lying to me about brother's burial for all these years, the haunting and baffling nightmares that I had every year about my brother's broken body being stolen away before he could be buried.

As it turned out, the two-month lapse that occurred between this brutal conversation and my son's actual visit gave me the time to prepare myself for my brother's interment. Although I made few preparations on the outside beyond choosing a spot, inside I was slowly making a radical adjustment. Betrayal birthed gratitude. My beloved soul twin was coming home to rest in a place that he would have loved. And this was the only thing that mattered.

2

The day is overcast. My son follows me to the spot. We both kneel on the wet ground and carve out by hand a small depression against the gray creviced stone. The Great Bear Goddess moves through the leaves that crunch under my knees, her solid presence reflected in the humpbacked moss-covered granite looming in front of us. Trillium rock. We are surrounded by water and woods; the stream slowing my heartbeat as I merge with each leaf and twig and the heady earth scent of early spring in the mountains. I am still on my knees when I open the box. The bones are fragments. Their fragility surprises me—the richness of texture and color like desert sands and the crinkled eyes of the peyote cactus glowing from distant stars. As I sift his body through my hands and pour him into the rich moist ground, the fine white dust caught by a puff of wind swirls for a moment and settles around us, casting chalky shadows over papery brown beech leaves. The soothing sound of the rushing water behind me pours through the veins and arteries of my body, loosening the rigid cross that had lodged itself in my back, my conscious surrender a healing. Each of my cells feels my brother's visceral presence as I gather the last precious fragments from the bottom of the box, getting up to move to the water's edge to release them into the stream's clear water. Scooping water into a cup, I pour it into the depression, letting the water flow over the remainder of his ashes, softening thirty-two years of brittle and parched bone scorched by summers of attic heat. And still on my knees I bow my head as I gently press the moist soil back over him—weeping—closing a heart circle in time.

3

"His death has haunted you all your life." I hear my son's words as if from a great distance, along with my wordless reply. The need to touch him one last time. To say goodbye. I feel my son's hand touching my back for one precious moment. The two Davids. Both of them Beloved.

4

That night I dreamed that my face, fragile as an eggshell and made of fine white bone china, was cracking. The fracture was jagged, running from under my left eye and descending like steep steps, the fissure walked across my face to meet my lower right jaw.

5

One year later the memory remains sharp and clear. April 22, 2004— the spring day when time stretched herself out like a rubber band to touch infinity. The power of nature's grace—the crack opened so effortlessly. Even the woodland ground was soft. It was as if the earth had been waiting to receive my brother's body—the bones that had hungered for the light of being held in the arms of those who could love. I had just planted trailing arbutus with fragrant pink blossoms that would soon creep over the ground towards the spot where his ashes would become new soil. Two days into his burial the trillium cast their nets for me and I dug three across the road to plant at the grave site, asking the earth to receive these gifts in his memory.

That first week, turkeys scratched through pine needles and brown leaves searching for tasty seeds, the ducks waddled by on their way to the birdseed, and the deer came and pawed up new ground. When the red-tailed hawk swooped down out of the air that first night and perched on a branch just over the place that he lay, regarding me with one fierce yellow eye, I knew my brother would never be alone here, for this bird was my brother's totem. How could I have imagined then that this hawk would be only the first of so many to visit? For ten days after my brother's homecoming the shrill "keeeeing" cries of red-tailed hawks soared over my head and flooded the skies above my house, driving the other birds away. And whenever I looked out the window down towards the brook I was comforted by the sight of trillium rock rising out of the ground like a whale, warming him as she basked in the sun. With both of us caught between worlds for decades, it still amazes me that my brother and I eventually met on this edge between stream and wood. For a moment we rested, even as we gathered strength for the next part of our respective journeys. The veil grows thinner between us with each spiral turn.

Sara Wright

Mama on the Street

After Mother died and I was back home in Mill Valley, I was walking down the street, and I thought it would be nice to have Mother with me, so I invited her, she was there already, and I did not have to slow my pace except for the dog, and that was nice for me, nice for me, not to slow my pace, not to slow my pace for Mother. I remember when I had to hurry up for Mother, had to hurry, hurry, hurry, to keep up with Mother, and then she got slower, and slower, and you know, I kind of enjoyed that slower pace, keeping down with Mother.

So I was walking down the street with Mother and my dog, and Mother was like a figure in a Chagall painting, kind of up above me, kind of drawn with a French curve, dreamy. And I was talking with her, not so anyone else could hear, and she was definitely there. She was with me and she was young. She was young, and a lively spirit. That's who she is. I liked being aware of her presence, but then I got busy, my mind got busy, walking down the street with my dog, and Mother faded away, just got out of sight, I lost sight of her then.

Walking down the street, I wasn't quiet enough, imagine, quiet enough, to be with her. I suddenly realized she was gone, that she was gone, and I missed her, walking down the street with my dog. The street with my dog in California. But she is around.

We must have been some sight, the three of us, the dog, tethered to me on a springy leash, and me, tethered to a floating woman, floating just above me, graceful as anything, and quiet.

Libby Chaney

Swannanoa River

Photograph, Blue Ridge Mountains, North Carolina

Terese Armstrong

Requiem

for Daniel Michael Flynn, 1960-2004

In the pale light I brought him a mound of earth, dank and dark, and he, tall, taller than when I knew him, stood before a vast valley. He showed me a golden river which ran effortlessly, eternally, and he danced through the valley as if to tell me that now he lived in magic. He was giggly, full of faith, the sky bright, the gray road behind him.

He grew quiet.

"Sister," he said. "I haunt the old life still. It was not my wish to die. It weighs on me."

"I hoped you had alighted into this place of endless valleys," I said.

He swept his arm to encompass the great expanse before us.

"Oh yes, I do belong to this. But I do not melt yet into the golden river."

"What calls you from it, brother?" I asked.

"You call me from it," he said, and I knew he meant all of us who love him and mourn him.

"Should we relinquish you?" I asked.

"Not too soon," he said. "There is something still undone," and he turned towards the grassy hills and began walking.

I hurried to keep up with him. I had never seen him walk with such surety. Gone were the tobacco-filled lungs, the ailing heart, the wounds of his psyche. He walked whole, as if he and the earth had no difference between them. He grew taller still.

At the top of a hill he looked down to a valley, the golden rivers running. In a place below the trees, beneath the clouds, were two children playing with sand. His red hair gleamed and curled as it always had. My dimpled hands patted the mounds and hills of the little world we built. The boy lay down suddenly and stared through the trees to sunlight above. He showed this to the girl, pointing up as light poured down unto them. And the girl, now five, and the boy, just three, returned to the sand, for there was no other world than the one they made.

At the top of the hill, he pointed now to another place. In it a teenaged girl stood with her brother, both stranded on an urban street. Her legs in knee-high boots and short skirt were raw to the cold. It was just below twenty degrees. The boy, twelve, too, was cold. Very cold. No overcoat, no hat. His knuckles red, he warmed his hands with his breath. Her back was to him. They did not speak. She watched for a car to arrive. Together we witnessed the two that we had been.

And now he stood above the clouds on the tall hill, me just below him, looking up into his eyes.

"Look out there," he said, "look." And I turned my eyes from him to the multitude of infinity living in the living hills. Our ancestors were there among the bushes and grasses, he seemed to tell me, and then I saw them, creatures who appeared but had always been there, lined along the golden river and among the trees.

Our great-grandfather Will stood among the standing dead, by the arching oak. His suspenders laced his great chest like a man who had once plowed the earth heavy and hard. Others were among them, ancient Irish kin, and the dead from other lands. And he who stood with me on the hill glanced down along the way, and we saw still more, an infinitude of souls among the tiny acorns and the tallest trees.

"Here now, here," he said to me, that tall man who once giggled naked next to me in the wiggly tub on cold nights when our mother thought to protect our warmth. He stood again above the clouds and pointed to a place close to the river, open to the sun. There two boys dug in the moist earth with sticks and small shovels. One, the older, pulled up an old rusted coin. The future sang in his eyes—he wished to live in the world of earth and sky and find its treasures as he traveled. He showed the coin to the other boy, smaller, blonde of hair and cheek. And the other, who carried life with a great knowing heart, stopped his digging, and examined the coin, and gave his approval, and returned then to his work digging and looking for treasure remaining in the good, good earth.

Up on the hill we looked together towards the tall man's sons, and here I saw his true heart breaking. Then, too, I saw a golden glow come to the boys as if the endless river rose up to join them. Around and around them the tall man spun the golden light. And though the boys continued their digging, they paused in their play, and looked up, and looked around. There were no words between them, but they seemed to know without speaking that the air and light about them had become warm. And he was there.

"These are my methods now," he said to me high on the hill. If it were possible he became taller still. Not so that I could not reach him, but closer to the sky. He pointed down into the valley, and put now the golden light around the little girl and boy playing in the sand, and around our younger selves standing out in the cold. And they too looked up for a moment to the light as if called. I saw that the dead, once they have come to a place such as he, bring healing to those they love, even the girl and boy we ourselves had been—knowing as we both did the wounds they would, and did, sustain.

He turned now among the hills, moving faster along the brush at the top of the ridge. Again I saw that we were accompanied, that rows of the dead lined the ridge and mountaintop. Each wore the golden glow that makes the earth hum and shimmer in certain light. I saw that the earth sings with the light of the dead, that a soul cannot leave the place of its creation. Like the spirits in blades of grass, stones, rivers and sacred trees, the dead have lives among us.

He brought me now to a place unknown to me, a cave among the highest hills. He was inside before I understood his intent, and I could only follow into darkness too impenetrable to speak, so thick it felt I walked within a living presence. The man who led me was nowhere that I knew, and I walked a dark passage unsure, even, of my direction or the path to return. I touched no dank walls nor could I feel that perhaps he was calling. If I did not know that he had led me here, I might doubt my quest and vanish among the strange figures who seemed to distract me in the dark. There was no knowing if I moved towards him, or if my steps took me away. I felt no nearness of being or spirit. The only map I had was my heart, which seemed to nudge me, here, then here, slowly, hesitant, often fearful, here again.

Suddenly among the darkness I saw his purpose, and knew there would be such times for myself and for all of us when the light was gone and the guides seemed to vanish. And somewhere in my heart I saw again the man who led me here. He was not in the cave at all. His quick movement at the opening had only made me think it so. He stood on the hill and said to me in the dark cave, "Sit there, sister. Sit." And thus I did. I halted my quest and cancelled all beliefs. I removed myself from trying. I slept. In the womb, I remembered my remembering, and the moment of my birth. I remembered the long darkness that was my making. And suddenly I stood, and walked out of the cave as if I'd always known the precise turns of its wandering bends.

At the top of the hill he greeted me. He was older now. I saw that his mustache was white, his red hair lined gray. Around him I saw the golden light he had spun around the living. It spun around him, and saved him, and rectified him. In that light I saw our grandmother Annie. She spun a golden thread upon him, for he was still new to his dying and in need of an elder. Annie seemed to be an angel, mostly light, and he settled into what I now saw was a physical substance, the actual feel of love. He warmed.

"Tell her," he said, and I knew now he meant his beloved mate. "Tell her she is forever mine." And he showed me the married couple, up late among the kitchen lights, laughing and talking. We could see the spirits who sustained them, their ancestors, the unborn, the spirits of their sons. "Tell her she is forever mine," he said again, and here too, I saw his heart break, and his leaving pain him. Then, as if it grew from his love and his ache, the golden river came to the woman, at the kitchen table, alone in the deep night, the house silent. She too looked up, as if beckoned.

And here now, as he grew upward towards the sky and seemed to merge with our grandmother's light, he spoke as if the ancients sang through him, wisdom above what he'd known in life, or even yet in death. He, too, learned as he spoke.

"The living are called to the great river of reaping and loving," he said. "Tell her, tell them all, to go to the great river, to share the great life. When they love with a clear heart, they love me. When they see others in light and beauty, they see me. The tree they speak to, the night bird that visits them, when they hold dear these precious things, they too hold me dear."

And I knew then, all of a moment, that my brother spoke as well to me, and harkened me unto life, as if the endless stream would not quite live its true being if I did not but enter it fully.

"Go now, go," he said, and I saw that his light had shifted unto the sky. It was time now, I saw, for the valley and the golden river to be his. He returned to me the mound of earth he'd held in his hands. In a way, I did not want to let him go. "No, no," he said to me. "I am all around," and as he climbed further into our grandmother's light the morning sun shifted. The candle that had burned all night in his name still burned. But the flame seemed to encompass all things. When I turned again to the hill, he did not stand upon it. I knew suddenly that he was it, he was the hill; and the golden light of his becoming gleamed. I felt the golden river surround me, and I too received his blessing. His love spun around me, a physical thing, something real on the skin, a warming.

"Tell them," he said to me, "tell them to love." And in this moment when his passage had been through four seasons and wound back to the fateful morning of his leaving, he blessed us all—we who mourned him and held him to us: his beloved wife and his sons, his sisters and brother, his nieces and nephews, all whom he had known and cherished in life, and the unborn of all these people, and his own coming grandchildren—he blessed us all.

"Long live the fateful light," he said, and then he was the light, and he was each hill and blade of grass. And I walked then into the forest and to the great stream and vowed to love, only to love.

Carolyn Brigit Flynn

To My Beloved Husband of Fifty Years

My dear one, it was one year ago today you died.
My year of mourning is complete.

Mourning *m o u r n i n g* and morning *m o r n i n g*—
only *u* makes the difference.
This year I looked backwards.
Last year we were together.
Now you are gone.

That way of living my life is full of You—*U*—mo*u*rning.
Mourning your death, your sweetness.
Mourning my loss, what was and is no longer.

And if the *u* is removed,
as you have been removed from my daily life,
I am suddenly left with Morning.
Dawn—new beginnings.
Light out of the darkness.

When I look towards the past, you are present.
When I look towards the future, I AM present.
Each anniversary was a letting go of the past—
and a hello to the present.

I AM all that I have.
I AM that I AM that is present.
I AM me. I AM now.
I AM dawn. I AM light.

I AM moving with life's currents.
Goodbye my dear.
I AM that I AM.
Present, here, now.

Barbara Thomas

Tiger Swallowtail

Photograph, Blue Ridge Mountains, North Carolina

Terese Armstrong

Song at Sand Hill Bluff

I. Cotoni, an Ohlone ghost

The day you brought winter back to the cove, my daughter, I was drifting inside the song of the season. Spring had come to Sand Hill Bluff; a fragment of my spirit floated between mustard blooms. Part of me lingered in a den where a mother bobcat panted as she birthed a kit, the little one's first breath echoing around us. Another portion drifted beside a cricket, sounding his fragile wings to call a mate.

But then your Uncle Seal cried, an anguished squeal that called the shards of my body back together. I took shape, a solid form born from the fear in his song, and sped to the cliff edge, wondering what had harmed my friend and relation. What, in this mating and birthing season, could fill his mouth with such grief?

I didn't know, my daughter, that it was actually your desolation that brought me back. I couldn't see the truth in that tune when I looked down the face of the cliff. For there, under a spring sky, the cove had suddenly grown frigid and wintered. A storm raged, swelling the waves, turning them gray. I gasped to see hail pocking the faces of sand dollars. The shells broke apart on frosted sand, scattering up the beach in a sweep of muddy foam.

But there were no clouds in the sky. Why was it raining? Why, when I lowered my head, did the poppies still bloom under my feet? To the north, to the south, spring sang its proper song, the tumbling laugh of the season. Why here, in this little scramble of rocks and water so beloved by our people, had time turned back to bite its tail? Seal cried again, diving under a wave that crashed behind him. I watched ice diamonding the curl and saw the reason he felt so afraid.

Seal surfaced, his snout pointing east, toward a shadow on the trail in front of me. "It's her," he shouted. "One of your kinswomen. She's the one who is twisting time."

I saw you then, a living descendant, holding winter tight against your chest, strong arms beaded with sorrow. So much grief oozed from your small body that the cove had turned to ice. You'd trapped the cold season in the hard muscles of your legs, the cage of your ribs, a jaw that squared defiantly against the afternoon's sunlight. And daughter, I could barely make out your heart, shriveled and edged, like a fragment of chert I'd chipped off to shape a spearhead. It had hardened, firm as a piece of flint that now struck ice to life instead of fire. Wherever you walked, the blue-eyed grass beneath your feet shriveled, sang a dying song from cold.

Seal bleated as a swallowtail, still unused to its new wings, faltered in the wind and brushed against you. The touch of your skin, a cold it was never meant to know, brought death. I wept for so many eggs lost, larvae taken before their season. Like the yarrow frosted at your feet, so many seeds withered, unable to root.

You couldn't know, of course, the destruction you were making. Our people had lost that vision, taken from us by the brown-robed ones carrying crosses, so many years ago. You couldn't even see me, your ancestor, standing right beside you on the cliff, my hand reaching to brush your shoulder. "Listen to me," I begged, hoping at least that your blood would hear.

But then I faltered, struck dumb by my own loss of the power of our people. How could I explain to you, so separated from the old knowledge after all these centuries, that you were not alone? Your heart, daughter, was linked with all the species in this cove, everyone a member of your family. I didn't know why you were twisting time, but the capacity, untrained and blind, was causing you to kill.

"You must stop," I pleaded, knowing that you would not understand me. I watched as my words skittered across ice, slipped along the frozen rivers of your veins.

"No!" Seal shouted, unable to accept my failure. He glared at me, then lifted his snout and began to sing.

II. Harbor Seal

I sang the shore. I sang the lift of the wave over my back, the stroke of the sea, a fan of kelp clipping my flipper. I sang hunger, I sang fish, moist morsels, a lust and lunge, snap of teeth, juice and bone and fin. I sang the spring hunt, the feed, the smell of one warm evening. I sang the sky, the ocean, the truth of these birthing days.

My music battled the human's, Cotoni's kinswoman, whose throat made winter. I tried to shout past her cold music, to silence her icy tune. But her voice was louder, she who sang steelhead back to life, wearily trying to slither past me once again to spawn in Laguna Creek. She, who made mussels tear from their rocks and starfish lose their arms. She sang lightning, she sang shark bite, teeth and mouth and biting. She sang the great white's slash and blood, my brother's last wave, his final breath and rotting pile of bones.

I sobbed again for his loss, for the emptiness of his place in the surf beside me. I cried for the comfort of his body against mine when we hauled out on rocks to sleep. In my weeping, I let a swell carry me closer to the bluff so that I saw the human better. And there, beneath the fury of her storm, I heard something else.

A cry so high and faint that not even Cotoni could sense it. Small and weak, a flutter of notes: the faded music of her flinty heart.

I swear by the sea, I swear by the sky, this is the truth of the story. I quieted, I softened, I chanted a whispered harmony like it was summer solstice day. And that heart listened, beyond the squalling of furious winter. The human kept bellowing the winds of the cold season, but her heart lifted up from her body and flew off like a bird.

I only meant to free it from ice, but that heart took flight, dove into the clean kiss of water. It surfaced near me in the swell and looked boldly into my eyes.

What else could I do but bow, but flip, but dive in shivering welcome? It was clear to every being in the cove: this tiny muscle had chosen me. So I shivered, delight flooding my body. I raised my head in a loud and joyful song.

III. Cotoni

When Seal began to sing his new tune, the evening sharpened. The sunset glistened with power, as if it had been torn from the face of Sacred Time. Coyote sat back on his haunches and lifted an ear to listen. Hummingbird stilled her flutter. Eagle plummeted from the sky and closed his wings.

Silence, the sound beneath sound, gripped the throat of the world.

As if I was a hunter again, I heard the breath of birth, the sigh of dying. I felt the quiet which must flood our bones before we kill. Seal smiled at me from the sleek cloak of the water. "Did you want to become one with me again?" he asked. He was ready to give himself to feed our lost tribe.

I laughed at his offer, the joke soaking the silence between us. Neither of us were sure anymore just how much "human" still walked in my bones. Even during the quick days of my lifetime the division confused me. I couldn't feel what separated the man in me from the seal who swam.

You haven't been taught this, daughter, but when our people hunted, the stillness of Sacred Time drenched our spirits. Dressed in furs or feathers, we would carefully move into the heart of the animal we sought. When we felt one with the creature, we gave ourselves, dying under our own spear or arrow. But unlike others in the tribe, when I woke again I could still feel a beak in my face or hooves at the end of my limbs.

It was my own pelt I skinned afterward, lifting the hide free from a white thrust of muscle. I thanked my own flesh as it sizzled fat into the grateful fire. I became so confused that every night my dreams threaded themselves with creation's silence. I spent my days wrapped in the quiet of the first stars.

The elders took my stillness as a gift and called me Cotoni Shape Changer. The way I hunted, they said, echoed the wisdom of Sacred Time. Our people tell that whatever died then, became another. Death walked in a new coat on the shaggy hills. The tribe declared I had been born to make flesh of this memory. The power of that age spoke through my crowded bones.

They grew thick with the feathers and gills of those I hunted. I couldn't speak for the fur that lined my throat. The creatures I killed fed my people a meat made rich with an ancient wisdom. But all the dying grieved me. The sour taste snatched words from my mouth.

I became Cotoni, the Silent One. Cotoni, the Great Hunter. Cotoni, whittled thin by quiet during the autumn of his arrowed life.

And then one day I truly died, taken from the tribe by the wind of a bitter winter. Sobbing, they carried my body to burn beside the waves of this narrow shore. I rose, ash and air, into the gusts of a December evening. The wind carried me straight into the mouth of a song.

Surprised and gasping, I was swallowed into truth; I learned the heart of my own story. For the first time, daughter, I heard the music beneath the silence of Sacred Time. It springs from the joy of our Mother of Many Waters. She beats melody into the world with her Body of Land.

I listened and understood the voices of Seal and Coyote, Eagle and Hummingbird. Deer, Elk, Otter: the animals in me rushed out, singing to her tunes. And I found words, pelting and sharp, that roared in the rain Mother sent to comfort our people. After decades, I spoke finally, strong and brittle as the wind.

My tribe bent their heads to the wet, pebbled sound of my small wisdom. They leaned forward to catch the tune of my rusty voice. I watched how the song, the storm, softened their lean faces; I could see it cup the sweetness that curled at the nub of their grief. In that moment, Mother revealed to me her greatest secret—at the heart of the world, the notes for love and grief are the same.

Love and sorrow, silence and song: this is the beat of our Mother's music. This is the joy that Seal threw back his head to sing. And I listened, traveling centuries toward you, the living descendant who squatted at the edge of the cliff beside me. Your heart had flown; winter was melting from between your fingers. I hesitantly placed my hand on your arm.

Your flesh was smooth and cold, like the rainstorm you carried. Lines etched your face, wounds from the battle you had fought with time. You looked empty, daughter, like a deer speared without the proper prayers, unable to return to life. With your heart gone, I thought, you will fall from the bluff and die.

"Give our daughter back her heart," I called to Seal, who was playing with the home of your spirit in the spring waves. The muscle, a dark spot in the water, rested like a tease on his bobbing snout.

"She has to value it enough to ask," he replied and flipped your heart up into the arms of the evening. It laughed. I peered into the silence of your face to see if you had heard.

Your eyes flickered, but still you said nothing. No smile cracked the mask of your lips. Seal wanted joy, but you could not reach into yourself to name it. I understood then that pleasure was a language that you no longer knew.

"It's no use," I called to him. "You can't change her. In the name of our family, return the heart."

Seal shook his head. "Listen to how it sings, here in the water." I heard the thin happy music as they dove together under a breaking wave. "What she doesn't know, she can't miss."

"But she will die," I protested.

Seal shrugged. "I have died many times, leaving life to enter the song of our Mother. Maybe that is what the human needs."

"No!" For the first time since my own death, I couldn't find the words to explain to your uncle, the sea creature. I reached for my spear and quickly stood. I, Cotoni, would hunt the heart, as I had hunted so many others. Cotoni would snare the muscle and return it to your chest.

"And isn't joy what you hunted all along, killing the laughing spirit of another to feed your people?" Seal asked. "You were so skilled, you prevented others from learning of the rapture in the hunt for themselves." He shook his head and your heart nestled close to him in the dark water. "This human will starve until she learns how to throw her spear accurately. For once, let this one stalk pleasure on her own."

I rested my knife in the long grass of the cliff and faced the truth of Seal's wisdom. He was right. During my lifetime, I had clutched at the delight of the hunt as tightly as you clutched your false winter. I had fed the tribe but did not allow the cheer of the catch, the hidden music in it, to feed me. Oh, how I ached to tell you: "Set your traps for joy. Feather your arrows. Do not become so lost in the hunt that you forget how to eat."

You shifted back on your heels at the cliff edge, and I tried to speak, but I was silent. The words fluttered like a flock of winter geese, crowding my nervous mouth. I made myself talk, but what emerged was a plea, not the wisdom and strength of a story. "Play with Seal," I finally begged. "Let the Mother's joy enter your song."

And for a moment, I thought that perhaps you'd heard my true meaning. You surged up beside me and opened your arms to the wind.

IV. Maria Reyes

It was the strangest thing. When I stood, my feet anchored themselves to the ground for the first time since Maggie's death. I could feel the soil under my heel. What I mean is that, finally, between my skin and the earth was more than just my hightops. I had made contact; it wasn't just Mag's voice that called as the grasses blew.

I could see again. Through the dusk, I noticed the burst of pink mallow that dotted the cow pasture. Orange poppies flamed among the green. Even the water beneath me had changed color. It wasn't gray anymore, had slipped into the turquoise of spring.

For six months I had been traveling the dark corridor of my loss. I hadn't even noticed when the season changed. As far as I was concerned, the world was still in the middle of an El Niño winter. It was November 1st, the last time Maggie and I had walked down to this, our favorite cliff. The first day of the eleventh month had been gray, huge waves swelling the rocks below us with a storm.

"The sea is hungry," Mag declared, loosening her parka. She whipped her hat off so the spray could tangle her braid. "Such a forward girl! She wants a lover so bad she's just throwing herself at the land." We laughed and sped back home to act out the ocean's desire. The next day, a nail, a rock maybe, some sudden flat slammed Maggie's life into a rainy highway curve.

I heard her voice in every wind that howled around the house that winter. The rain sheeted the fields with her words.

"All we have is right now. You know I never said I was willing to make you any promises. We've had a damn good seventeen years. What more do you want from me?"

"I want you right here," I cried to the silence. "Forever. Maggie, why did you leave me? Please come back," I knelt on the earth and begged. Each wave, every bird answered my sorrow. The whole world echoed her stubborn *No.*

So what kind of life is this, I thought, so beautiful and so empty? We're supposed to do all the work it takes to love just to have it snatched away?

I clenched my hands into my jacket pockets. "Listen," I cried out loud into the evening. "I want forever or I want nothing. Mags, what do you say?"

She answered with a breeze scraping the husks of last summer's cattails. A wave rattled the empty rocks on the shore.

Each evening I trudged to our favorite haunts, hoping she would give me a different answer. I knew I wouldn't get what I really wanted; it's not possible for the dead to return. But I'd forget sometimes, while my feet dragged down the long hallway of our life together. The entire world stretched into a tunnel, no windows, no guarantee of that supposed light at the end.

Until today, until I came back to this cliff for the first time since Maggie died and stood up into the wind and my foot scuffed the crust of a living soil. It startled me. I actually felt the pulse of the earth under my toes. Maybe you'll think I'm crazy but this is what happened. At that moment, I looked out across the fields and I saw them breathe. Just as I do sometimes, in the lonesome shade of early evening. It gave me such comfort. The world sighed, almost as if, like me, it didn't want the day to end.

And then I noticed the old Indian man standing quietly behind me. Maybe I should have run but I didn't. He looked so much like Granddad that I guess that's why I wasn't more afraid. But the man was a stranger, and I felt my chest clench at the potential danger. Then I thought, "What's the matter with you? Maggie's dead. The worst has already happened." I shook my head and peered out to the ocean. "Nothing this guy could do will ever hurt you like that again."

And you know, I was right not to leave because the old man leaned forward and whispered, "I'm proud of you, daughter." At his words, I felt my spine lift up as if I had actually done something worthy. There I was, thin and worried with a ripped flannel shirt under my jacket. Nothing was any different. I was still as cracked and hollow as Maggie's favorite mixing bowl. But the man spoke with a soft voice that was as firm as granite and I believed him. He swept his arm out toward the water. "Do you hear the sunset song?"

I did. A music that vibrated every cell of the cliff rose up into the dusk. I'm telling the truth now. Rye grass, yarrow, even the ice plant opened its heart and sang.

And for the first time since she died, it didn't matter where Maggie was because of the song that shimmered all around me. Each stalk, each curl of wave played its own tune. I couldn't help myself—something made me sing with the lovely evening. The old man smiled. Before I knew it, my mouth was shaping some kind of melody out of Maggie's life.

I sang everything: all our years together, the fights, the surprises. The love I thought I'd lost made notes from my bones.

For a moment, I had a wild hope that my song would bring Maggie back to me. I'd look up and there she'd be on the path, plaid shirt and brown sweater: Maggie, with her graying braid, sure-footed and strong. But the path remained empty; it sang its own story. I understood then that each of us is given only one song.

Only one song. The old man pointed to a seal and I heard it say, "Listen!" One song: but whoever arranges the music never takes any notes away.

The seal lifted his head out of the water and tossed something at me. "There's your *forever*." I felt as if some small rock had hit me in the chest. Then he cocked his head and looked me in the eye. I swear that he smiled. I heard his teasing voice, "What more can you want?"

I threw my arms out and yelled, "Everything!" And then I sank down into the grasses and starting weeping. I can't explain what happened except that, this time, there was something different in the tears. Maybe my ears could finally hear the music in them the way I'd heard the sunset. Anyway, I was crying with the same force that I had wept all winter, but I didn't feel so alone.

For one thing, there was the old man who placed a firm hand on my shoulder. He squeezed. When I looked up next, he had disappeared. He was just plain gone.

But there was still the seal, a thick wedge in the darkening water. I watched as he dove one final time and then swam away from me.

The stars sang me home along the scuffed trail. "Thanks for the music. See you soon, Mags," I promised as I let myself into the welcoming house.

Marcy Alancraig

Jasmine

It is jasmine I smell. The scent that brings memories to mind.

Jasmine. Every morning, my grandmother picked new buds from the bushes surrounding her house and sprinkled them in bunches inside her linen closet. It was her ritual. The new buds would pour their perfume, wilt, die and be transformed.

When I was a little girl, staying over at my grandmother's house, I would watch her arrange her freshly scented, crisply folded whites in that closet. What always attracted my attention were her bath towels. They were large and plenty. The kind that covered you from head to toe like a shroud. They were white and had fringes all around their sides. Some had an added gold embroidered design; a design that was fit to be seen and admired, most probably by the ladies in the Hamams (public baths) soaking side by side with my grandmother.

I looked forward during my bath to the moment my grandmother would hand me one of her prized towels to wrap my toasty, steamy, freshly scrubbed body. I would grab the towel with great excitement to quickly contain the heat escaping the surface of my skin. The towel wrapped around me became alive again. Flowery smells were revived by the steam and humidity. Feelings of gratitude and delight would overwhelm and humble me at once.

I often waited a while covered with my white bath attire, to rest my tired body and for my temperature to normalize. As I would begin to put my clothes on, little butterfly-like creatures pressed against my skin came flying out in the air and slowly fell to the ground. Startled at first, I stepped back to examine the creatures closely. They were lifeless and seemed to take on a different posture lying on the Persian-carpeted floor. After picking one up, I finally determined their identity. They were the jasmine my grandmother had picked earlier in the week, carefully placed in her linen closet, passionately tucked in between her sheets and towels.

Jasmine. The smell makes me long to be with her, to be tickled by the butterflies that blessed my bed sheets and the flowers that filled my nightly dreams.

Reem Hammad

Portal

Acrylic

Barbara Thomas

The Ancestors

They form two lines behind me, women on the left, men on the right.
The grandmothers reach back in undulating lines. They bend
and straighten, bend and straighten. The grandfathers sway,
moving side to side, like upright reeds. They come
into focus, then fade. They ripple out from me like angel wings.

Bits of light follow me on this dark night like a diaphanous
cape clinging to my shoulders. The grandmothers
and grandfathers whisper in my ears as I move through
the short day and into dusk. For just this moment
I am in front of the parade. Soon I will join them
in their haunting dance, moving in and out of the shadows,
step, dip, turnabout.

See the lineage, the multiplication of souls weaving
in and out, glowing. There are the Dutchmen building towns,
the Irish and Indian great-grandmothers beating rugs
and scattering corn. The dreamers on both sides, the workers
and traveling men. All moving on. Moving back. Their soul force
beating on the veil like a black-winged bird trying to be free.

I move on, just out in front, singing a wordless dirge.
Behind me the steady *beat, beat* of the raven's wing,
and the hushed and luminescent glow of moving souls.
They are my family, my prototypes, my dead.

The generations wait to move to the front—my children,
my grandchildren. And I will be the bridge from ancestor to progeny.
I will learn to listen to the ancestors. I will listen closely,
bear witness to their stories, pass along the words
of comfort and warning. I will practice their dance.

Gretchen Sentry

Unto the Hills

My Grandmother's Grandmother

Julia Veazie, the miller's wife, pulled a sock taut over her darning egg. She threaded her needle and pulled the thread across the hole in its heel. On the other side of the table, by the light of the same lamp, her husband Benjamin was teaching their sons.

"Daddy," little Walter asked, "how did Noah catch all those animals?"

"Of course he couldn't catch them. This is a fable, like the stories in your primer." He looked over the top of his glasses at the boy.

Julia finished the first sock and reached into her sewing basket for another. She remembered the story of Noah, the animals herded into the ark to rescue them from the flood. She pictured Noah's wife saying goodbye to her family with tears in her eyes.

Benjamin told the boys, "Look, this word for God is plural. This is a different story from a different time. At some point the priests just cobbled the stories together and claimed it was a Bible."

Her husband was teaching their children to read the Bible in the original Hebrew and Greek, so they would not be fooled by such superstition. Julia could read only the English Bible, the book with its cracked leather cover that her mother had given her. She was raised up Christian and married in church. She knew she missed the sewing circle, the bake sales, and all the community activities she had shared with her family. But she didn't know what she thought about God.

When her sons read the words, she listened. There were harsh laws and terrible bloodshed. She didn't think that God could be like that. But sometimes there were words of comfort, reaching a place deep inside her. Rising in the morning to stoke the stove and start breakfast, she would find these words lingering in the air like her breath in the cold house. As she adjusted the draft on the stove she let the words come together in her mind: "I will lift up mine eyes unto the hills, from whence cometh my help." She thought of the green hills to the west of them. Surely a God could live in those hills.

She never questioned or contradicted her husband. Not in public, not in front of the children, not when they were alone together at the close of the day. Save the arguments for important matters like their daughters' schooling. On religious questions, she dropped her eyes, shrugged her shoulders, and made a noncommittal reply.

She didn't have time to work out what she really believed. There were babies to tend, clothes to wash and mend, floors to scrub. She only sensed, sometimes, something holy, something that didn't come from a book. And sometimes from inside her a prayer came up, stripped to its essence. "Please," she would breathe into the air, or "thank you." And she knew from how it felt that it was prayer.

When her sons left home, she folded their shirts, rolled their socks, and packed food for them to take away with them. At the door, she put her hands on their arms and looked up into their faces, and the word she silently raised to heaven was "Please."

Each of her sons, schooled by their father and prayed for by their mother, became a minister. And when Julia died, her son Walter was at her bedside, to frame her final prayer into the kind of language that ministers use as she closed her eyes into peace.

Cara Lamb

Shabbos Prayer

(Hungary, 1860s)

The fire is built in the hearth, tended, and banked with dense logs that must carry their heat through the cold night and morning, to Havdallah, the end of Shabbos at tomorrow's sunset.

The family gathers at the cottage table—a long, smooth plank of oak from the Bavarian Forest, set on legs carved into simple swirls by the village craftsman. The pride of the family, it is altar to their nourishment and communion.

As darkness overtakes day, two white candles are lit and the blessing emerges from the great-grandmother's lips. She is the first to speak them, and the others join in eagerly—*Baruch Atah Adonai Elohaynu melech ha'olam asher kid'shanu b'mitzvotav v'tzivanu l'hadlik ner shel Shabbot.*

Four generations convene weekly, like clockwork, awaiting this moment of celebration. *Blessed is the Eternal One, the Source of Light; through your guidance to kindle this light, You fill us with the holiness and blessing of the day.*

Another cycle has turned—another week of study, of labor and chores, mundane concerns and worldly decisions, of aching muscles and arthritic fingers. Until the sun again sets, no work will be done. The food has been cooked, the bread baked, the wine uncorked, the oil lamps lit, the warmth assured—for at least a few hours. The children may play without prodding to gather kindling or feed chickens.

As the wine is blessed, spirit is called in. Laughter becomes the unseen but vocal guest. Overtaxed brains and bodies sink into blissful surrender. *Baruch Atah Adonai Elohaynu melach ha'olam borei p'ri hagafen. You abound in Blessings, Adonai our God, source of All, Creator of the Fruit of the Vine.*

The bread is blessed, the braided egg challah. Its scent has infused the cottage with earthy aroma. *Baruch Atah Adonai Elohaynu melech ha'olam hamotzee l'chem min haoritz. Blessed are You, Holy Source of Life, Who brings forth bread from the earth.*

The bread is pulled apart with exuberance. They feed each other small pieces with wishes for a good Shabbos. A simple, delicious soup of potatoes, turnips, and beets is ladled out and consumed with gusto and gratitude.

The parents and grandparents have bathed and scented themselves. When the meal is finished and the candles burn low, they will embrace. They will enjoy and remember each other as lovers, as it is a welcome and prescribed duty to pleasure one's partner on Shabbos.

The great-grandmother will drift into the night in the chair that once cradled her beloved husband. She is cocooned in the faded blue and cream *tallis*, the woven shawl he draped on her before his strength left. She fingers the silken fringes and they comfort her. She will sing and she will pray. *Yit gadal v'yit kadash sh'mey rabah...* The words will be there, the Mourner's Kaddish, all the sacred syllables intact. She remembers them effortlessly, though she forgets why she is at the butcher shop. She communes with Shekinah, the Divine Presence. Through giggles and lovemaking and snoring and crackling embers, she makes her music. This is what she came from. This is where she is going.

Marigold Fine

Grandfather

You go during one winter of wilderness.
The years have flattened your grave with the earth,
wind wiped your name from the granite stone.

You had woods and weather,
rising bluffs and arching sky,
mountains that lift clear to the ocean.
The apple orchard you set on the green hill.
Sons and daughters all born
at your old mountain home.

You worked year after year,
plowing back and forth with your shaggy maned horse,
clans of birds, tribes of beasts in the forest.
I can see you working cattle since daybreak
then home by nightfall, supper and sleep.

No tree or stone or fence the same,
since you left.
The brown barn leans like an animal,
the apples are small and bitter.
Hungry deer straggle in leaving bits of hide
on barbed wire.

I remember your promise of a hike in the woods,
a swim in the pond, the trout we might catch.
In dreams, you tell me to rake the dead stalks,
clean the earth bare again, scatter the wild grass.

Lara Gularte

Resemblance

Mixed Media Collage

Diane Roberts Ritch

A Cry in the Night

Fear slices sleep:
a dream breaks through.
Last night, again
my grandmother was with me.

When I was a child
I cried in the night
and she came
to her daughter's
daughter.

A thread of mothers links us.

Someone once asked me
who had loved me so well
that I could afford to feel the edge
of fear going back toward the core
of what we are—

Who transmitted the thread,
gave me the way
to my source?

A thread of mothers
flows through me.

Last night my grandmother
was with me in a dream—
herself in miniature
sheltered in my arms.

It was her cry
brought me to her.

Connie Batten

Samhein

As days shorten and darkness lengthens,
we celebrate the seed under the earth,
a new year growing in winter's womb,
the beginning and end of life
stirring in the dark.

The veil thins between the worlds,
those who died are welcomed home.
Rituals of water and mirrors
reflect the light of fires across the void
that separates living from dead.
Cailleach, the blue-black goddess,
begins her reign of wintry night.

I have placed my altar and my candles
in the western window as a guide
for my mother's spirit journey home.
As she comes closer, I see she has lost
the trappings of her later years,
the walker and the wheelchair.
She moves lightly, a young woman,
dreaming down the beach in search of shells,
lilacs from Iowa in her hands.
Her blue eyes look far away within
where perhaps a poem even now begins.

I am unable to imagine
what she might say to me, or I to her.
The vision remains without a voice.
Even when we lived together,
it was hard for us to know each other.
I have no wish to interrupt her reverie.
For both of us, the poems are enough.

Sylvia Bortin Patience

Invocation

I park in the gravel lot at the corner of S.E. 35th and Highway 101 and leave Dave fidgeting in the passenger seat while I walk downhill on the asphalt road. He hadn't wanted me to take this trip to Lincoln City. Nothing short of dying would've kept me from going. He couldn't deal with me going alone, so I said fine, come on, but I don't want to hear about it. Not a word. This is where my great-grandfather died twenty years ago, the rat bastard. He's been haunting me ever since and this time I'm gonna get rid of him for good.

The March wind gusts, whipping my hair like long black snakes around my face. I breathe in the salt smell of the cold air, the wetness and weight of it so much like home and refreshing after the long predawn push from Portland. The rhythmic roar of the ocean and the high-pitched cry of gulls call me. Pines and firs, vines and ivy grow wild along the side of the road, where the grassy earth slopes down and frames one side of the D River, where the water bubbles and skims over brown rocks heading out to sea. Wood houses line the other side of the river, all of them different, the last green with a white picket fence backed up against the cliff where the road dead-ends. I take the muddy concrete stairs down to the beach fast, ignore the safety rail, land on both feet at once in the thick sand, like when I was a kid.

I've never seen the Pacific. The waves heave over sharp, black rocks, rippling like muscle as they break into foam, layers of water stretching onto the sand. Blue streaks the cloudy sky. On my right, the D rushes through a rusted grate into a wide, rocky pool that meets the ocean. Ahead of me, two girls in jeans and hoodies walk the shoreline, collecting shells in a white plastic grocery sack. There's a couple walking further down where the beach curves, a black and a blond Lab weaving around and between them. The woman whistles and a terrier leaps from a heap of driftwood by the steep rise of the cliff.

I've always been what my friends call "sensitive." Not that I know stuff will happen before it does, 'cause if that were true I'd have spent a lot of time at the horse track back north of Houston making a killing. I can't see dead people or even hear most of 'em, but I do hear one of my dear departed relatives and that's a problem. It started when I was eighteen, set up in Denver in the burgeoning business of telemarketing, living on commission and twenty-five cent boxes of macaroni and cheese and dreaming about Grandpa at night. I was trying to ignore him and he was trying to get a message through. I only told Dave. He thought I was nuts until stuff started breaking in the house: TV, pipes, balcony rail, can opener, toilet. Couldn't have been the cats, was all he said.

Footfalls pound behind me, and shallow, labored breathing. I slow, the sand trying my balance. Dave pulls up beside me.

"Thanks for waiting," he says, sucking air. His short brown hair is spiked where he's slept on it.

I glance over my shoulder, kind of surprised to see a couple hundred yards of boot prints. "Change your mind?"

"I'm still not helping you," he says. "I just need to move some after all that sitting."

I look at the water, spray dotting my glasses. "About what I expected."

He zips up his windbreaker. "We can still go home."

"He'd just follow us back," I say. "Like he did from Denver to Houston."

"He's a little old man who couldn't keep his mouth shut, Shel. That's what got him killed. He got what he deserved."

I raise a brow. "You think so? I'm not sure anyone deserves to be robbed and murdered."

"He was an asshole," Dave says.

"So're you. So am I."

"I thought you hated him, Shel."

The wind creeps through the weave of my sweater. I fold my arms across my chest. "I do."

Dave gets us a room at the Sand Dune motel overlooking that same stretch of beach. He takes a ride down to the grocery store at the other end of town for supplies and I go for a walk. Grandpa shows up five minutes in. At least I'm outside. It's always better outside because of all the space. Two people in my head at once makes me feel claustrophobic. Grandpa Freiberg: Gray-haired, mostly bald, cold blue eyes, never smiled at me, not even once. Camel jacket, Italian shoes always shined. He read the paper and grunted rather than talk to me whenever he came around, and he played favorites, always pitting my aunts and uncles against each other, doling out money to one but not the other, paying attention to one but not the other. He thought he was so smart, so Machiavellian.

"Look where it got you," I mutter, climbing up the hill to the highway.

"The point," he says in his two-pack-a-day rasp, "is where it got you. You're here."

"What do you want?"

"You keep asking, but you never listen when I tell you."

I roll my eyes. "I won't be listening much today either. I didn't come here to be lectured."

"You came here to help me," he says.

"Can we not go 'round and 'round about this?" I ask. "'Cause I've only got until tomorrow night to do what I came here for."

"You're going to do a spell, little girl?"

I'm thirty-four years old, eat way too much chocolate for my own good and my hips show it. Little? Not in any way I can think of. "That's the plan."

"You can't make me go away," he says.

"We'll see, Grandpa. We'll see." I make it to the highway and stare longingly at the blue book shop with the mermaid painted out front. I dearly want to browse, but not like this. Not with the voice in my head.

"You should go in," he says. "You like bookstores. I like bookstores. What's to lose?"

"Grandpa, if you wanna go, go."

"Shel, why is it so important to you that we not have anything in common?"

Which, hell, that's the point, the question that shoots straight to the heart of things.

"Because you destroyed my mother." I give the blue mermaid store a last look before I turn on my heel and walk down to the beach.

"I thought I'd find you down here," Dave says. He hunkers down by where I sit with a dime-sized circle of sand in the palm of my hand.

A light mist is falling, so I've slipped my glasses in my jacket pocket. At about ten feet out, the world eases into a blue-green blur.

"It's different from back home." The sand on the Gulf of Mexico is light brown and fine. This stuff is orange and black and brown, gritty flecks of rock.

He scoops a handful to study. "Did you call your mom?

"Interrupted her solitaire game." That's how she spends most nights, dealing out solitaire one hand after another on her scuffed-up coffee table, smoking cigarettes and channel surfing. I keep buying her books, but she won't read 'em. Reading's too much like thinking, and too much thinking always leads her back to the disaster of the family, which she figures is all her fault.

"Tell her anything about why we're out here?"

"Are you kidding?" I shake my head. "I did that, it'd be bad. I'd have had to hang up on her."

I know she loves me and she's proud of me, she tells me all the time. But there's an edge under her words, like if I trespass too far over the line she does everything in her power to get me back where I belong. And that comes from love, too, because she doesn't want me to screw up. But I can't be what she wants.

She doesn't understand what I do, or my brother and sister for that matter. But I'm taking care of myself, making a decent living as a secretary, doing what makes me happy. Even if what makes me happy makes her mortified. We were all raised Jewish, my brother and sister and me, but no one stayed that way. Mom always says, how the hell did I get two Christians and a Witch? It's a mystery to me, too.

Dave settles in the sand beside me. "Not telling her, not asking her permission, it's not entirely ethical."

"I'm not doing this for her."

He cocks his head. "Point taken. But it might have an effect on her. She might not be able to handle it."

"I'll be responsible," I say, knowing it's not that simple.

He draws circles in the sand with his fingers. "So can we talk again, Shel, about what you're planning on doing?"

"We can talk."

"I'm not trying to change your mind," he says. "We're beyond that now."

"I'm glad you realize it."

He flashes a wry grin. He always says I'm the most stubborn person he ever met. Not above listening to reason, but stubborn.

"It's illegal to burn the driftwood on the beach, you know," he says.

There's a lot of it, too, the driftwood, from the twigs that show where the tide's gone out to the big logs up near the cliff. "I was thinking of having a cauldron fire."

"I don't know what the law is on that."

"Don't worry, I won't get caught if it's a problem." There were ways of dealing with that kind of thing.

"Do you know what the ritual plan is yet?"

"Not yet. We have the two nights here before we head back to Portland so I'm thinking it'll probably happen that last night, I'll know by then." It'll come to me, that's the way I work. If I made a plan ahead of time, it'd just change.

"I'll hang around the room tomorrow then," he says. "That way if you need the car to go for supplies or whatever, it's there."

I stretch out, lay my head on his lap and listen to the waves come in. He strokes my hair, brushes it out of my eyes. I met Dave when I lived in Denver, a couple of jobs after my telemarketing stint. We started out as best friends, going to Happy Hour for the free buffet, asking each other's advice about all our relationship problems until it occurred to us we'd been avoiding a relationship of our own. We've been together ever since. I don't know if he'd say the same about me, but no one understands me the way he does.

"According to the tide tables, you need to be off the beach before midnight," he says.

"Okay." His voice has that tone that says the other shoe's about to drop.

"I want to be there," he says.

I raise up on one elbow and look at him. "You don't want me to do this, you think it won't work. And you're not helping me. What gives?"

"I want to keep an eye out, Shel. I trust you. I don't trust whoever else might be on the beach. And I sure don't trust your grandfather."

That makes two of us.

After a healthy breakfast of frosted strawberry toaster pastries and coffee, Dave goes with me to buy some Epsom salts and rubbing alcohol to make the fire. Near dusk, I go down to the beach to reconnoiter. The clouds are backlit gold and orange, the sea darkening along with the sky, the wind rippling through the short trees and brush that grew on the cliffside. In the distance, silhouetted gulls bunch on the rocks. I slide my hands into my jean pockets, my fingertips brushing the precious stone offerings I've brought for the spell.

There are still a fair amount of people out and about. I waffle between ignoring them and trying to seem inconspicuous while I find the best place by the river to work my spell.

I want to do it by the river mouth because it's a place where things meet, a melding of energies. And water carries the energy of emotion, of tears and sweat, of dream. It's the shadowy place where the blood of the subconscious flows.

It's not that I know exactly what happened to make my mother turn out the way she did. I have only glimpses, mostly what her sister told me. We talk about it with each other, but never with Mom. How she ran away from home when she was twelve and was gone all day and no one noticed, how her sister always had a new dress for the dance and she had to go without, how no one ever told her she was pretty, or smart, or worth a damn. How now whenever she passes a mirror and catches her reflection, her brow furrows and her eyes narrow, like she's given herself a white-glove inspection and failed miserably.

I sit in the sand and do a quick Tarot divination to make sure I haven't overlooked anything, that I don't have any ulterior motives in using magic to get what I wanted. The Magus: you have all the tools you need. The Hermit: trust in yourself. Art: the flow, mixing, synergy.

The hairs on the nape of my neck rise. I glance over my shoulder and even at the top of the stairs, not seeing anyone there watching. I feel Grandpa a heartbeat before he speaks.

"Shel, are you prepping that spell?"

I don't sense any panic in his tone, only curiosity. "Yep. I'm good to go a bit after dark."

"If you think you know what you're doing, you're a fool."

"Wouldn't be the first time someone told me that," I say, fool not being a bad thing, necessarily. In the Tarot, the Fool signifies new beginnings, and that's what I'm making, a new beginning.

"Do you know what it means to spit on your ancestors?"

I dig my fingers into the sand. "Do you know what it's like to have someone in your head when you didn't ask for it? To have it be someone you despise?"

"You never knew me, Shel."

"Thank Goddess."

"You wouldn't be here if it weren't for me," he says. And he is right.

Mom and Dad married young. He grew up in New York in a family of carnies and spent his evenings pulling his father out of bars. So he and Mom tried as hard as they could to raise the perfect family because if everyone acted the way successful people were supposed to act, joined the right organizations, dated the appropriate people, and looked like successful people were supposed to look, then what had happened to both of them growing up would never happen again. If they could force their children to be what they themselves had always wanted to be, to be what they should have become, that would make up for everything. What a shame that all that careful planning backfired like hell. Hindsight told me why, clear as the river water. They had fed us their ghosts and we swallowed them whole.

"Shel, exactly what do you think you can accomplish?"

I get up to fetch a long piece of driftwood. "For starters, summon a few ghosts."

Dave brings the cauldron and supplies down around nine, flashlight bobbing at his side scattering halos over the river. "You think you'll need anything else?" he asks.

"If I need anything else, I'm not doing my job."

Dave sets the cauldron down on its stone base so it doesn't inadvertently burn anything when it gets hot and pours equal amounts salt and alcohol inside, sets the long-throated lighter beside it. He turns off the flashlight. It takes a few minutes for my night vision to return. He takes my hand, twining his fingers with mine. I'm glad he's here.

I meet Dave's gaze, his brown eyes seem all pupil in the dark. "Do you want to be inside or outside the circle?" When I call all these ghosts, I want a container, something that'll hold in the energies I'm working with and keep any unwanted influences out.

He mulls the question a moment. "Outside. That way if there's any trouble, I can deal with it without disturbing your work." He squeezed my hand. "If you get in any trouble, I'll be inside in a flash."

"I know," I say. I don't say there won't be any problems. That'd be double-daring the Universe, and that'd be a damn fool thing to do.

I pick up my driftwood, walk a few paces to the north, draw a circle around my space, building the container, marking a boundary in the name of the elements of life. "By Earth, Air, Fire, Water, and Spirit, the circle is cast and we are between the worlds. What happens between the worlds changes all the worlds."

My consciousness shifts, a deepening into who I am beyond day-to-day survival. My critical, analyzing brain takes a seat. My intuition, my subconscious, is in charge now.

I take a deep breath. "I call you, Grandpa. I invoke all of who you are now in whatever realm of the dead you inhabit. I invoke all of who you were when you last lived."

I feel him there in the circle. Not only in my head. For once, he doesn't have a word to say. He just waits.

"I invoke all the parts of my mother that vanished, that faded, that became lost to her because of something you said or did. I call back the pieces of her own power she gave away to you."

One minute passes. Two. I'm checking, checking, my intuition wide open and receiving. The circle begins to feel thick. They've come.

I kneel by the cauldron and light the fire. It flares orange and blue. Flames leap with the wind, casting my shadow. A hundred other shades stretch across sand and water.

They all look exactly like my mother. Curly hair. Strong arms. Wide hips. In their shadow faces I read hope because I'm going to give them back to her. I'm going to show them the way home.

Aren't I?

Grandpa steps forward. "I don't think she can handle it, Shel."

"It's her power," I say. "Not yours."

He nods. "And not yours."

That stops me. I hesitate just long enough to lose a fraction of my focus. Just long enough that all the parts of my mother begin to tremble. I'm losing them.

Losing control of the circle.

Grandpa takes a step closer. If I reach out, I'll be able to feel the nap of his jacket. The fire reflects the shine of his shoes.

"They don't belong to you, Shel," he says. "They're not yours to use like this, to throw in my face."

If I make an offering maybe they'll stay. I pull a piece of rough rose quartz from my pocket and lay it on the sand. Rose quartz for love and open heart.

It seems to hold them. It won't for long.

In my mind's eye I see my mother on her sofa, down pillow propped under her head, flipping the cards. Card after card. Solitaire. It's not enough to distract her from how much she hates her own company. She hates her own skin.

She fed me her ghosts and I swallowed them whole.

"You're right, Grandpa," I say. "And you're wrong, too."

I look at the shadows gathered here and wonder if any of them belong to me.

Five, six of them separate from the others. Lost parts of me, coming home. All they need is an invitation. I don't know what they are, who they are. But I say, "Yes," and breathe them in.

The others fade. I can't help them.

"I can't help you," I say to Grandpa.

He doesn't reply for a few minutes. "You can't make me go away," he says finally.

I still want to. "Next time, ask before you start talking."

"And the time after that?"

"Then, too," I say.

He nods, backs away, melding with the darkness outside the fire's glow. I think he understands.

I rest the lid on top of the cauldron, smother the flames. Give my ongoing gratitude to the elements, release the circle. Wipe away any trace of it. The sand feels solid beneath my feet.

Dave hands me a bottle of water. "Did it work?"

"Not the way I expected." I take a good, long drink.

He rubs my shoulders. "You know, I couldn't see you too well. You almost disappeared off the beach."

"I'm more here now," I say.

Leslie Claire Walker

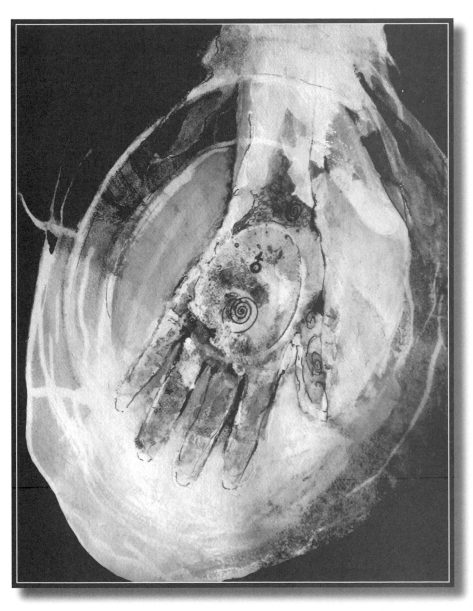

Invisible Hands

Watermedia on Paper

Joyce Eakins

A Common Archaeology

In the dream the original clans gather,
dried stalks of the separate races.
Each knows the long way home,
across famine fields and dust bowls,
plantations and reservations, railway stations.
Memory before womb, before naming.

Shards of beings flaked by ancestors
are thrown into the night brews.
I step into their light and join the sacred
backbreaking work, pulling out blood suckers
before they enter the soul's memory.
We hold each other up before makeshift fires
blanketing ourselves with muttered prayers
that we walk through before the sun comes up
and we shuttle off to separate lives and continents.

In the beginning, before shame,
was a peaceful savanna and one woman
married to the world of trees and grasses.
Each of our histories crowds on top of that layer,
an archaeology of the soul, not to be confused with history.
I stand on one leg while the dried stalks mumble prayers.

At dawn no matter how severe the potato famine,
our grieving for stolen land, the pain of a lynching,
in the midst of my own death in a mass grave,
we throw off the threadbare strings of old blankets
and embrace on the ground by the liquid heat beds.
We slide along the fluids of sex that give us birth
until hope comes trickling out of our back pockets.

Hope is the seed; sex and flowers the perennials.
Poetry: the liquid sounds the lovers make.
These signs of nature are holy; they blossom
into a community of belief. I learn how to exist here.

Before bright daylight returns, I will string
the teeth of poetry through our night intelligence
so none of us is struck dreamless.

Sandia Belgrade

Family History

This story began centuries ago
with the stubborn scrape of burial tools
against chalk ground, or with the
ox-like moan of the final birth push
that brought a child, wet and clambering,
like those first Devonian amphibians onto
the beach of its mother's belly. The moon
was there to see it all, pouring its milk
over your ancestors' upturned faces.
Forebears of the dog posted now at
your side were there, rubbing against
the legs of the ones who were
making the story then.

This epic is punctuated by departures
and arrivals: final embraces and predawn escapes
to the ship leaving the docks, the man she
wasn't to marry, the God they weren't ready for;
the children born out of love and force, demanding
more room, fresh bread; strangers, who appeared
walking up the hill one day and stayed,
knotting themselves into this life with mysterious
threads. The sun shone, sometimes like a
flashlight through a gray woolen blanket,
sometimes like laughter from the heavens,
scattering gold and silver sparks off the washbasin
set by the door, always as a command to rise up
from the depression worn into soil, straw, horsehair
mattress, to write one more line.

It is your story now. We are all reading along.
We know your childhood games, the people
you have loved and lost, the dreams
you hold tight under your sternum, the way
you talk to the mockingbird in the dark
morning when you do not sleep. We

have seen everything fall apart, rivers grow wide
between parent and child. Standing on the banks, we
call out to you, knowing you cannot possibly hear,
wishing for the return of our breath, for another chance
to speak our dying words, the strength
to pull two living hands together.

Or we are waiting our turn, praying
the doors to open, the magic words to be uttered,
sweet courage to rise up like an unseen spring, bringing
songbirds to roost, blessing our beginnings. The stars
are burning holes in the sky; from the marrow
of your bones, newly formed red blood cells
are streaming out in search of oxygen. Open
your mouth wide and pull down a breath, take us
in your arms as you would a newborn grandchild
or your mother's ashes. Carry the story along.

Vivian Gratton

SONGS OF
MY SISTERS

Song is at the core of all poetry, liturgy and sacred texts. From the dawn of human time, music and ritual dance have been a primary means to reach the gods and the spirits. These sacred songs and incantations include prayers for healing and wholeness, the blessings of love, the beauty of the earth, and praise to the sacred mother. All are fully notated for voice and instrument. They are offered to be shared in living rooms, concerts and sacred circles, and to be sung to oneself as private sustenance. These melodies and heart-songs move us towards the sacred in a way that transcends language—soothing, healing, transfiguring the heart.

Spirit Love

Coleen Rhalena Renee

Arranged by Pamela Gerke
Copyright © 2004 Coleen Rhalena Renee

Guide Me

Kate Munger

Guide me through the dark-ness. Guide me through the light. A-bide with me through seas of doubt and in the sa-cred star-ry night.

Rain Fall Down

Bayla Greenspoon

1. Rain fall down on me, ___ heal my bod - y.
2. Rain fall down and feed ___ all the crea - tures.

Rain fall down on me, ___ heal my soul. Rain fall down on all
Rain fall down and feed ___ Mo - ther Earth. Rain fall down on all

___ of cre-a - tion. Rain fall down on me, ___ make me whole.
___ of the chil-dren, tell - ing them of life - and re-birth.

Let It In, Let It Go

Marie Summerwood

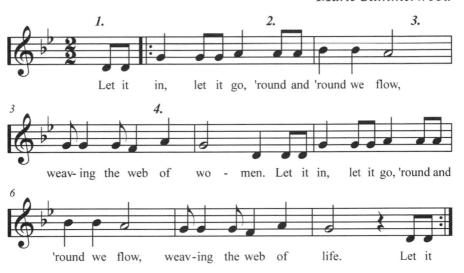

Let it in, let it go, 'round and 'round we flow,

weav-ing the web of wo - men. Let it in, let it go, 'round and

'round we flow, weav-ing the web of life. Let it

The Beauty of the Woman

Marie Summerwood

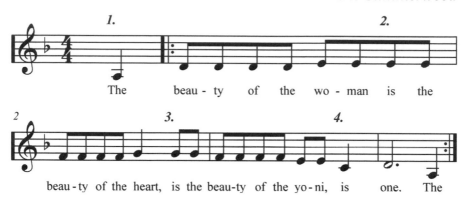

The beau-ty of the wo-man is the

beau-ty of the heart, is the beau-ty of the yo-ni, is one. The

Song From My Soul

Jody Healy

I grant you the free - dom____ to be your - self,
to love and hon - or____ your in - ner wealth.
I'm here as a wit - ness____ to watch you grow,
to o-pen to the pro - mise____ of all you know.

She Walks with Snakes

Marie Summerwood

crown of stars to bless the night.___ Mo - ther Ma - ry,

give me sight_____ that I may see... She

Ma - ry, Ma - ry, Ma - ry, Ma - ry, Ma - ry, Ma - ry, Ma - ry, Ma - ry

stands on the moon.

Elle Marche Serpentine

Elle marche serpentine, se lève sur la Lune.
Elle marche serpentine, se lève sur la Lune.
Elle marche serpentine, se lève sur la Lune.
Notre Marie se lève sur la Lune.

Lumières des mains remplissent mon âme
Couronnes d'étoiles bénissent la nuit
Marie me donne la vision.
Que je connaisse et puisse voir...

Translated into French
by Sappho Morissette and Marie Summerwood

To the Islands

Lynx Quicksilver

When I lay down to＿sleep,＿＿ all of my mind＿in a deep
＿tur - moil,＿ I pray You my soul＿to＿keep.＿＿ So
if you're not smi-lin' just think of the is - lands, the
waves wash your trou-bles a-way.＿＿ The gift of the o-cean, she's
al-ways in mo - tion, the waves wash your trou-bles a-way.＿ So we say,
"Lay lay lay lay＿lay＿lay＿＿ lay lay lay lay＿lay＿lay

In This Body

Mary Blaettler

1. In this bod-y I am learn-ing how to love.
2. In the spir-it I am learn-ing how to be.
3. Through this song I am learn-ing how to sing.
4. In this mo-ment I am learn-ing how to live.

Through this bod-y I am learn-ing how to love. In this bod-y
Through the spir-it I am learn-ing how to be. Of the spir-it
Through this song I am learn-ing how to sing. In this song
Through this mo-ment I am learn-ing how to live. In this mo-ment,

I am learn-ing, I am learn-ing, I am learn-ing, how to love.
I am learn-ing, I am learn-ing, I am learn-ing, how to be.
I am learn-ing, I am learn-ing, I am learn-ing, how to sing.
in this mo-ment, in this mo-ment, in this mo-ment,

in this mo-ment, I am learn-ing how to live.

The Turtle Remembers

Becky Reardon

The tur-tle re-mem-bers a dream in De-cem-ber, a-lone _____ with God, _____ a-lone with songs of the whales, re-turn - ing, re-turn - ing. The

Arms of the Mother

Rhiannon and Jami Sieber

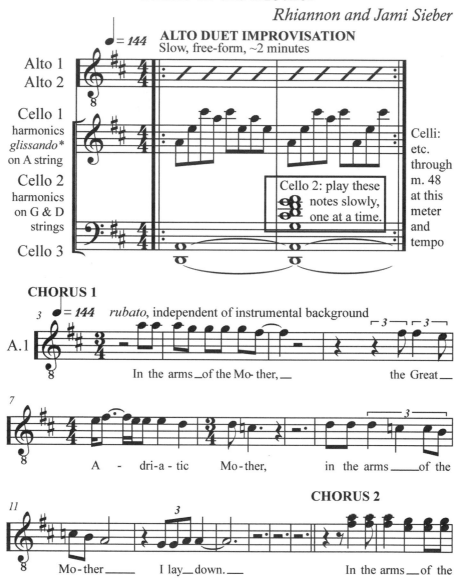

* The Cello 1 legato glissando between the harmonic notes shown will cause other, higher transient harmonic notes to sound intentionally. This piece is most often performed live using a single cello and an electronic sequencer as follows: record two measures of Cello 3; initiate repeated playback; record two measures of Cello 1 and initiate repeated playback; play Cello 2 live.

Lyrics and Music by Rhiannon
Cello Instrumentation by Jami Sieber
Copyright © 2003 RhiannonMusic

Mo-ther, ____ the Great_ A - dri-a - tic Mo-ther, ____

in the arms ____ of the Mo-ther ____ I lay ____ down.

CHORUS 3

In the arms ____ of the Mo-ther, ____ the Great_

_____ A - dri - a - tic Mo-ther, ____ in the

rit.

arms of the Mo-ther I lay down. _____

IMPROVISATION   **CHORUS 4** - *a cappella*

Rhythmic, ~ 2 minutes   ♩ = *100*

In the arms ____ of the

♩ = *125*

Mo-ther, ____ the Great A - dri-a-tic Mo-ther, in the

arms_____of the Mo- ther   I lay_____ down.

CHORUS 5

In the arms_____ of the Mo-ther, _____   the Great_____

accel.

A   -   dri - a   -   tic Mo - ther,   in   the

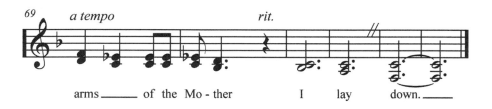

a tempo   *rit.*

arms_____ of the Mo - ther   I   lay   down._____

We Are All Our Mother's Children

Jane Nyberg

1. We are all ___ our Mo-ther's chil-dren. We are all ___ our Mo-ther's
2. We are all ___ our Mo-ther's chil-dren. We are all ___ our Mo-ther's
3. We are all ___ our Mo-ther's chil-dren. We are all ___ our Mo-ther's

chil - dren. We are fire ___ and wind and wa-ter and love ___ up-on the
chil - dren. We are love ___ and grace and beau-ty and light ___ up-on the
chil - dren. [end]

earth. We are fire ___ and wind and wa-ter and ___ love ___ up-on the earth.
earth. We are love ___ and grace and beau-ty and ___ light ___ up-on the earth.

Note: This song can be sung either as a round or sung with the designated chords for accompaniment.

Copyright © 2003 Jane Nyberg

Earth Is Woven Through My Body

Kate Munger

Earth is wo-ven through my bod-y. O-ceans flow in me as blood.

Wind and breath, in-spired,__a-rise. I greet the earth with ev-'ry step.

Copyright © 2000 Kate Munger

Sacred Stones

Shawna Carol

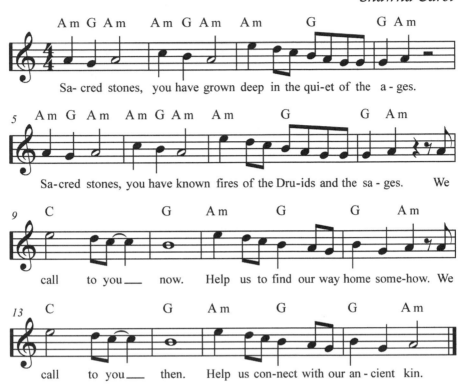

Sa-cred stones, you have grown deep in the qui-et of the a - ges.

Sa-cred stones, you have known fires of the Dru-ids and the sa - ges. We

call to you __ now. Help us to find our way home some-how. We

call to you __ then. Help us con-nect with our an - cient kin.

Somos Tejedoras

Rhiannon

Oo_____ Oo_____

Mm_____ Mm_____

So- mos_____ te - je - do - ras. Weav - ing to -

geth - er,_____ Wo - ven to - geth - er.

Cir-cled by the gol - den threads ___ of the sun ___ we dance._____

Moved_____ by the rhy-thms we har - vest from our souls.

We are the wo - men who glow briHiant,

Song inspired by a poem by Monica Lozano
Copyright © 1992 Rhiannon/ASCAP

dan - cing as ___ we weave, ___ dan - cing as ___ we weave, ___

dan - cing as ___ we weave. ___ So - mos, ___ so - mos, so - mos

te - je-do - ras. Weav - ing to - geth - er, ___

Wo - ven to-geth - er. Cir-cled by the gol - den threads

___ of the sun ___ we dance. ___

Moved ___ by the rhy-thms we har - vest from our souls.

We are the wo - men who glow brilliant,

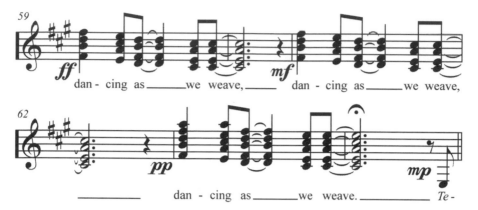

dan - cing as ____ we weave, ____ dan - cing as ____ we weave,

____ dan - cing as ____ we weave. ____ Te -

[The following two-measure phrase may be repeated many times as background for spoken word. In improvizing this song, seven voice parts enter, one at a time, in the order shown to the left of the staff. Each part enters at the "𝄎" symbol, and is sung twice before the next part joins in. Additional parts may be vocal or body percussion. Once all seven parts have joined in, some may come and go from time to time.]

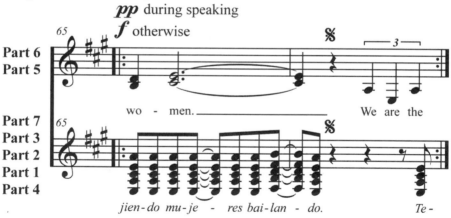

pp during speaking
f otherwise

Part 6
Part 5

wo - men. ____ We are the

Part 7
Part 3
Part 2
Part 1
Part 4

jien - do mu - je - res bai - lan - do. Te -

[These are personal stories told by the women, stories of times spent with other women that are memorable for all kinds of reasons: joy, sorrow, difficulty, transformation. One story leads to another. It is vital that our stories are told, remembered and connected. Understanding that aspect of the song increases the power in any circle in which it is taught. When the storytelling is done, the above phrase ceases and everyone sings the following last line together.]

We are the wo - men. who glow bril - liant!

Laughing Maiden

Ruth Barrett

Laugh- ing maid-en is a-born-ing. Laugh-ing maid-en is a - ris - ing.

Laugh- ing maid - en is a - fly - ing. Spring is come. Spring is come.

Suggested Format
Verse 1: melody only, sung by a soloist.
Verse 2: melody only, all singers in unison.
Verses 3 through 8: a two-group round, where each group sings both melody and harmony.
First coda: simultaneously both groups sing measures 7 through 8 with harmony, twice.
Final coda: both groups sing measure 7 with harmony.

Somehow or Other

Bayla Greenspoon

1. _____ I woke up _ this _ morn - in' on the
2. Well, I'm find-in' out ____ that liv - in' this
3. _____ I'm not a-bout _ to say that there is____

first day of the ___ year.   The snow was fal-lin' all a-round,
life of mine is ___ fine, with my _ friends _ shar-in', work-in', play-in', ___
no-thin' here _goes bad. You know we've got real strug-gles and at_____

_____ so bright and clear it _was. _ I smiled at my be-lov-ed be-
_stronger all the time. _We've_got such beau-ty all a-round us and our
times I feel so sad_____But I_ guess I should ex-pect that, since I

side me in my ___ bed   and then this new year's_ song_ start-ed
lives_are so____ full. Why, with all the strength _ we've got here it makes
live my life _for change. A whole world is real-ly_____ not an eas-y

CHORUS
(Vocal harmony above melody)

spin-nin' 'round_my head: I give thanks for the moun - tains. I give
so much-pos-si-ble.
place_to_re-ar-range.

Testimony

Ferron

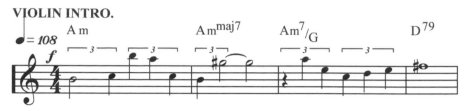

16

F   G^add11

_____ and had,   like ____ we ___ know. ____   But

_____ and doors   and doors   of ____ locks. ____ But

     to the jad - ed _____ jew - el. _____ But

May they take   their ____ own   in ____ turn. ____ And

CHORUS

18

Am   G   F

by   my ____ life   be I ____ spir - it   and
by   my ____ life   be I ____ spir - it   and
by   your ____ lives   be you ___ spir - it   and
by   our ____ lives   be we ___ spir - it   and

22

Am   G   F

by   my ____ heart   be I ____ wo - man   and
by   my ____ heart   be I ____ wo - man   and
by   your ____ hearts   be you ___ wo - men   and
by   our ____ hearts   be we ___ wo - men   and

26

Am   G   F

by   my ____ eyes   be I ____ o - pen   and
by   my ____ eyes   be I ____ o - pen   and
by   your ____ eyes   be you ___ o - pen   and
by   our ____ eyes   be we ___ o - pen

by my _____ hands   be I _____ whole. _____
by my _____ hands   be I _____ whole. _____
by your _____ hands   be you ___ whole. _____ Listen*.
by our _____ hands   be we ___

_____ whole. _____

Violin:

* "Listen" is whispered.

Godfather

Nancy Grace

teach me how to___ live._____ Oh,___ lift me

up___ and show_____ me: to love___ is___ to for-

give._____ Now I don't need a per - fect___

dad-dy._____ The one___ that I had was just fine. __

___ All I need is the love that comes____from my

Heav-en-ly Fa - ther di - vine. So___

Light of My Light

Ferron

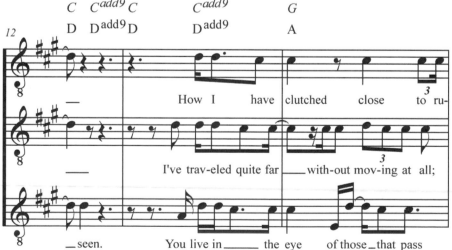

CHORUS

Mother Mercy

Alysia Tromblay

_____ move __ a moun- tain _____ with the hum-b - lest __ of

seeds, dare to whis-per I'm __ wil-ling to __ re - ceive, ___ move a moun-

- tain with __ the sim - p-lest of needs. Oh mo - ther,

VERSE 2

love __ me. Mo-ther com-pas-sion, can you teach me how to find ___

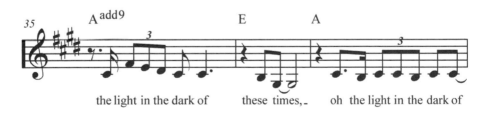

the light in the dark of these times,__ oh the light in the dark of

__ these times, __ oh the light in the dark of _____ my mind?

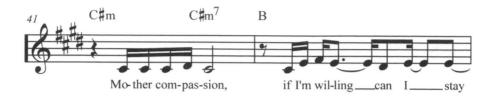

Mo-ther com-pas-sion,   if I'm wil-ling ___ can I ___ stay

___ and learn to love ___ your way   one more day,   oh ___ one more

CHORUS

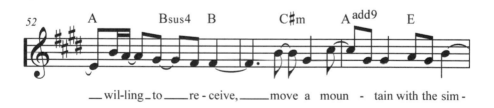

day,   just ___ one more ___ day,   so I may _____ move ___ a moun-tain

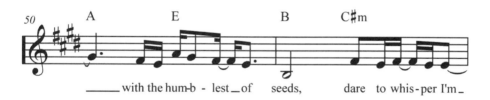

_____ with the hum-b - lest ___ of   seeds,   dare to whis-per I'm ___

___ wil-ling ___ to ___ re - ceive, _____ move a moun - tain with the sim-

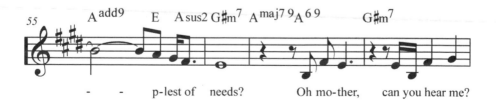

- - p-lest of   needs?   Oh mo-ther,   can you hear me?

Chords Used in Songs

Jerry Paul

Examples of the chords used in this book are shown at the right, for chords whose root note is C. You may play any of the notes in a higher or lower octave if you wish. Note the distinction between CO (diminished 7th) and CØ (diminished half-7th). If a slash appears after a chord name, add the bass note whose name appears after the slash. For instance, "Cm/B" means add a low B to the Cm chord shown at the right. If the "slash bass" note proves too difficult to play, often you may omit it, or get another person to play the bass line.

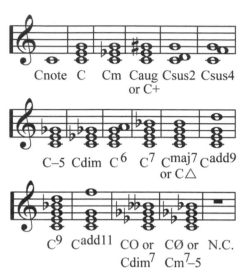

Cnote C Cm Caug Csus2 Csus4
or C+

C–5 Cdim C⁶ C⁷ Cmaj7 Cadd9
or C△

C⁹ Cadd11 CO or CØ or N.C.
Cdim⁷ Cm⁷–5

Guitar fretboard diagrams of some unusual chords:

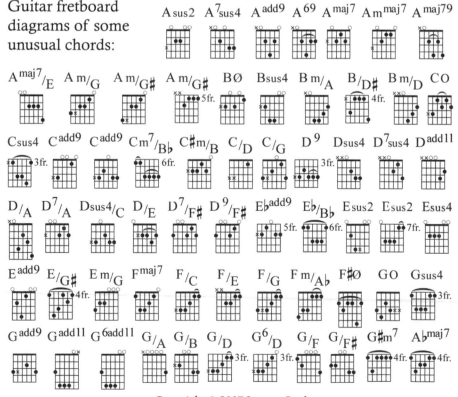

IN THE

OAK GROVE

Everywhere in prayer and poetry we find the human way of touching the sacred in nature. In the ancient Hebrew tradition, the goddess Asherah was said to be embodied in a grove of sacred trees. Celtic druids practiced their holy rituals in oak groves, considered the most sacred of places. These poems, stories and art speak of touching one's holiest self in the wild places of the earth. There are praise songs to trees, to flowers and fields, to the desert, the great mountain, our beloved Gaia. Here, too, is the simple act of putting one's hands in the soil: the lush garden where the earth sings and life flourishes before our eyes.

In the Oak Grove

Oak trees of untold age
extend curved branches
clasp each other overhead,
the bark of their forearms dressed
in scales of gray lichen
and miniature forests of moss.

They whisper and moan
as the wind's convoluted passage
gives them voice.
They speak the language of trees,
the dialect of oaks,
which you begin to understand

if you listen, as they do
for a hundred years.

Sylvia Bortin Patience

Grand Oak

Photograph

Sara Friedlander

These Woods

Walking in springtime
along the river
eager young leaves
burst from branches
my spirit rushes
to sheer delight.

Everywhere
sweet fresh moss
like lacy lingerie
intimately clothing
the patient trees
flares iridescent chartreuse
on curved limbs
in splashes of sunlight.

With a new lover's touch
my hands explore
ever so lightly
the soft green velvet
body and soul tumbling
in exquisite love
with the verdant life
from which I spring.

I am not a stranger
in these woods.

Andrea van de Loo

In Praise of Dandelions

I admire dandelions.
They rise up unbidden,
dotting the lawn
with spots of gold.

You can't get them out.
For every one
dug from the earth
legions sprout
in their stead.

They stand up for their right
to be where they choose,
defiantly yellow in the grass.

They are subversive,
taking back wildness
from the cultivated bluegrass,
audaciously disrupting
the mowed evenness.

When dandelions turn
from gold to gray
they send their daughters
on the wind to reclaim
the feral earth.

Diane Corbin

Fairy Circles

White mushrooms in fairy circles
dot the field
where new grass springs up like green fur
Coming upon the circles suddenly
they surprise me
like remnants from an ancient time
rounded chunks of marble in the sun
fat pearls in a green nest
With bald contentment
they disregard me as I pass by in clumsy boots

Later the mushrooms will be buried
beneath the tall, rank grass
I won't see them change
in the green gloaming
No doubt their perfect caps will break
their soft brown undersides disrobe
Back to earth they will go
before the advent of hot, windy summer

Thanks be that this field
is not of my making
Thanks be that even the garden
surrounding my home
is not purely of my design
Finally, great murderer that I am
I have begun to listen and watch
as seasons turn
How many times have I
subjected pansy to dry blast
and petunia to dull fog?
At long last, I come to read
the changing light

Now, with rare mistake
each living thing
in window box or pot
shows me when to move it
from leeward to windward
We shift positions
following planetary motion
responding to the light

The fields and wood I leave alone
to work their own magic

Elizabeth Tozier

My Neighborhood, My Garden, My Self

When my husband's employer sent us to the South of France, I enjoyed getting to know the place as no tourist could have: learning plants of another climate, discovering a different attitude toward use of space, and every day gazing around me at the most strikingly beautiful place I'd ever lived.

But I also enjoyed our annual trip back to the U.S. for "home leave." Keeping us temporary relocatees in touch with home, the company had found, was good for our morale.

We had left in August; it was May when I arrived back the first time. I looked at the color of the spring woods, the shape of the tall New England trees. I felt the thick mulch of leaves and needles springing underfoot; I smelled the hemlocks—and my body reacted with a sigh, a feeling of being cradled in familiarity, of being in my place.

My awareness of my own self was different, in different surroundings: to be "back home" felt like returning to myself. "Ah, yes," said a part of my mind, "this is reality, this is the real me." Suddenly it seemed I had been cramped for room by the short ceiling of the trees on the Côte d'Azur. Now I could breathe freely again, stretch out ... have elbow room. Under the taller trees, I felt taller ....

But in the next few weeks, even as I enjoyed being back, I started to miss our new home midway between the Mediterranean and the Alps: the flowerbeds in every corner of the towns, the steep, terraced hills overlooking the sea, their ancient, gnarled olive trees still producing. And when I returned, I felt that deep recognition again, this time to see the scarlet wild poppies in bloom—along the roadside, in hedgerows, along the terraces of the hillsides, even whole fields of them in unmown meadows. Coming back to the poppies made me feel—again—"home."

My mind was torn. I felt disoriented, with a very physical sensation that my sense of identity, my sense of rootedness and relation to the earth, was flipflopping back and forth between the two very separate geographic positions.

Finally the discomfort forced me to take a mental step back, or up, somehow—so that I could relocate "me" in a sense of place that encompassed the two "homes." New England and les Alpes Maritimes became two parts of a much larger neighborhood.

After we repatriated, I started gardening more. First thing in the morning I liked to walk out early to say good morning to my garden, strolling through all the beds, front and back and woods, checking for skunk damage and savoring the unique qualities of each plant. One day, instead of heading right back indoors to make breakfast, I paused and lay down on one of the paths, the better to gaze at some violas tucked away in a corner. I found myself wondering why I didn't get down to ground level more often; I couldn't remember doing it since I was a kid. I felt little and the garden felt big, a wonderland that both sheltered me and surprised me with glory every way I looked.

Standing up again, I looked around from a taller perspective, taking in the whole of the garden. There was plenty that could be done, of course: weeding and supporting tall plants and moving others that weren't in the best location—but all in all, the plants were in very good shape and cooperating well with each other. They were happy.

I still felt sheltered, invigorated. I realized I was identifying with my garden. I was happy because it was happy. There was no separation between us, we were all one entity, happy.

When I found myself expanding my neighborhood to include both the New England woods and the poppies of the Midi, I felt my self-perception growing out of my relation to the land. But here, in my garden, now the feeling penetrates to a deeper part of my sense of self. My love for this place expands not just my neighborhood, but me. My neighborhood is the land I know and live in, but my garden is the land I nourish, shape, cultivate, celebrate. It is my larger body.

I do the best I can to nourish health in the body inside my skin, but it has some handicaps, and gives me a fair amount of pain. I think about Buddha's solution to suffering: learning to perceive the self differently. Buddhist Joanna Macy talks about the world as our self. The self does not stop at the boundary of the skin. The self does not stop at any boundary. Who we essentially are is the whole universe.

Well, I'm not there yet, but my garden has taught me the first step. When I breathe in the fragrances of the foliage of chamomile and calamintha and lemon thyme and Russian sage and asters, I sense the leaves transpiring in the sun, giving me delight simply by being who they are abundantly, and I give them back my love and my carbon dioxide. Together we are one organism, one give and take.

May all human beings realize their largest self.

Catherine Holmes Clark

Mountaintop Goddess

Clay

Susan Rothenberg

Earthia

Earthia, Goddess of the Earth
Earthia, Goddess of the Earth
I call upon you,
Come and be with us.
I feel her presence,
Her nurturing energy
Surrounding and filling our being.
Earthia now speaks the wisdom of the feminine.

She says,
Have reverence for your body.
Once a day lay your body upon my body.
For I am your true Mother.
It is I who gave you life.
It is I who nurture You.
Remember, remember your roots,
Your connection with Mother Earth.
Remember, remember your roots,
Your connection with
Mother Earth.
Remember.

Marcia Moonstar

Bare Hands

In February when I was a child
I would kneel
On Ash Wednesday
At the altar rail
So the priest could dip
His thumb into the ashes
Of last year's palms,
And make on my forehead
A soft gray cross
As he said the words:
"Remember, oh man, dust thou art
And unto dust shalt thou return."

This year on Ash Wednesday—
All day digging,
Bare hands in the garden—
I smear my muddy fingers
On my shirt tail
To clean them enough
To touch the doorknob.
This February I smell the truth—
A woman remembering that earth she is
And unto earth shall she return.

Connie Batten

In the Garden of the Heart

Beside the gate this epithet is lightly scratched in stone:
I was a seed. I was a rose. Grandmother now, tree-rooted I am.

In every season, in all kinds of weather, my changing body has stories to share with you in the circle between earth and sky.

Between sky and earth, gardening comes down to bare essentials that reach up for light from fertile ground. Once, when I asked how to prune a camellia tree, an old Japanese gardener told me..."Step inside, look up into the canopy. Follow branches from trunk to twig. Go with them toward the light, until from within you see lace patterns against the sky, until from within you feel branches moving in the wind."

For a garden to feel alive there must be moving foliage and flowers and young limbs breathing in delicate breezes. There must be old trees that hold imprints of storms that bend and sculpt them.

For a garden to feel alive there must be music: sounds of water echoing nuances of changing light and wind in a passing day, sounds of communicating birds and bees, sounds of two- and four-legged creatures scurrying through vines and vegetables and playing in dirt.

For a garden to be alive there must be sex, lots and lots of sex: flowers, promiscuous and selective, opening their scents and colored throats, exposing hairy pistils and freckled petals to invite passing pollinators into the sacred dance of fertilization.

A rose is a rose
opening to morning light.
Fragrant labyrinth
embroidered in petal delight.
Yoni warmly asks a bee
to pollinate her center.
Who knows the rose?
Arabs do. Indians and Chinese too.
Soft wind
She elephant
Flying dragon
Moon gate
Dark pearl
Golden tongue

Velvet chamber
Palace of delight
Happy valley
Heart of darkness
Hairy fire
Valley spirit
Whoever enters 'the Rose' unfolds the soul.

Whoever tends a rose, also knows how much careful attention they require. Such legendary beauty demands high maintenance: regular feeding, seasonal spraying, routine pruning to outward growing canes, to outward facing buds. Roses want the very best: full sun, rich soil, heavy feeding, deep watering, constant cleaning and inspection to reduce fungal disease and insect infestation. After all the summer grooming to encourage bloom, they need a rest under winter mulch gently mounded around their crowns. In every season, roses must be treated specially, like royalty.

This is why I prefer trees. In the garden of the heart, if we grow as strategically as trees we become models of "old growth" maturity. Our coming of age naturally reflects dignified individuality within community. We stand our ground while adjusting to change and weathering seasons. Inevitably with longevity come wounds and scars and limbs lost, but an old tree can grow a callus around a scar to stop disease from traveling deep within. She can staunch weeping from a wound.

Growth through and beyond wounding gives a tree its existential character as it expands from heartwood to bark, season after season. Roots in earth, branches in wind, listen to the voice within. As the author Tom Jay says, "In the heart of truth, there is a tree."

In the crotch of that tree there is a message written on a paper bag: *Gardeners are caretakers of wonder. Water the tree…*

Inside the paper bag is a poem pieced together by many hands, for gardeners of the heart never work alone.

What do you want in your garden?

Visible and divine
Learning from trees

Being fully shaped
By a wildness of vision

Wanting to grow
In light
In rain
In air

Hungry and trusting earth
eating the fruit
with wonder
inside the circle

Between growth rings
Water the tree of life

Step inside
Reach for light
Feel music in the wind.

Katie Metcalf Nelson

A Rose by Any Other Name

Photograph

Karen Koshgarian

The Roses

Roses, Roses, Roses
I praise the roses, my flowery friends
roses, roses, roses

I praise all the colors of the roses
roses, roses, roses
sturdy   soft   and   thorny
these roses, roses, roses

I praise Rosette and Rosina
Rosemary and Rosemarie, Rosie, Rosa, and Roe
Roseann, Roselle, Rosalyn, Rosalind, and Rose
Rosaria, Rosalia, and Rosalie
these roses, roses, roses
these poets and lovers
these mothers, godmothers, stepmothers, grandmothers
fragrant, fragrant, fragrant   roses, roses, roses
these teachers, singers, cooks, and bakers
luscious, luscious, luscious   roses, roses, roses
these musicians, painters, storytellers
roses, roses, roses
these daughters, aunts, nieces, and spouses
dew-kissed   sun-kissed   perfumed
roses, roses, roses

Roses on the walls   roses in the yards
roses in the offices, classrooms, and malls
these roses, roses, roses
roses in and on and with the hearts
roses in and on and by the beds
roses in and on and by the roads
these roses, roses, roses

I praise and I bless my flowery friends
these roses, roses, roses
I call the Great Ladies of the Roses to bless

the roses, roses, roses
Sweet Saint Rose of Lima with your roses
bless the roses, roses, roses
Doctor Little Flower Saint Therese de Lisieux with your roses
bless the roses, roses, roses
Powerful Saint Rita of Cascia with your roses
bless the roses, roses, roses
Our Amerindian Lady of Guadalupe with your roses
bless the roses, roses, roses

Bless all the roses, roses, roses
Bless these demure, daring, and dazzling
roses, roses, roses.

Maria Fama

Gardens I Have Loved and Lost and Loved

Grammie Foss sent her wedding gift by United States Postal Service. It was long and thin and when I opened the package dirt fell out. I gingerly pulled out two rose canes, root ends wrapped in damp paper towel and caked with rooting hormone. I could see my grandmother bearing down hard on a shovel, breaking off these canes from the Seven Sisters rose bush, tended by generation after generation, beneath the living room window of the farm. I planted the canes carefully, wondering how these Maine transplants would take to city life in the Pacific Northwest. The rose bloomed beautifully, alongside lovage and rosemary, sage and lilac. After twenty-five years of wandering I was putting down roots.

Eight years later, we sold our house in Seattle. As we walked around our home with its new owners I pointed and said, "I love that rose bush. If you ever decide to get rid of it, please let me know. We've taken cuttings, but I'd like to know I could come back and get more if I need them." Ted, the new owner, an aspiring naturopath and gardener from a long line of gardeners, agreed enthusiastically.

Our cuttings did not survive. It's okay, I thought, whenever I wondered about contacting them about the rosebush. There's plenty of time to get cuttings later.

This February I dreamed about our house in Seattle. In the dream I walk into the house and do not recognize it. I go outside and turn to the south side of the house, towards the garden. There is nothing there. Instead, darkness leans out of the house. In my dream I scramble on my hands and knees into the darkness, determined to find the roses, but I find nothing.

Later that day I e-mailed Ted. I'd like to come over, I wrote, and take a few more cuttings of the rosebush.

A month later he e-mailed his response: "You're welcome to come over and see if the rosebush is still alive. It's beneath our new deck."

I took a bath and cried. "How could he?" I sobbed into David's shoulder. As I cried I remembered them all. The rosemary, planted our first spring there, grown into a sprawling, partying tree of a shrub, sprinkled with purple-blue blooms and relishing any excuse to perfume the air. The fennel, laden with seed heads outside the window, swaying as I nursed Gabriel in our sunroom.

David's right shoulder was damp with tears and shiny with snot when he asked gently, "What is this about?" I pulled away to blow my nose and, hiccoughing, I told him everything I remembered. When I was done and leaned my head onto his shoulder again, he said, "You talk as if it's all gone, as if it never happened, as if Ted covering up the garden makes it all go away." He touched my cheek gently. "It isn't all gone." I cried harder.

I fell asleep with a pounding headache. That night I had no less than three dreams about going to the house to find the rosebush. In the first two dreams I found the rosebush: both times it was dead. In the last one I found the rosebush alive. I saw the dark crown of the root and two straggling canes creeping upward. I woke from the dream in the gray dawn and dragged myself out of bed.

I determined to go to the house and discover for myself if the rose was alive. I packed gloves, a pot, clippers, dirt, and cornmeal in the car. I didn't know if I was going back to the house to honor my dead or transport the living.

Walking up the steps to the house, the first thing I noticed were the cedars. They were the same—beautiful, tall, full. But at the top of the second set of stairs I gasped. The camellia was gone. The lavender was gone. The lemon balm was gone. The lilac was gone. I stepped onto the porch and knocked. Ted answered, and we went around to the back. I made no attempt to hide my displeasure. He made little attempt at conversation. "If it's still alive, it'll be here in the corner," he said, tapping his foot on the shiny metal deck he was working on that afternoon. "You'll need to go down over there."

He pointed to a space between the privet hedge and the deck, about one by two feet wide. Branches scraped my back as I lowered myself down. Squatting, I barely fit underneath the deck. Once I got past the beams there was about a foot and a half clearance. I shoved a black bucket in front of me. On my belly, I felt the cold press into my gut. My eyes adjusted to the shadows and I oriented myself beneath the deck by locating the fireplace.

The rosemary, the first living thing David and I planted on our property in 1995, grew there. Now there was only a bare patch of ground. I tracked to my left, and my hand brushed against the soft feathery down of young fennel. The rich smell caressed me, and my heart lifted with the song of the chickadees. I looked further to the left and saw it. It was exactly like my third dream. Two long, pale, pinkish canes lifted up from the ground. I scrabbled over to the rosebush. It was alive. Starved for sunlight, but alive.

Two sacks of cement mix, hardened with rain, lay over the bush. I grabbed one of the sacks and pulled hard, inched both of them off the branches and minutes later unearthed the brown core of the main root of the bush. "I'm here," I said, "I'm here. You called me and I came." I dug around the core, arms and shoulders aching from maneuvering in the cramped space, while Ted walked back and forth on the metal planks inches above my head. When he ran the electric saw the sound reverberated in the space between the metal and the ground. I took what I could, and decided to ask David to come back later in the week and get more. I held handfuls of cornmeal and prayed above the shorn dark root.

I crawled to where the rosemary had bloomed, sprinkled cornmeal, and remembered the deep throats of the purple-blue blossoms and the fresh taste of rosemary in my lemonade. I heaped a pile of yellow next to the fennel and offered thanks and gratitude. I half sang, half chanted a deep-throated song. Then I slowly backed out, dragging the planter toward me as I carefully inched my way back to the privet hedge. When I got there I extracted myself gingerly, putting the planter with its bits of rosebush on the deck first, then the clippers, then the cornmeal, and finally hefted myself up.

Ted paused in his work and asked from the sixth rung of the ladder, "So is it still alive?" "Yes," I said, "starved for sunlight, but still alive." I wanted to tell him how mad I was, how disappointed. But I wanted David to come back for more of the rose later, and I didn't want to piss him off. He might tell us not to come back.

As I left I saw the wooden bucket of Kentucky Colonel mint. I took several clippings from it. The sage I planted from seed was thriving. I took clippings from that too. Ted stepped down the ladder and stood behind me. Neither of us spoke. When we got halfway down the stairs I put everything down and disappeared beneath the cedar canopy. I touched the wood and leaned into the tree that towers over the remains of our two kitties: Puck and Pesha. I looked up into the tossing, frothy boughs and whispered, "Blessed be." When I reappeared out of the tree Ted was standing, waiting for me to leave.

Four days later David returned from the old house with two large pieces of root. I planted them both in the last light of the day. At their bases I put nine coins and a handful of rice. I whispered my intentions for our lives in this still-new place, where David and I have chosen to raise our children. I don't know how long we will live in this home. But I will plant a garden here, too. It will be full of flavor.

Hours later, as I prepared for bed, I felt blood flowing between my legs. For the first time since Danny's birth my period started with a gentle flow rather than a series of painful cramps. I closed my eyes and smiled.

Debbie Carlson

Lady of Wild Things

Downtown L. A. *penitentes*
stump on their knees to Guadalupe, some say
her old name, *Lady of Wild Things.*
In Santa Rosa, a bleeding pine bough
in the cemetery reveals her,
thousands flock by Greyhound, limo, field truck,
to touch her face in the weeping wood,
burn candles among the roots,
leave snapshots, braces, rosaries,
business cards, love letters, Bull Durham
in little pinches, Mexican marigolds…
Migrants with a few centavos
chinging in their pockets camp out
in the graveyard, their gypsy fires
bring dogs and nightsticks.

Me, I'm the caretaker's helper
in the landlord's garden,
there's a tree here we've tended
for decades, I don't know the name—
flowers, minute white flowers fall
from her continuously,
each petal precise
as a newborn's fingernail.
White flowers fall, have fallen, will fall
on the altar stone
we rolled in from the field,
on urine-soaked straw
hauled from the stable,
on the burial mound
and the shovel rusting all winter,
on the beer bottle
tossed from a neighbor's window,
on the rotting wicker throne
and the maypole with its filthy ribbons,
on the swallow's mud slick

the lizards' playground
and the ants' acropolis,
on the brass bells
and the rain barrel's black water,
on the passion vine where once I kissed
the caretaker's eyelids.

Maia

Just Brushing the Lips of

Everything on earth
   kisses everything else

Grass kisses sunlight
Wind kisses your face
Just brushing the lips of

It happens all the time

Birdsong flies through air
An axe chops wood
Freckles appear on your arms there
Clouds pass over the blue afternoon

A pen glides over paper
Just brushing the lips of

A painter dips her brush
That bird over there takes wing
While its baby waits for its next meal

A new mother's milk flows
   down to her nipples

A green lizard skitters
   across the land
Ducks mate in the lagoon
Eggshells crack

The river recedes
   and rises with the tides

The pull of the moon
   kisses the lakeshore

Mosquitoes realize it's
time to hatch

The earth turns
round and round

Just brushing the lips of

Jean Mahoney

Seeds

She reaches into the pocket of her apron. It is her special apron designed just for this occasion, made of sturdy cotton, utilitarian beige. Extra-long sashes tie around her waist to form a large bow in back. In front she has placed three pockets, large enough for her hand to fit comfortably and feel around. To please herself, she has attached pins from her jewelry collection to the front: a round rhinestone-studded 1930s brooch, the "Born to Talk" pin her son made for her when he was eleven, a 14-carat-gold stick pin that was her mother's, a bronze acorn lapel pin from a friend, "Farms not Bombs", various baubles of costume jewels that she loves. More are added on whim. This is an important apron and must be treated like an altar.

She takes herself to the garden. The early summer sun is warm and burns through the floating clouds. She is focused. Her intention is clear. Today she will plant her garden.

She pulls her tee shirt over her head, places it on the wicker chair next to her. Removes the scarf from around her neck, puts that over the back of the chair. Unbuttons her pants, steps out of them, folds and places them on top of the tee shirt. Removes her Victoria's Secret high-cut briefs. Flings them; they land behind the chair. Black lace bra goes. She steps out of her orange flip-flops, wiggles her toes as her feet connect with the earth. She ties the apron around her, low on her hips, covering belly and pubic hair, resting on her upper thighs. She inhales a big full breath. Feels her belly expand, pushing the apron up. Lets the air deflate as it rushes out of her nostrils. Takes another breath, then another. She's learned that things come in threes.

She slips her hand into the pocket on the right. Her fingers sift through the contents. There are seeds inside. She doesn't remove them in advance, but trusts her fingers to select the correct seed. Where to start? Her eyes close so that she can listen better for instructions. Start with the heart. Of course.

She fingers the seeds. Ah, this is the one. Removes it into the light. It is pale green, a large plump kidney-shaped seed. She examines it, turns it over, holds it up to the light, then places it on her heart. Immediately it melts into her body.

She wastes no time and places her hand in the middle pocket. Fiddles around briefly, selects two similar tiny round BB-shaped seeds, deep chestnut in color. Places one on each nipple, where they disappear into her breasts. Her hand reaches into the remaining left pocket. Her fingers choose an oval flat seed the size of a penny, ivory with a thin band of black circling it. She immediately places it on her belly, under the apron below her belly button, just at the bottom of the curve of her pooch. It is sucked in with a slight whoosh sound.

Let's see, she ponders, where else. Hmmm, my forehead, and on the top of each foot between the big and second toe. She fumbles around in the middle pocket. Removes a light violet speck of a seed. Touches it to her third eye. A faint tinkle, like Tinkerbell speaking, vibrates into the air. Now a hand into the left and the right pockets retrieves mismatched seeds, a garnet-colored pea-shaped seed for the left foot, a mung bean-shaped amber seed for the right. A jingle of bells reverberates as she lifts and places each foot on the ground.

Okay. She takes a breath and exhales with a satisfied sigh. She moves the wicker chair off to the side. Removes her apron, folds it in thirds to form a pillow for her head. Lies down on the earth. Scooches her body around to form an imprint. The sun begins to warm her flesh. She sinks into a yawning restful sleep.

Later, much later, she stirs. Yawns, satisfied. Stretches her arms over her head. Looks down the length of her body. Ah, there they are: my little sprouts. Small green tendrils grow on her body. From her forehead grows right thoughts. At her heart grows the foliage of compassion, love and kindness. Her bellybutton tickles with creative source tendrils. Each foot tingles with new life to dance, to step with the certainty of joyful action. Soon each will grow to maturity and produce fruit—luscious, juicy, delicious fruit.

She knows they will come. They will pick and eat and all will be right in the world. What a delightful use for her body, her garden of light and love. It is her pleasure. It is her passion to serve this confused world. Now eat! Don't worry, no need to push, there will be plenty for all.

Carolyn Davis Rudolph

Calla Kids

Gouache on Black Paper

Jane Reyes

Everglades

A paved path rises through sawtooth grass.
I have come to see the sun ride down long gullies of leaf
and birds call from their blackness,
exultation in red stripes of wing.
Here under the arcs of grass and flight
eyes skim on the water's surface.
Does my sight mute the land like a path?
Does my tread make firm its intrusion?
In a breath, leaf and wing and ancient eye
wash me with their light.
My eyes and feet are taken
and I too sing and glide.

Lawrie Hartt

On That Day
Santa Cruz Island

String out acorns, shells and bones on waxed red thread
Traverse chalk-stone miles up the cranny of a narrowing canyon
Count *one two three* past sheltering shade of eucalyptus trees
Four cross as dust settles into the silence of geologic time
Five swells as strata of tide lines
Six plunges breath back into birdsong
Seven stitches the three-tiered world
As *eight* beads wind the elements round

What did you chance to see?

sea anemone, green, pink and wavy-white;
mud-cluster of nesting swallow: fragile brown jars
swarm of cliff swallow, drift, turn and skim again
broad green leaves of kelp; leather curtain surface
limpet light on the wall, in the dark cave: touch it
red-needle bill of the oyster catcher: busy busy busy
soft chalk cliff, milky way of beings

What lent itself to sound?

gronk of raven
bleating of sheep, hill wind winnowing
grip of northwest wind reaching through the canyon
wind pressing-in through windows, only looking around
night-bellow of the bull sea lion
singing puddles of bright-green tree frogs
canyon whistle, call, call and gone
and inward, this shell-cup of silence

What did the depths of your body sense?

rhythm of the tides
sun as it rode bold across the sky
buoyant core wobbling, plumb-certain in water
increasing gravity of the moon
unspoken borders/forgotten songs
disappearance of skin
dropping in to all that ever was

What did you admire?

bark-play of the island fox
midden-glint on precipice: abalone
ash paste, shin bone, charcoal chunks, fragile fragments of fish
ironwood trees, *lyonothamnus floribundus*,
dropping finger-notched leaflets
acrobatic raven grace opening up to the sheerness of sun
glistening rise and rise of dolphin across the channel
astonishing continents of constellations

What do you long to see again?

wild horses clattering down the canyon
smooth hooves on river rock, burr-flowers in matted manes
sun lapping-water-sucking sounds, exuberant galloping rounds

What was most tender?

soft belly of a hummingbird
orange-red blossoms of monkey flower
tracing the womb imprints of Chumash huts
tadpoles after winter's downpour
succulent green hands of bunch grass
the swollen dudleya

What was most powerful?

the ocean and its thunder
channel patterns in dark currents
migratory passage for leviathan
two thousand feet down, down
in ancient wave-cut benches
cliffs, canyons, ravines
riven tokens of an earlier earth

Susan Manchester

For Holden: Grief and Hope in the Millennium

I wish I could give you
a drink from a river I knew.
It ran fresh and clear
from the core of the Sierra.
My first sip made me a river creature,
a wanderer of trout stream,
a listener to brook, a gazer of pond.
Today we can no longer drink from her shores.
We have poisoned the water.
I wonder how will you learn this lesson?

I wish I could give you
the farmland that ran along
San Francisco Bay.
That farmland gave homes
to pollywog, mayfly and weasel.
It was this land that beckoned me
to follow nature.
This land inspired me to wonder.
Now that it is gone,
how will you learn this lesson?

I wish I could give you a walk in the wild
hills of my childhood,
where I hid from judgment and decoded
the song of cricket.
Those hills gave me comfort
in the shelter of tall grass that held me,
in the hum hum of bumblebee,
in unmeasured time when my soul took flight.
Now the hills have been caged behind a giant gate
and flooded with houses.
How will you learn this lesson?

I wish I could give back the fish in the sea
for they, like the stars, kept our stories alive.
I watched salmon run from salt to fresh water
high in the mountains.
Their bodies became crimson miracles
that felt the pull of the moon.
Their internal compasses pointed them
away from the tide
towards the alluring scent of homestream.
Their journey gave me purpose.
They taught me how all of life is a cycle.
How will you learn this lesson?

I wish I could give you the knowledge
to clean rivers, a way to unpave farmland,
the desire to let the hills remain wild, the wisdom
to take only what you need.
But these are only wishes.
What I can give you is the gift of life
and hope you will listen to my teachers:
the mountain, the water, the hills and creatures.
Only then will you learn these lessons.

Lea Haratani

One Precious Moment

Joshua Tree Desert

Imagine if you will
hawk soaring high above Eagle Rock Peak
where yucca tree threesomes
sport bulbous white blossom stalks
atop pointed crowns.
Down below
crunchy gravel washes
dotted with spring flowers
purples, pinks, yellows,
oranges, whites, reds
dance jovially
as hummingbirds
and bees
partake of their sweetness.

And the birds, the bees
dance a dance of joy
flitting
from one succulent
to the next—
doing the busy work
to maintain the sacred lands
of the Cahuillas
who roamed here not long ago.

Hot pink tiaras sit proudly
atop the barrel cactus,
and brilliant reds
adorn the majestic ocotillo.
Juniper trees mingle amid
yellow-flowered sage,
while rabbit, mouse, and quail
take refuge
from the golden sun
beneath their much-coveted greenery.

Deborah Phoenix

Spider Web

Photograph

Terese Armstrong

Canyon de Chelly

A woman prays at Canyon de Chelly
the sun rises over
Spider Grandmother's sandstone spire

    distant starshine
    warm first light
    sacred rocks, juniper trees, sagebrush
    the wind is a presence
    one eagle flies overhead

spirit guides, come
animal mentors, come
a woman prays at Canyon de Chelly

    seashells of past ocean
    dry sands of the wash
    change and stay
    ancient Anasazi cliff dwellings
    present Navajo hogans
    change and stay

    hawk and owl
    sheep and herders
    cornfield and stream
    trees and scrub
    prairie dog and mouse
    change and stay
    sing the power of the pulse
    the holiness of sunshine on stone

a woman prays at Canyon de Chelly
changes   changes
and stays.

Maria Fama

La Luna

Para la luna en el dia de San Valentin
For the Moon on Valentine's Day

En el cielo	In the sky
la luna brilla	the moon shines
pero	but
en el cuerpo	in the body
ilumina	it brightens
el corazón	the heart
En el cielo	In the sky
la luna brilla	the moon shines
pero	but
en el corazón	in the heart
ilumina	it lifts
la alma	the soul

Linda Serrato

Tierra de Mi Madre

My husband does not fear losing me to another lover
as he fears losing me to this land,
these wide singing stretches of salt cedar and sand
these piñon-peppered mountains
the Sandias, Nacimientos, Sangre de Christos,
this air that strikes with such clarity.

With one breath I lose my profession,
I forget the sound of the ocean,
the smell of plum trees blossoming
outside my bedroom window.
I know only this singing that calls to me
Come back—Come home.

If my companion knew how loud, how insistent this desert siren,
would he ever let me return to this home
that first called me before I was born,
pulling my mother seven hundred miles across Texas
so that I could take my first breath here
in this place they call the "land of enchantment"?

He has sworn never to leave the golden hills of California,
the live oak, the madrone, the red-tailed hawk, the friends
that are worth more than anything we own—
and I have agreed—
but in this high desert I find the singing grown stronger,
the smell of juniper and pine overpowering.

I call back, in a language I never learned,
sending my own song out to the far ridges—
tierra de mi madre, my motherland,
my bare-skinned lover.
I am in your arms again.

Vivian Gratton

The Roar

The powerful force of my yell-shout knocked me backward to land on my ass. A moment before, I was standing in the mouth of a cave in the canyon wall—though it could not really be called a cave because the mouth was as wide as the inside. It was, rather, an enormous football field-sized opening in the canyon wall, created by sandstone falling away as eons of water dripped into crevices. Below me, thirty feet down, grasses, downed trees, and ravaged cottonwoods staked their claim in a flat area of earth, heralding October with brilliant yellow crowns.

I had come with eight women backpackers into wild lands with the promise of connecting to spirit. Little did I know that the sheer simplicity of doing something so unfamiliar would bring me to my knees—or ass, as it seemed in this moment. We had hiked all day after spending a freezing night in Kodachrome Canyon in Utah. Unprepared for the cold, I'd slept with two sleeping bags besides my own. That morning I had followed my sisters' easy flowing steps, slowly penetrating red rock by following a dry streambed. Whipped by branches, later fording icy water with legs unused to long hikes, we had arrived at the confluence of two creeks called Coyote Gulch. With the October weather colder and wetter than we anticipated, we began to make camp in this massive dry place.

As I unpacked my gear, a surge moved through me and brought me suddenly to my feet. This was not the same feeling that had dragged me up and over the rugged places on the trail. My belly sank back and rested on my spine. A bubbling filled that space, demanding movement and attention. My feet felt as if they'd grown into soil, my toes alive and curling into warm mud. Strength of purpose filled my legs like steel, ramrodding me into a colossal energy beacon. I felt my head could touch the flaky white and black seep-stained ceiling of the cave, some twenty feet above me. Something outside of me flung my arms out to my sides—I would ordinarily never be that bold or take up that much space—a sensation like a rusted locked door suddenly sprung, and the contents that had been inside, boiling against the door, pushing for centuries, surged out in a blast.

The spaces around my heart that had never witnessed air or breath or light sucked in these very substances, more nutritious than any food. A throbbing ran from my heart through my arms, tingled my fingertips and ran down my spine, meeting the steel in my legs and penetrating the stone beneath my feet, then ricocheted back up and slammed against my throat.

Throwing my head back, I had no choice but to let out the sound hammering to be released. My long-silenced, stifled, rusted voice became a cry, a wail, a growl, then a full *roar*.

The power of it left me sitting on the canyon earth, looking around, wondering how I had landed legs outstretched, cold stone penetrating my clothing. My sisters were off to the right setting up the kitchen, others were staking their backpacks to the wall or reorganizing supplies, one or two simply gazing—now each turned and stared at me.

In surprise and recognition, one by one they joined me where I sat on cold stone. The leaders hauled me to my feet with the craziest of smiles and laughter on their faces. In the October evening the combined sounds emanating from this deep canyon wall rumbled with the essence of knowing the one inside, the one outside, the one everywhere—which has no name or place or time, but lives pulsing in every one of us still.

Marci Graham

Banner Peak

Clouds half-cover
the face of the god I have known
since childhood. How soon will the veil
lift to reveal the dark cheekbones,
eternally gazing glaciers,
eyes of complete compassion?

Blue rain slants deep
in the canyon to my left. Mists
climb and curl gracefully
over the peaks. Fold upon fold
of crystalline granite, like
a giant stairway,
beckon up the canyon
back to the time
this god spoke silent
words of love and promise
to a listening child.

Standing tall on the steep slope
of pumice sand and lavender lupine,
I sing out my sorrows,
my prayers and praises. Reach
with arms wide, call across the canyon
my own name—

and the god replies
with perfect silence.

Linda Holiday

Cherry Creek

Photograph

Connie Batten

Sunrise at Dark Canyon

Rise up, run,
run across the sandstone,
cry out to the red
swallowing chapparal,
chase the piñon on fire,
run, run
before the owls' cries
get lost into minutes.

Leave behind shoes
and unfinished dreams.
Come quickly,
glide without muscles
and leave behind toes.
Climb higher
and watch pinnacles
ignite.

For the sake of your one life
wake up
and run,
don't give up
until you arrive
on the rim
of today's canyon.

This once,
don't shield your eyes.
Choose to stand
on the edge,
and be your full self,
melting.

Anne Mize

IN PRAISE OF WATER

Water is a wondrous blessing and a necessity for all life on earth. Rivers, streams, bays, inlets are the places where human societies form. These poems, stories and artworks praise the river and the stream, the ocean, the sacred well, the mists and the sea. They speak of the power of water to awaken and heal, the beauty of a quiet lake, and the prayer that the saving rains will come and shower the earth. Millennia ago, our ancient primordial ancestors emerged from the sea. Even now, our bodies are three-quarters water. Water is our birth, our essence, the healing elixir of life, and we sing praise.

From Where I Stand

From where I stand
I cannot see
how the river began
or when it will
fall finally into
something else.

It is enough to watch
leaves float beyond
the sound of my voice,
to see fish stay in the deep
while waiting for
some shiny promise.

This is what I always come back to.

The river doesn't need
to know anything,
find anything,
or forget anything.
I want to move inside it,
feel its song
opening around me.

The river can hold each stone
to its place, its purpose.
It will go to the lowest ground
before it finds the sea and
there become something new.

I listen for its silence,
know I can return
to its banks and it to mine.

Ziggy Rendler-Bregman

Baptism

Oil on Canvas

Robin Rector Krupp

Birthsong

I am of water, and of air.
At three weeks old
holy water bathed
my brow, and they say

I was an angel, that
I lay serene and calm while
the priest held me awkward
blood rushing to my head

along with God's water.
Sometimes angels stand
on the tip of a needle
or along the ridges

of a woman's comb.
Sometimes angels are at baptisms,
indecipherable chants
underneath the world, singing,

You are held,
you have always been held.
You come from sea creatures
who flew on ancient wings.

Your feet were fins,
your arms lush feathers.
Don't trust the land doctors.
Ignore the priests

when they intone over you.
You are more water
than land, and inside the cells
of your body lie great stretches

of uninhabited sky.
You can swim, or fly.
And when you are called
you will return, floating

into the opened legs of your mother,
where you were born
in a splash of breaking waters.
Sea mists will welcome you home

to a world as heavy and light
as the moment
just before the moment
you were conceived.

Carolyn Brigit Flynn

In Praise of Water

We are driving back through the rain, through the high passes. There is snow on the mountain and it is dazzling, as luminous and pure as the bright almond blossoms we saw the day before. Water and beauty and now this downpour. At the end of the play we saw, the two characters reach toward each other. They hunger for touch, for gentleness, for kindness. They drink water from each other's mouths. They enter the water body of each other. In the theater, rain washes over them. They are drenched as they cling to each other.

I had chosen to see the play instead of going to the mikvah, the ritual bath before Shabbat in which one dips three times in living waters. Instead I immersed myself in language, in poetry, in living words, because I am a believer in the possibility of words to heal us.

All through these days I ask myself: what shatters us, what heals, what are the sounds in which one can be immersed and rinsed and restored to wholeness? At the end of the play the characters take an imaginary ride to the ocean. They can see the vastness of the waters. My own tears begin then, as I see them onstage visualizing that journey home.

And an ancestor named Alma has come to me from the songs of my people and the waters of the Mediterranean, the body of water that my own body remembers. The songs of this water live in my cells. I am drenched in their beauty. And so the tears come again washing over me. At what moment did Alma recognize that she was a healer? When did she realize that her voice, her songs, her stories were themselves a kind of healing rain?

Back in town again I get ready to make my way down the coast. Though it is raining, something compels me to stop at my friend Sara's tiny apartment. The kitchen is warm and she is cooking as usual. Whatever she makes will be given away to whomever appears. She tells me how she translated a message for a Mexican man who does not speak English, who needed to tell his boss that he had to return home to Mexico because his pregnant wife was about to give birth. Sara tells me how she leaves food for this man while he works, sandwiches carefully wrapped, and water to drink. In return he leaves her his words in Spanish. Beautiful notes of gratitude.

Words, water, food, gratitude.

I am sitting in the Synagogue, in Shul, a bright room with a stained-glass image of the Tree of Life, the sephirot, a living symbol of how we come to wholeness. The Rebbe and his wife are singing. Their song has no words that I know with my mind. It is as if they have taken me with them to the great ocean. In this place there is only love and it is so immense, so fierce, so tender that as I sit there my body is dissolving, becoming water. Tears flow down my face and I cannot do anything to stop them. I am becoming a river, a waterfall. My body is weeping. I am drenched in healing music, healing rain.

Music and tears. Sara calls me on the phone. She is listening to the Opera Nabuko on the radio, live from the Met in New York. She is baking *biscochicos* and crying at the same time. I am thinking about these precious tears, how they heal us.

My little brother died at twenty-five. He was made of water, and harsh words shattered him. The cells were broken up and scattered. They could not find their way back home. Just like in the fairy tale, I was the little girl who sang at the fountain, trying to protect him from harm, from evil.

And this evil, what is it really? Isn't it the inability to weep for oneself or for others? Isn't it the way that hearts harden and dry up and shrivel and become bitter?

In this moment, I can see my ancestor Alma. She sits in the old Synagogue, in the women's section. She can distinguish the sound of her beloved's voice from all the others. She can hear his soul in his voice and it is as if she has been given eyes and ears into his heart. Listening deeply is one of the most precious gifts she has.

In that listening she is praying. She is mending what is broken. She is hearing the wholeness. Later when she wanders home along the path next to the river, she will remember and sing her gratitude that she can hear the soul of her people, both the pain and the longing. In the longing, she can also hear the depth of the love, and the possibility of meeting, of returning home. Inside the tears is the abode of joy.

Alison Bermond

The Return of Her Rivers

She came from the heat at the heart of things

Her rivers ran tropical
Slowly traveling south
Carrying a cargo of memory and leaves
Fulfilling the dreams of canyons and creeks

The artist longed to breathe her aura
To become still enough
To hear her relentless passages sizzle over
And under ancient stones and markers
Placed by peoples long since removed
From the bonds of their bones and brains

For to merge with her fractures of light
To sparkle in her diamond eyes
Blazing under flood lamps of sun
Is to be blinded
And made whole once again

Deborah Gorman

Nesting Place

Photograph, Rancheria Creek, Yosemite

Heather Lewis

Three a.m. at Lake San Antonio

This is only a lake

and you are only half a moon

and I am only one woman

gazing at you

lovingly

in the middle of the night

Linda Serrato

Beyond

Beyond ordinary understanding there is a woman on the ocean
surrounded on every edge by wavering, fathomless blue.
Her eyes are the color of the sea when the sun is lolling in midsky.
Her hair is the color of the sea when the light has lain down
behind the horizon's veil.
Her skin is salty and she dines on algae, turtle eggs, and kelp.

The woman makes her voyage.
She has a map encoded with red and blue lines on strands of DNA.
Her compass is the eightfold dream she has borrowed from the octopus.
She is drifting like kelp, or bone-colored wood, toward the answer
to the mystery.

She speaks with gestures and animal cries.
The jellyfish and the starfish speak her language.
Her voice sends out waves that tickle and ripple in all directions,
like tentacles, or love.

Beyond ordinary understanding is where she is at home.
She understands the singing of the coral.
She reads the etching on the turtle's scarred hard back;
like hieroglyphics, they tell her what direction to go.

Lisa Beaulieu

The Sound of the Sea

for Florence McNeill Wild

You see, there was this woman, a dark-haired beauty born on a farm in a green, green countryside. It was an island, so naturally the people thought often of the sea, and of what lies in and over the waters.

It was this way for the girl-child of a farmer and his too-quiet wife. You see, the girl-child's mother was like many quiet women in this place. The man in her life, this farmer-husband, took the wife's breath into his own lungs and used both their voices to live his life. His words were too quick—as if he knew the breath he used did not really belong to him, so the words would come out as if pushed by a high wind.

This girl-child and her younger sister would hide from the words, hide from the wind that belonged to their mother's breasts and dream of other places, of the sea and what lay under and across the water.

This girl-child, named for the flowers in her mother's quiet garden, and her sister, named for the sound of the sea, grew up with the animals and the seasons of farming.

They grew up with the softness of turned earth under a rain and the green of new fields. They grew up with spring calves and lambs.

There was always the short warmth of the summer, followed always by the glow of the fall fields and the red from the blood of the slaughtered spring favorites.

And there was their mother's silence and the wind of their father's words.

All this, year after year, as the island grew older around them until spring came into their bodies and their blood. They saw summer dancing to a pipe and fiddle under a warm moon. And there was the sound of the sea and the sight of the water at the edge of the world.

Then there was war across the water and the hot fire of explosions rather than summer storms. With the war came men, many men, with stories of places across the water, of times at sea.

The sisters listened. They heard the voices of men that did not exhale into their mother's face. They felt hands on them that did not hit first and then ask reasons for joy found unexpected and out of sight from the house.

And there was the sound of the sea that called to the water in the sisters—all the unshed tears of quiet childhood longing for the ocean.

The men left. They went back across the ocean. They left promises of things the sisters could not see on an island ringed with so much salt water.

And when the quiet mother was buried, and when her husband's voice lay beside her in the soil, the sisters said it was time. And they left. Each one hearing a silence that needed to be filled with the sound of her own longings.

But there was only the sea and the sound of water against the edge of their world. There was only the water and what lay under and across it.

And they left.

The sister of flowers went first, went to see if the sound of the sea was the same on another island called a continent. She traveled many days, coming again to an edge where the water touched the land, and there was rain and an occasional storm and the sound of a man's voice like her father's, pushed from inside a hollow place that echoed with breath like the wind she remembered. And so she stayed by the edge of this sea, looking back at the land she left.

The sister with the name of waters followed her off their island, to places where no one knew her name or how to call her so she could hear the sound of her own voice answer. This sister of the sea worked alone and met a man who was the silence behind her father's words and the silence of her mother's voice. And she married him and moved away from the edge of a land where the sea could still be heard.

But this sound of the sea, and what lies under and across the waters, remained in their memory. I know. I have heard it in their voices when they would tell me of leaving, and how it is to turn away from home.

Danelia Wild

Contemplation

Photograph

Michelle Sumares

Be Still and Know Love

Be still and know love.
Love comes in infinite forms.
It comes as a sacred presence, surprising and arresting you at the crossroads, taking your breath away, felling you to your knees.
It comes as a sudden thunderstroke, crashing, deafening, blinding and illuminating, blasting the citadel, the fortress, the castle, prison and temple you built to house your sacred dreams.

In silence, love comes stealing into the still dark and receptive pool where dreams form like clouds in water and fallow fields receive seed.

I was enclosed but not protected, versed though not defended. And, reverently though I bowed my head in the ancient crypt, trod the labyrinth, foot in ancient thong, and knew well the wrongs and rights of ancient script, love came crashing, cracking the nave like heaven's drum, imploding structure, exploding form, and before my eyes, raised and shattered were the seven stones carven with seven creeds. The twenty-two letters were lifted, liberated, split one from the next into burning skyrocket jewels that flew all akimbo, tumbling, reeling, and were dashed into sands of seven deserts and doused in the fathoms of the seven seas.
Love electrifies. Love strikes midstream and you are raised sailing to the highest peaks of ecstasy, as the world as you had known it blasts into oblivion and dissolves in irrelevance. An instant in love's embrace and your destiny changes course.
Then, without warning, love drops you out of the sky.
What has the power to raise the dead has the power to scatter remains amid ruins.
By love you are exalted, by love you are destroyed.

I perused the ancient grounds where love's firestorm had so lately shattered the flooring, pulverized the pavement painted by ten generations, reduced to rubble the ruts my people had trodden dreamlike for two thousand years.
The edifice crumbled, there was no more outside or in, no dark interior retreat from exposure. What was hidden stood starkly naked and re-

vealed without border, boundary, limit, shell, wall, roof, ceiling, name or enclosure.

All that remained, as far as I could see, was the sacred well, the holy spring around which it had all been built in the beginning, too long ago for any story to elucidate.

In the midst of ruins, I slumped beside the pool.

This pool. This water. This living spring. It ends then, here, where it all began.

After the maelstrom, after all that was built is cast asunder, there remains what was, is, and ever shall be.

Suns and moons passed as I sat by the well. In the starlight, creatures came to drink, raccoons, all manner of cat, opossum, and in the early dawn, birds, fox and deer. By day, fish sprouted and tree frogs mated. I, too, drank from the bubbling waters, and, after a fashion, I became fascinated.

The dark pool twinkled under winking stars, the moon's reflection crossed the surface and in the dark mirror I saw images of things I had known and loved and things I had refused to examine, visions from which I had turned away.

Do stars dancing in the water dance in the sky also?

Visions of those I had loved and lost floated just beneath the surface.

I saw in that pool the reflection of my world, my world itself the valley of the shadow of life, the valley of the shadow of death. I saw the image of a five-year-old child shredded by shrapnel, a young girl sold for the market worth of her body, a manchild forced to kill for a cause of which he knows nothing, a baby born with opiated dreams, a young mother mad with loneliness, a widow stoned for comeliness, an old man dead with one eye open.

In, around, beneath and through these images, golden fish cut the water rippling. They birthed tiny golden fish and swallowed them whole.

A cat caught a red-headed finch chirping at water's edge and broke its neck.

A shimmering lime-green snake slithered into the fluid and silently gulped a translucent silver fish full with progeny.

I looked into the well and saw life eating life as if all of life was mouth and belly. Belly and womb. Womb and tomb. The pool doled out life and reeled life in, gave birth to death.

Light gave way to dark, dark to light, light to dark in the passage of days, and as I contemplated, it began to seem as if the nature of the reflecting pool reflected the nature of life itself. The amniotic sac was all death, but all life also, full and empty, thick and thin, wholly pregnant and savage.

The reflecting pool teemed with ends and beginnings—perhaps in equal measure.

Plants grew up at the perimeter, green, growing grasses doe and fawn grazed upon. Cottontails leapt up out of mint fields and monarch butterflies lit on yellow buds of fennel.

In the water, gelatinous bags of black seed transmuted into iridescent black fish that grew legs and became emerald frogs, who crawled out of the pond singing.

Mayflies grew diaphanous wings and flew upright out of the water.

In the trembling ripples, I saw an image of children dancing in a meadow.

In the ripples, I saw a vision of a child's face, my child, my own baby.

My heart leapt then, jumped like a frog in my chest, fluttered like a fledgling robin jumping at the edge of the nest. And my lungs filled with a sensation I can only describe as tender jubilation. It was a feeling so sweet it pained me.

Suddenly it was as if the sorrow and the joy of it all stood so intimately commingled that they were inextricable and could not be rendered separate. Sperm dies into egg. Egg dies into fish. Fish dies into embryo, and so life ends—and begins.

Listen, said my heart, *All that is born dies. All that is formed passes. The sorrow of that, and the sadness of that, and the mystery of the swallow swooping out of the clear blue sky and consuming the mayfly in first flight, is more than your small philosophy can comprehend.*

My heart said, *Feel the joy of the mayfly rising! Feel the perfection in the swallow's swift glide!*

And I did feel joy when the mayfly flew. Indescribable. But, torn—it was like my own self was plucked by the swallow's gluttonous beak just in the moment of triumph—and I had to ask, what, then, this belly of the bird? Is it then death? Or some other stage of this strange transformation?

How could something so accurate, so acutely perfect, be *wrong*? And, yet, I was a sieve. The meaning flowed through me and I could not contain the sense of it.

I perceived the pool as a great and wise lady, infinitely greater and wiser than I would ever be. Her eyes were full of sorrow. Her eyes were full of joy. They sparkled with the commingled emotions of love and release, nurturance and terror, for they are, are they not, every one of them, her children?

I, too, sat like the child at the edge of her skirts. I, too, like the others, felt the immensity of sustenance, the power of creation and dissolution of form, and I felt a sense of veneration. This holiness. Grander than the artist's imagination.

I saw death everywhere, and in death, life. I saw life everywhere, and in life, death.

And I felt compelled to grasp life, to hold and protect life while it lived, even to give birth though it imperiled me and meant death to my offspring. I felt impelled to create, to pour life in the mix, even though, yes, even though all creation, *my* creation, will meet its end—or change form.

I sat in awe—in sorrow and joy—observing continual metamorphosis, the poignant issue of what seemed to be life and death twirling endlessly into each other all around me.

And suddenly I realized that what I thought was life, what I thought was death, was not life, was not death, but was what *is*, living the pathway so ordained by the great ordainer that flows through all.

I saw life in death. Death in life. The baby dove, not knowing this world or the next, in faith and impulse, breaks the shell.

This I saw as I sat by the wellspring in silence.

Dropped into ruin after love's riotous jolt, I felt this place in sorrow. And now, after bearing witness for fifty-two days and nights, which seemed like fifty-two weeks or fifty-two years, though the images of sorrow remain, they came to be laced with a gratitude so powerful that it filled me with a sense of hope, promise and fate.

Love blasted the sheath, allowed me to see beyond the veil. I saw then as the first ones saw, truth before form, truth as it was before they cast creed into stone, made the sacraments and built the structures to house them. The truth, I saw, was between the lines. At the source, life and death are one and the river that runs through it all is love.

For love, and love alone, life makes life.

My impulse was to seize the moment, to cry out *Yes!* To cry out *Love!* To fall in love, to lose space and time in love, to make art, to plant fields, to give birth, to carve a creed, to build a holy shrine.

I gazed into the well, drank deeply, and what was dark became light. I saw my own image shimmering with crystal clarity.

The mystery in my eye was vaster, deeper, more conjoined, desultory, blissful, empty, sorrowful, and filled with life than the smallness of my letters could contain.

That pupil—a twinkling pool of love. These tears—love's sphere for golden fish to swim in, love's anointment for the journeyer's transmigration.

Who journeys? Love.
What does love seek? Love.

Love is the traveler, the journey, the point of departure and the destination. Love is the way and love is the means.

Love is eternity in the current of the stream.

Pamela Eakins

River Rocks

Photograph

Connie Batten

Walking the Creek

Waters from the snowy, sacred mountain,
Place of perfect balance, say the Chumash,
Once seeped down into the creek all year, cold
Even in August's fire season,
And then afterwards, into September,
Even until the first rains of thanksgiving,
A trickle of the old stream, flowed.

Walking the creek this July morning,
Gray river stones mark the graves
Of reeds alongside corpses of trees,
The brown dust of dry leaves,
This year's season, amber on the ground
Where we have known loam.

I dreamed Fire came in all her raiment
Over the ridge, and a petitioner
Took his drum and began praying,
As if on his knees,
Praise to the Great One, as She descended
Among the torches of great oaks
And the fireworks of pines.

Fire is a god,
The hidden one, her power
Contained in stars,
The nuclei of strange particles and
The sacred magma at the core of planet earth.
We cannot drink it,
We must not take it in our hands.
It does not serve us
To breathe it in.

Michael, the Archangel, Water
And Gabriel, the Archangel, Fire
Together they are peacemakers,
Who form heaven, *Sh'mayim*,

Through the gathering
Of the holy letters,
Shin, the eternal flame
At the core of fire, *Esh*,
And *Mem*, the essence
Of the sacred water, *Mayim*,
Sh'mayim, heaven,
Includes *Yud*, the Divine itself
And *Aleph*, the silent one,
At the beginning of beginnings,
Ever present in the word.

Fire season, we call it,
Not knowing, not wanting to know
The Holy One. Instead we make
A furnace of our world,
Separating the sacred from the sacred,
Water from fire,
Splitting the atom of paradise,
Fulfilling the prophecy of ultimate sin
Written this century
In the burning bodies of the holocausts
And the oldest ancestor's oily bodies.
The world is no longer
The Temple of the Sacred:

It would be a sacrilege to call for Rain.
Yes, it is a sacrilege to call for Rain.
Thus, we can only pray for the Rain.
Pray for the Rain. Yes, pray *for* the Rain.
Please pray for the Rain.

Deena Metzger

IN THE NAME
OF RAVEN

Animals have lived on the earth many millennia longer than humankind. Owl, horse, seagull, fox, wolf, snake, cat, deer—these are our ancient kin, and we have never known the world without them. Animals have been connected with the human urge to pray since ancient times, and have long been part of sacred scripture, texts and holy art. These writings and art sing of the profound and deeply rooted spirit connection between humans and animals. We see the ways humans live with animals, learn from them, dream of them, and are blessed by them. We see also the heartache of what has been broken between animals and humans, and the prayer for how that relationship can be made whole again.

West Cliff

Small black birds filled three cypress trees
and chattered, so that the trees themselves seemed to trill.
We craned our necks to see the small black dots.
Suddenly dozens of birds took flight together
rose in a cloud, then whirled,
letting the wind take them,
and I laughed aloud at the miracle of wings—
laughed, and cried a little.

I tried to tell you then:
prayer shawls, prayer books, incense and candles
are only helpers if you've lost the way.
The destination is a flock of black birds
chattering, rising, wheeling in the air.

Cara Lamb

The Blue Embrace

I am here on the garden swing
lazing in the sun on the same spot
where the cat lay curled in dreams
of clouds and embryonic peace
before I came,
but, please, don't look for me now.

I am entering the cat's world for a while,
losing myself in the scent of eucalyptus leaves,
resting, with unhurried grace,
under skies pregnant with treetops
and the flapping wings of birds,
dreaming of the gentle Mother's
silent, blue embrace.

I am concentrating on the cat now—
not on its departure,
but on the absence of its calm repose—
and I wish not to be disturbed
when I am feeling myself into a soft ball of fur
and shutting out everything but

the sun penetrating my hungry pores,
the leaves whispering lullabies to me,
and the wind breathing like a lover on my closed lids—
blowing my weariness into the heavens
where it is caught and converted into
birdsong, heart-piercing and eternal.

Lori Levy

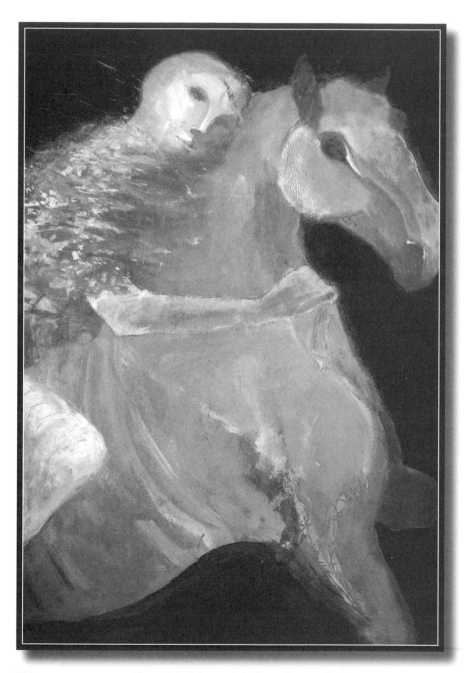

'You may not realize this,' he said, 'but I can fly.'

Acrylic on Masonite

Cathy Williams

Seagull

Every day the ocean calls me.
In reply I walk the shore,
and open myself to Spirit.

This June day at Seabright Beach
feet in sand, water kissing toes
a warm breeze soothes my shoulders.
The tide is so low
a hidden beach is revealed
beyond the rocky promontory.
River pours into ocean
past boulders white with barnacles.
I stretch out and up, breathe in sky.

A young boy walks toward me
a broken bird in hand—
he lays it on a boulder, wing askew.
The seagull lifts its head, opens its beak
lets out a tiny cry
    and again   and again
triangular mouth and thin tongue exposed.
One yellow eye, wide and round, looks my way.
Cries continue but no sounds come.

I walk close, send my prayer to the gull.
Let your Spirit go with grace
breathe
Let your Spirit go with grace
Exhausted, the gull lowers its head.
I begin to walk on.

Then the sound—a frantic cry.
I turn, astonished to see the seagull
head up, mouth open, summoning me.
My jaw drops, pulse surging.

I walk close again,
and the broken gull relaxes.
Inaudible cries come from its angular
mouth
    slowly   more slowly.

I direct my prayer
Let your Spirit go
Let your Spirit go with grace
Let your Spirit go
Let go

The gull's head drifts down to the boulder
neck softens, wing moves in slightly.
Body expands with breath once more
then relinquishes.
Let your Spirit go

A breeze blows over the small torso,
an arc of feathers stands solemnly—
and then releases.
One last prayer of awe
before the body of bird on stone
returns to the elements.

Thank you, I say,
for guiding me here
to touch this Spirit.

May your Spirit go
May your Spirit go with grace
May your Spirit go
May it go

Coleen Douglas

Bread Offerings

Making bread offerings
To the Gulls,
God's hungry angels,
Week after week,
Became a way
Of calling the invisible
Into a feather
That afterwards
Could heal
Even the broken wing
That happened to be
My own.

So that when
A gull took the crumbs
At the sacred island
And walked along the wall
So close we held our breath,
A male landed,
Annunciation
In a flurry of raised wings
We gathered stubborn faith from
This sign and from the pelicans
Flying around and around
The cliffs in a corona of light.

The simple repetition
Of an activity,
Like the old woman feeding
The pigeons in the city park,
Or the old man on the boardwalk
Emptying his lunch bag
For the most ordinary creatures,
Rats and random birds,
Becomes a prayer tie,
One and then another,

Leafing a tree that reaches
What we cannot see.

We want a chorus here:

> A heidi ho
> Or a yaha yaha yaha yaha yaha
> Ahoo ahoo ahoo ahoo ahoo

The songs of gulls
Shrieks and sibilant vowels
And watery consonants
And the pauses in between
Where the waves break
The triuned letters on the sand
And the eddies in the air
Calling, calling, calling out in prayer.

Deena Metzger

Owl

It was a dark summer night in the Arizona desert.

I stood alone in the center of a large animal rehabilitation cage with my back pressed against a slatted wall. I made myself as small and flat as my soul could bear.

Picture me on this hot desert night trying to make myself invisible. There was a heavy silver microphone in my hand that amplified and recorded all night sounds. I was a channel for sound. It poured into my cupped ears with breathtaking clarity. Everything was sound…the crickets, the wind, the crunch of footsteps. And one other…the one I was there to record that would stop my heart.

Inside the wooden enclosure it smelled of hay and dying heat. It was perfectly still, deadly quiet, except for the fearful *scritch-scritch* of talons on wood.

Silence. Waiting, *scritch*, waiting…and then a sudden explosion of wind and focused power. The great and beautiful creature was moving fast across the cage. And oh god how glad I was that I am not invisible. An infinitely powerful wing smacked my breastbone like the sharp cane rapping of a Zen master upon the flesh of a lazy student. The great wounded owl landed a solid blow precisely where I slept and said, *Wake up! We are running out of time.*

The whole world was the sound of power beating through wind and the sound of feather and bone on body. I was dizzy with sound. And just as it became *scritch-scritch* on wood once more and I tried to catch my breath, it exploded again, with a solid thwack and a breathless breaking open of my chest.

It has been almost fifteen years since that night.

I now have two baby boys, eleven months apart, who are native to this stark, magical land. A great horned owl calls outside our bedroom window at night. I dream of owls watching over them while they sleep, like burrowing owls do, curled and content in the warm, dry earth.

During the daytime, their baby arms flap and thump like bird wings against my chest saying, *Wake up! Are you present? What will you do with our precious time?*

I hear the sound of strong wings pounding through wind.

Then pure, peaceful silence.

Holly Metz

Incubation

Acrylic and Handmade Paper

Carol Gaab

Holy Longing

I am drifting in my canoe. It is an early summer morning on Long Pond, the sun's warmth infusing the cool night air, quickening into a soft boil of breath moving over the water, a reunion of warmth and cool, dark and light, stillness and movement, a moment where one blessed thing lives beside another before giving itself over completely.

The wind troubles the waters like the old gospel song, slowly spinning me, the canoe, my control into itself and out beyond the shelter of the island. Needing release from an unbearable longing to know God, I have come seeking Her here.

I am drifting in my canoe. Listening to the wind whisper fog into the trees surrounding this chalice of lake, my thoughts a rosary, I finger each bead, praying for the release of ecstacy—to melt into a world that is moved by deeper imperatives than mind or plastic desire. She is thinly veiled here among the beaver, the otter, the heron, the hawk, between water and sky.

I am drifting in my little boat, held in the Mother's watery palm with trees, sky, clouds, and the reflection of the loons flying above me, pumping and shushing in from Nichol's Pond. White bellied, brushed by the peach light of early morning, appearing over treetops, one by one, heavy in the air, like storm clouds ponderous with the weight of water.

The cedar waxwings undulate and dart, fall into the currents. Little bandits showing off, the sky is home to them. But the loon's element is water, taking awkward flight in a long and perilous migration in order to mate. Such open-hearted willingness to leave the safety of the sea to follow the imperatives of instinct cracks open the husk of my heart. What we must do to follow our desire to live. What we must suffer to again and again come home to our elemental nature. The loon is willing to risk her life, desperately earnest, flapping as fast as she can in answer to a greater calling.

Can't I at least do that?

I count, there are nine loons gathered this morning. Never having seen more than two adult loons on this small pond, my blood quickens. I leave the spaciousness of the drifting, the wind, and the sun. My mind, dropping through the water, lodges itself among the old stones. My flesh, thin and luminous, stretches over bone and becomes horizon cupping the now-still waters, sleeping boulders, and circling loons.

In this precise and shimmering moment, Nine Sisters of Brigit tend the eternal flame, nine Shape-shifting Priestesses guard Cerridwen's Cauldron of Wisdom, nine Loons circle. Two—one West, one East—arch up magnificently, spread their wings wide, like starlit capes, and glide over the water, dancing the distance between them in an ancient choreography, ululating as they go. Seven Wing-Spread-Sisters whoop and holler them to greater ecstasy, as again and again they dance across the water. Have I entered into the eternal spin of the great migratory round, or some other mysterious rite marking Her cycles? Whatever I have been privileged to enter, whatever veil has parted and allowed me entrance, I am grateful.

It is sweet now inside my skin. I am rewoven into the clan of my longing, the whole of life. And then, as if this sweetness is too much, I look away. My hands, stiff and cool, clutch my paddle; my mind makes its way back to me at the edges of this magic—all in just a few brief seconds. When I turn back, they are gone. The ceremony is over.

I am anxious now to go home to the cottage where, in silence, I will climb to the second floor loft, get into my bed overlooking the water and finger this new luminous bead—the gift of an answered prayer. This is my practice, this is my liturgy, for I know that it is in moments like these that life gathers me back into itself, reclaims me the way the weeds and trees reclaim the scarred earth.

Giving thanks, I paddle my little boat back to the dock.

Nora L. Jamieson

Fox Calling

Thanking Lucille Clifton

I will walk out to you tonight fox,
past the closed glass door. *Now*
I see you, red patience so long
a sentinel at the breach between us.
It was this that kept me—
I thought you were rabid—
that I would lose my life to you.

Who are you? How did you stir
such patience in the face of my refusal,
when all that while your white moon
writhed and rocked and pulled me
in my dreams? You are sentinel
to my belly full of ochre, pitch and fur,
teeth and brine, gall and white sage
burning. That you have stood
guard all these years cuts me sharp
and clean across my heart, loosing
a shrike that calls the dead to live.

Sharon Rodgers Simone

Green Onions

Peppery scent of green onions
wild in fields behind my Midwest childhood home.
Horses graze on the slow slope,
beckon me up and over the wood rail fence.
I visit the palomino,
approach cautious, offer an apple
dug out of my corduroy jacket.
He accepts the sweet gift
from my open hand.

His warm wet lips, his big square teeth,
the smell of him like sweat and grass
his saliva on my skin—
feelings I've not yet known.

Nighttime I swirl into horse dreams
ride bareback, legs flung wide,
embrace his powerful back,
rest the most private
delicate part of myself on his spine.

In the day, I become him.
Snort, throw back my head,
paw the ground with my foot,
gallop recklessly through backyards.
Exhausted, I collapse to the ground,
heart thumping. I hear my life
pounding in my ears.

Lying on the ground, grass cradles my body.
I search the soft blue sky,
clouds woolly white and impossibly huge,
the familiar, pungent aroma
of green onions invades me,
foretelling a wildness—
the untamed life
that moves through me.

Carolyn Davis Rudolph

Easy E

Acrylic on Masonite

Elizabeth Williams

Lily and the Deer

No one looked out the window because it was snowing. Teenagers in the house across the road stuck a pizza in the oven then flopped down for an afternoon of videos. No one saw a small Indian girl walk through the village alone, while her babysitter napped in front of the TV.

At first, the snowflakes were fat and lazy, drifting down like feathers. The afternoon was almost warm. Lily went to the frozen creek that led into the forest. She loved to slide on the ice. For a while she played there, sliding back and forth, singing a little song. She stopped against the creek bank after a wonderful, long slide, and saw deer tracks in the snow. The tracks were sharp and deep, as if the deer had just passed.

Grandma often took Lily hiking through the woods. At each new track, Grandma and Lily would stoop down and examine it. Skunks and raccoons, fox and deer, all left their footprints behind them on the path. How Lily and Grandma longed to see the shy little animals.

Lily climbed up the slippery bank and began to follow the deer tracks. Tall, slender trees creaked as a breeze came up. Cold branches clicked against each other far above Lily's head. All around her, evergreen boughs bent low beneath a pile of snow. The whirling flakes whispering through the woods sounded almost like someone talking.

"Hello, Mrs. Squirrel," Lily said, and a curious squirrel popped back into her tree house. Lily laughed because the squirrel looked so surprised. Then a rabbit jumped in front of her, and Lily laughed again. This time the rabbit surprised her!

The pretty deer tracks were joined by another smaller set of tracks. Then larger tracks appeared, and Lily felt sure she was trailing along behind a whole family. It was very exciting. She hoped the deer family was just ahead, around the next puffy green pine tree. She hurried to catch up. The snow was deeper now, so Lily couldn't lift her feet as quickly, or perhaps she was getting tired.

"Wait for me," she called. "Please let me see you, just once."

Crows cawed overhead, flying back home for the evening. When Lily looked up, the sky had turned dark gray. The snow came down in tiny, darting points of white. Squirrels had stopped scurrying along the branches. The woods seemed to whisper and sigh, whisper and sigh, in the falling snow. Lily shivered. She hadn't seen the deer family yet, but she decided to go back home. She turned around but the path was gone and snow had filled all her little tracks!

"Grandma!" she called as loudly as she could. "Grandma!" All she could hear was the soft hush of snow drifting down, gently brushing against the trees as it fell.

Lily had never felt lonely before. At home, her mother and father and grandma and grandpa and cousins came and went, busy and friendly, so Lily and her baby brother felt safe to explore and climb things and weren't afraid to be alone in the dark. But this was different. This was cold and strange and she didn't know what to do. She stooped under the branches of a soft, round evergreen and sat down next to the tree trunk. She felt better within the circle of branches touching the ground. It was like a small room with the nightlight on, bright as stars.

"This is my secret house," she said softly. The snow made a fluffy blanket around the tree, so Lily pressed her shoulder against the rough bark and curled up to keep warm. The evergreen felt solid and comforting as Lily looked around the inside of her house in the snow light. A sweet slow warmth enveloped her like a quilt and she fell into a deep sleep.

Something cold and wet suddenly bumped Lily's cheek. She huddled back against the tree under her snow quilt. She had slipped far away into dreamland and wanted to stay there. It was too cold to wake up. But the icy wet thing bumped against her face again and Lily had to open her eyes. It was a deer nose! A very young deer stood so close that Lily felt the steam from its chest. It was panting, for it had bounded under the tree in a rush. Beautiful dark eyes stared at Lily intently. The little deer seemed to be talking to her, urging her, telling her something.

"What?" Lily asked in a sleepy voice.

Glad as she was to see the deer, she just couldn't keep her eyes open. The deer suddenly reared up and stamped its tiny black hooves. A spray of snow splattered across Lily's face and she jumped up in surprise. The deer whipped around and slipped out between the heavy branches. Lily stumbled after it, tripped over a branch, and fell into a snowdrift.

The little deer flicked its ears impatiently. It leapt in among the trees, looked over its shoulder to see if Lily was following, then leapt again. The deer's white tail seemed to glow with a guiding light. Poor Lily waded along as fast as she could, but her legs were so short and the snow was so deep! She was tired and hungry, and tears ran down her round red cheeks.

"Wait for me," she cried. "Please wait for me!"

It was too much. Icy fingers of the night caught at her breath and she couldn't breathe. For the first time, a cold shadow of fear fell across her heart. The young deer turned, gazing at Lily with bright brown eyes. She felt it call, but her feet seemed frozen to the ground. At that very moment, a great animal stepped beside her. His legs were like slim pine trees. Hot breath streamed from his shiny black nose high above her. His antlers spread out like branches and his great strength lifted and warmed her. He also scared her, so she began to push through the snow again as hard as she could.

Another movement caught her eye. A lovely doe was walking on the other side of her in a slow, graceful way, like Lily's mother when she danced at the pow-wow. Together, the three deer and the girl wove through the trees with quiet steps. As if by magic the child followed the young deer, its white tail bobbing like a lantern ahead, held fast in her path by the two deer beside her. They were so beautiful that Lily forgot the cold wind and the endless struggle to walk.

At last, the four travelers neared the edge of the woods. Flashlights poked and peered among the trees, and voices called.

"Lily!"

"Lily, Lily!" they shouted.

"Mama!" Lily cried. She began to run toward the dancing lights. Suddenly she remembered and turned back to the deer, but a lacy curtain of snow had fallen and she couldn't see them. A moment later, as her mother and father hugged her close, Lily told how the deer had led her home. The people flooded the snow with their lights, searching for tracks, but none were found.

Laughing happily, the people returned to their comfortable homes. Lily looked back over her father's shoulder. The forest was silent once more, except for the snow whispering and brushing against the trees and the chill creaking of branches in the wind.

"Thank you," Lily whispered as she stared into the darkening woods.

Pavita Decorah

Arctic Wolf

You stand there on the rise,
white and sleek,
intent on some far dream,
a meal perhaps or something greater,
an ancestor or guardian.

Naked in a bay of the Arctic Sea,
I am vulnerable to your gaze.
Have you seen such a hairless swimmer
in your summer travels,
or am I your first encounter?

Your companion, gray and thin from the long winter,
shows no curiosity. Ready to travel,
she softly brushes you with her tail
and moves on.
You follow her but are called back
to study this two-legged animal.
Your eyes clear and yellow
gently penetrate me.

We have only a moment together
before you turn back to your mate.
In this brilliant arctic light,
you lope gracefully
over sodden tufts of tundra.

How long before the planes
filled with men
come to end your days?
Will you lie down with your thin companion
and leave her with the seed of your fathers?
Will there be time for you
to savor your first summer meal?

On this endless day
of no darkness or sleep,
where loons and sandhill cranes
suffuse the shores,
I walk on spongy turf,
watching for your traces,
waiting,
longing for another glimpse.

Anne Mize

The Huntress

Silkscreened Scarf

Carmella Weintraub

Taking The Tail

I can still feel the handle of the knife in my hand as I bring it down on the joint of the squirrel's tail. Blade meeting fur, cartilage and flesh join with the sound of pine needles shifting beneath my feet as the pressure of my own weight is transferred through the knife blade and into the tiny body. But her fur doesn't part easily and the flesh of the squirrel's tail beneath rises up to meet the too-dull knife. She is resisting the cut.

I feel a momentary longing to end this whole business. But I don't. Something tells me that to stop now because it is too hard to cut through the matted and stiffening fur will dishonor her life even more than had I left her in the middle of the empty road where I'd found her two days earlier.

Getting out of my car that autumn afternoon, I was taken back three months to the first time I came upon a squirrel on this road. That June day, minutes after leaving a weeklong retreat with my teacher, a Medicine Woman with whom I apprentice to learn the ways of healing and peace-making, I had murmured a quiet prayer for the tattered squirrel and carefully maneuvered the car on. But this September day was different. Approaching the turn in the road at the same hour, I was moved to stop my car at the sight of a second squirrel lying in the identical spot and to make my way toward her lifeless body.

I hesitated to touch her, yet couldn't shake the urge to move her out of the road. Tenderly, tentatively, I picked her up and carried her to shaded ground. In the short time it took to move her those few feet, time seemed to slow. And with it my heartbeat grew louder. I wondered if the squirrel and I were somehow connected, and if, as in the old ways of native peoples, I was meant to take part of her body to honor this connection. I felt my heart break open with questions I had been carrying for years: How does one live this earthly life completely in service of Spirit? How can each action risked be a truly authentic and beautiful offering of benefit to all?

Now, two days later, having carried the squirrel more than a mile to my teacher's land, I kneel alone beneath the shade of a pine tree overhanging the edge of the dried creek bed. I am surrounded by the smell of sage and burning matches. The dry, tight air is filled with my questions even as it is so empty of moisture that my skin feels like it will burst into flames before the sage. Each breath I breathe upon the sage bundle carries my fervently whispered prayer to the fire spirits, "please catch, please catch and show me that what I am doing is blessed and right."

This place seems to have chosen itself, bringing me to my knees to lay out the meaty smelling squirrel with blood dried on its belly and tail. As if guided by something I know though have no memory of ever being taught, I carefully pour saffron and pink rose petals over the body and gently release my knife from its leather holder. The handle is heavy in my shaking hand as I press it into the tail joint and flesh.

I desperately do not want to dishonor this life, so I lean hard into the dull blade and the bone beneath it. A voice I know from a long time ago is singing a song to the Mother. The singing is like a warm hand on my back and the feel of it jars my memory. It is my own mother's voice reaching out to steady my hands in ways she couldn't during her life. I hadn't known she knew such a song.

Without looking up I feel the presence of my father on my right side. My father the butcher, who day after day cut bloodied flesh from the bones of animals he hadn't admired as they roamed the land, who had never knelt into their steaming breath as it left their bodies so he could offer prayers of gratitude for the lives they had given. My father who spent his days among cow carcasses suspended from meat locker ceilings, cutting prime beef for the public. A man who returned home in silence each night to wash his hands clean, not of the blood as much as the emptiness of the exchange.

On my left, I feel my Uncle Ducky settle in as my fingers continue to pry apart the fibers of fur where they insert along the knife cut. Uncle Ducky, my mother's brother who despised my father as much as my father returned the feeling. He was a furrier on the west side of New York in a day when "fashionable" women adorned their bodies with a family of foxes or a village of minks as part of a complex ritual of preparation for draping themselves over the arms of the "right" men, men of power, money and substance.

There was a time when men prayed with their community to be blessed to make the hunt for skins to swaddle newborn babies and to keep their people warm through the cold winters. Thanks were offered to the spirits of the animals, and just enough was taken for the people to live while the herds continued to prosper. There was such a time before my uncle sat in front of tables piled high with the skins of animals raised to be adornments of the powerful, and his diabetic fingers were infected by misplaced sewing needles no longer guided by the old ways. There was such a time before my father stood anonymously among strangers with whom he shared only the stale air of dank subway cars, his empty hands smelling slightly of blood, death and loss.

Among indigenous people it is known that when you take a part of an animal's body, you accept responsibility for learning and carrying the knowledge of that animal as medicine for the people. I don't know if I was graced with squirrel medicine as I knelt in the fading light, or if in that moment I became a medicine woman. What I do know is that there are times when the dead and the living reach out for one another, and together they make a kind of peace that heals.

Now, under a pine tree somewhere outside of time, an unexpected alliance is forming as four beings hover together over matted fur and sour-smelling flesh. Two wounded old men, tethered together in life by both their mutual loathing and the loss of some essential mystery they may not have known to name, link their vaporous body weight to mine as we press the knife deeper into fur, cartilage and finally flesh. My mother's song, empty of strength in life, firmly propels the knife through to the pine needles that lie beneath the bloodstained body of the simple squirrel. Together we take the tail.

Elenna Rubin Goodman

The Offering

A Dream

I enter the cave, and the Bear is waiting for me, holding my bearskin up to slip into–which I do, dropping down on all fours and nuzzling him affectionately. The joy between us is reflected in each other's eyes. *Where are the cubs?* I ask. *They are coming*, he replies, and then they are here, tumbling over me rambunctiously, frisking, wrestling, attacking one another in mock ferocity.

Take them to the meadow, he says quietly. It is an imperative, not a suggestion. I look at him searchingly, and he meets my gaze with strength and peace. I nod, knowing I have to go, knowing everything will change if I do, feeling the change already gathering all around us. I look into his eyes one more time, feel the great love between us. Then I herd the cubs forward out of the cave.

I amble down the mountainside to an open slope of spring grass and new flowers. The cubs are glad to have space to climb and run but I warn them that although it is not hunting season, there are those who hunt anyway so we must stay alert. I watch carefully while they play and explore, but a part of me is listening for something else. I do not hear it, only feel it. *We must go back*, I call to the young ones urgently and they come running fast. We turn back and climb the mountain quickly.

Not far from the cave I spot the first drops of blood–fresh, bright red against the dark earth. I tell the cubs to stay there, wait for me. I move up the trail quickly but cautiously. I step into the cave and find my mate laying on his side, his back and sides filled with bullet holes, the blood flowing fast. He is still alive but we don't have much time.

I lay down beside him and tenderly lick his face.

The hunters will return soon, he says haltingly, *and they won't handle my body in a sacred way. They never do anymore. So you must pray and do ceremony on my behalf.*

Yes, I promise. *I will*. I hesitate a moment then speak. *You will be back?* I ask him urgently as I see the light fading from his eyes.

I am the bear, he acknowledges with a strained smile, *I die and I come back again*. One last look at his beautiful face, then I rise and turn to leave.

I will find you, he promises fiercely. I give a low growl, knowing what he says is true. We will be together again. I leave the cave, gather the cubs, and descend the mountain.

Valerie Wolf
Grandmother White Bear

Eco Warrior

Acrylic on Canvas

Elizabeth Williams

Oh Great Spirit

In the name of Raven. In the name of Wolf. In the name of Whale. In the name of Snake. Who have taught us. Who have guided us. Who have sustained us. Who have healed us.

Please heal the animals.

In the name of Raven. In the name of Wolf. In the name of Whale. In the name of Snake. Whom we have slaughtered. Whom we have feared. Whom we have caged. Whom we have persecuted. Whom we have slandered. Whom we have cursed. Whom we have tortured.

Please protect the animals.

In the name of Raven. In the name of Wolf. In the name of Whale. In the name of Snake. Whose habitat we have stolen. Whose territory we have plundered. Whose feeding grounds we have paved and netted. Whose domain we have poisoned. Whose food we have appropriated. Whose young we have killed. Whose lives and ways of life we threaten.

Please restore the animals.

In the name of Raven. In the name of Wolf. In the name of Whale. In the name of Snake.

Forgive us. Have mercy. May the animals return. Not as a resurrection but as living beings. Here. On earth. On this earth that is also theirs.

Oh Great Spirit. Please heal the animals. Please protect the animals. Please restore the animals.

So our lives may also be healed. So our souls may be protected. So our spirits may be restored.

Oh Spirit of Raven. Oh Spirit of Wolf. Oh Spirit of Whale. Oh Spirit of Snake.

Teach us, again, how to live.

Deena Metzger

PRAYERS FOR

MY WORLD

In the end, like the Great Mother, we all hold the world in our arms. Around and within each of our lives is the greater world, which today is suffering with violence and war, and shared fear for the earth's future. These astonishing, shattering times bring us to our knees in heartache and in prayer. The writings and art in this section speak to those moments when numbness is broken and we feel the ache of the world, and when we allow this heartache to flow into poetry, prayer and art. Here are dreams of peacemakers and blessings to soothe the earth to peace and healing. These writings and images speak to what it means to live in a time when one's country is at war, and evoke the thousands of individual prayers for peace which every day fill the world.

Prayers for My World

I stand on a hill
      arms wrapped about a pine tree
      hanging peace prayers on a hidden branch
City lights
      shine beneath the sunset
      golden orange in the dusk
A gentle breeze
      calms me
      delicate in its freshness
My peace prayers are wrapped in tiny parcels
      made yesterday in sacred ceremony
      five peace prayers whispered
      into each fabric patch rolled around tobacco
      tied with red yarn and strung together
Yellow, red, black, white and brown fabric, the colors of earth's peoples
      prayers for peace among humans
      prayers for forgiveness for past wrongdoings
      griefs cried out to be made known
Green fabric for women and the earth
      prayers for protecting the earth from pollution
      prayers for forgiveness of harm done to women, to me
      forgiveness for women who have hurt me
      prayers for peace and justice
Blue fabric for men, sky and wind
      prayers to stop our pollution of air
      grief for my friend hurt cruelly by a man
      forgiveness for the man who wounded her
      forgiveness for men who have wounded me
      prayers for peace and respect between earth's men and women
Purple fabric
      spirit prayers
      soul prayers
      prayers that we live in respectful peace
          with one another
          earth, fire, water, air
          animals, plants, insects
      prayers to be in loving kindness with all

Forty peace packets
      tied in rows with red yarn
      like quilted ammunition
Two hundred prayers
      now rest around a hidden branch
      parcels of peace and forgiveness
May we and our descendants live in peace
      for many years to come
May wind, rain and sun take these prayers into the world
May my grief be dispersed as learnings for others
Peace and blessings
Ho

Jane Nyberg

Necesito un Milagro

I Need a Miracle

Necesito un milagro
the faces of tired children
sink like rocks
in my battered heart

Necesito un milagro
I am stuck in the horizon
earth cannot hold me
sky swirls around me
I have nothing to rest within

Necesito un milagro
a burning star
in the middle of the day
long rays of the sun that
turn red with passion

Necesito un milagro donde
los niños son los maestros*
with words golden and straight
with hearts light and strong
only men question such strength

Necesito un milagro
for myself   for my children

Abuelitas dance in the dawn
and wait for us

* the children are the teachers

Linda Serrato

Milagros*

Francis of Assisi took off his shoes
Threw down his fine clothes
Walked into the fields by his home
To speak with sparrows, tender birds who
Picked at his hair, perched on his shoulders
Shared his bread

The Buddha looked over the garden wall
Saw beggars, sightless children, hungry dogs
His wealth could not save him
He walked through the doorway of his broken heart
Into the world

Starlings swarm the apple tree
Leaves from the chestnut need raking
Light fills the November sky
Fingers of rain reach into earth
It is a milagro to be here

Little saints of our neighborhoods
Your shrines are everywhere
Blown gutter leaves, roses translucent with frost
Calligraphy of branches against the dusk
The lake below us
Shining blue bowl

* *miracles*

Beth Coyote

The Scent of the Lemon Trees

The scent of the lemon trees in the cemetery
At the monastery in Ein Kerem—
Death never smelled so sweet.

A Palestinian mother, Yamit, puts out halva on a plate
For her son Ahmoud
Who will be home soon.

And an Israeli mother, Yaffa, adds rosemary to the soup
For her son Avi.
He too is on his way home.

But Avi and Ahmoud, they never do come home.

The fathers identify the bodies.
And the names of the sons appear in the newspaper
And are heard on radio and TV.

At the funerals, both bodies are draped in flags,
Albeit different ones.

But Yamit's sobs are no different than Yaffa's.

Those lemon trees
In our country;

When will life smell as sweet?

Bakol Ruben Gellar

Persimmon Orchard

Photograph

Connie Batten

Sakaya Yallah

No one will answer. No one will say.
Why do they stop me? For what reason am I here?

Words wing from my mouth
but land on invisible ears.

Voices whisper as I'm walked
down a long row of cells.

Later, after the cops,
an angel appears, as is her custom

in high heels and tight dress,
deep cleavage revealed.

Lifted into a big, airy natural
is her beautiful hair. She smiles

that gap-toothed grin, the mark
she refuses to let a dentist touch—*sakaya yallah*.*

All night we sing *free-ee Nel-son Man-del-lah.*
Free-ee. The whole night long we sing

for freedom. Over and over.
From our cages. Our voices clear.

** Sakaya yallah means "opening of God" and refers
to a gap between the front teeth, in some cultures
considered a sign of wisdom.*

Lisa Espenmiller

A Prayer for the End of Greed

May the ravenous one
who lives inside me
and inside all those who dwell
with privilege
in this land of plenty
dare to unbind
the terrifying grip
she has on everything—
food and drugs,
wealth and fame,
the people she most loves,
beliefs.
May she gently let go.
May she open her heart
to everything that lives.
May she know the brevity
of all that breathes.
May she surrender into joy.
And may she greet each day
with the willingness
to be awake.
If she does not do these things,
she chooses death.
And if she does—
and one hundred follow—
then all will live.

Martha Boesing

Finding God in the Dark Places

I'm finding God in the dark places
The old age home with its stench of feces
A truck's shadow concealing an oil-drenched rainbow

Shiny supermarket fruit have no flavor
Give me an orange persimmon bruised brown
The avocado's rough rind reveals creamy green
Things are not what they seem

Disaster is a gift wrapped in grief
Loss is an addition of great value
Look at the one who weeps
And see their wealth
Beg them to share it with you

Still, when pain weights my lap
Like a malodorous black cat
It's hard to accept her with grace
If I can follow her down
Urine soaked alleys
To the blind one suffering in the corner
If I can entice her home
Enshrine her at my dining table
Join her in a feast of my heart
I will know the riches of a queen
And the ecstasy of a saint

I was once blind like she who bore me
We were stumbling drunkards, angry ranters
She mistook her daughter for a rival
I confused her pain with my essence
From that black compost
Comes my harvest

We are wearing crowns of candles
Yet we hear poverty barking at our heels
Things are not what they seem
Look in sour dumpsters and find gold hidden
God is in the dark places

Kimberly Childs

Nada Brahma*

If the world
is truly sound
then it is falling
apart
for lack of
a woman's
voice

Sanskrit: the world is sound

Danelia Wild

A Measurement of Grief

Clay Art Installation
(Each four-inch clay figure represents a person fallen in Iraq since 2003.)

Kathleen Crocetti

Women's Work

Silence tends to make me fear rejection.
It's an old female fear,
as old as an unanswered smoke signal,
the irrational belief that somewhere in the empty sky
a man is angry
instead of simply out of firewood.

But this is a different silence,
silence in a darker sky.
Today is another day without word
and there is a breath that is not breathing,
a heart that is still,
a subtle self on hold.

Last week I trusted he was safe.
I came home to four emails,
news that they were nearly finished,
heading back to Bahrain,
stateside by June,
that I could write back now, and should,
and send poems and stories.

I had heard how vital mail is in a war zone,
the tie to home,
the boost to morale.
I sent three stories, two poems, a letter and two notes.

Then silence descended like night.

Thursday morning I woke to a *New York Times* article
on the number of soldiers who have died since the war ended,
from both incident...and accident.
So many were heading home.

Wild fear is naked silence.
The ears go first

the blocking of sound and thought,
the ocean pounding of the heart, drowning out everything.
It pushes at your back like wind
while you do dishes, call friends and clients,
make the bed, scrub the floor.

I have talked myself through statistics.
How many people die in accidents at home every month?
How many happen to be soldiers?
I talk myself through faith.
If it is his time,
if this is the full measure of his life,
he doesn't have to be in a war zone.
I know this.
It doesn't matter.
This is old stuff, wet and earthy.
This is the cellular memory of women,
the fear of men and dirt,
of the earth taking them back.

Friday night, another article.
Three more deaths in central Iraq, a total of ten this week.
The words swim across my computer screen:
this week.
But he was in Kuwait, heading to Bahrain.
It doesn't matter.
In the silence, orders change.
People are dying.
Families are grieving.
Love didn't protect them.
Or prayers.

And I can't help feeling this—
though I don't know why, or why now.
I wasn't this scared when he left,
when he arrived in Iraq,
not even when he was near Baghdad.
Yet here it is: the ancient path of women,
to worry and pray and wait.

Sunday morning, another headline: *Names of the Dead*.
I looked at the screen for a long time,
wondering if I should click on it
or call someone to do it for me.
Reason would not have him there.
But fear is not reasonable.
Love is not reasonable.
Nor is war.
Or life.
Or most of what changes us.

I closed my eyes and prayed,
Dear God,
Bless all of them.
Bless their families.
Let them find comfort in their grief.
And let him come home safely.

I said it two or three times before I clicked,
whispering,
aware of how many people (how many women) were whispering the same.

He wasn't there. But ten still were.
It was a tempered relief, like the pouring off of Passover wine.
How can we drink a full cup?

That night I looked for an old photo, one of the few I have.
It's 1989. He's in Italy or Greece, vamping
behind the headless, armless bust of a Roman statue,
arms as outstretched as his grin.
I took it upstairs and placed it on my altar.
There was resistance to the gesture.
The cliché of it, the drama.
But there are things that we do, the heart requires them,
and this was one.

I propped it against a triptych I bought on the Via Appia,
a small Madonna and child.

"I put him in the hands of the mothers," I told her,
and also called on his and mine.
"Bring him home safe."

The day he left I put him in the hands of God.
This moment was woman's work.

Deborah Edler Brown

Through the Storm

It's an ark of sorts
    where all the women live.
A creation
    of their coming together.
A container, a cup, a bowl
    a holding, a hand.

They have far
    to travel, the women,
through high waves
    threatening, always threatening
to overturn them.

A large door
    in the floor of the ark
drops open,
    like a man's hungry mouth,
to the deep seas below.

To keep from being swallowed,
    the women use all their powers—
eye in the ear
    ear in the heart
heart in the hand
    hand in the eye.

Through the storm,
    there is a light I can see.

ॐ

Lisa Espenmiller

Holy Land

When the lines of pews and creeds have gone,
we will be left as we always have been,
without shoes,
to hear the earth with our feet
calling us down at last.

Lawrie Hartt

Belonging

Acrylic and Oil Pastels

Carol Gaab

Spirit Sisters

Deep at the axis of the earth lies a raised mound of dirt sheltering a secluded cave. Inside the cave live a band of women watching over the forces of love in the universe. They stand in a circle with arms wrapped around each other's shoulders. White long-sleeved blouses drape their upper torsos. Long flowing black skirts fall from their waists, touching the soft dirt surrounding their bare feet. A large black cauldron suspended from the ceiling by an invisible cord sways stealthily in the center of the circle. The contents of this aged stone pot have remained secret. But the spirit sisters know that from within the curves of the pot love radiates throughout the universe.

All remains still, except for the flames forging their way from the earth to heat the cauldron. The sisters fix their gaze on this cauldron and in silent unison repeat prayers. Not even the spirit sisters know what alchemy occurs in the cave, but they understand that if they turn their eyes away from the center of the circle, love will evaporate. The mystery of love is not for them to fathom. Their thoughts keep a respectful distance. They exist not to comprehend love, but only to perpetuate it.

But they are not alone.

Slowly, over eons of time, the sisters fade and are absorbed into the black belly of the cauldron. They merge with the secrets swirling inside the pot, never knowing they are part of the mixture. As the women disappear, a band of men rise up from their shadows and form their own circle surrounding the cauldron. White long-sleeved shirts hang limply on their upper bodies. Long loose-fitting black pants slide down low over their ankles. They are spirit brothers, and like the sisters they embrace the vigil of the cauldron so love doesn't die.

But the men are not alone.

Within their silhouettes are the outlines of the sisters. As the brothers fade in time, the sisters again take their places in the cave. And so it goes throughout cycles of creation and dissolution of the universe. The spirit brothers and sisters sustain love and keep it circulating and radiating out through the layers of the atmosphere.

Spirit life exists in each of us. It is an indiscernible ingredient in the formula for preserving love. When men and women keep vigil, stand united and pray, love continues. We watch over what is good and know others will follow.

Attention, like breath, feeds life. When doubts of sustaining love taunt your soul, remember the cave mound in the axis of the earth.

Within the cauldron lies the source of the mystery. The austerities of the spirit sisters and spirit brothers act as large bellows, fanning the continuation of love. No one knows how or why this cave was created or how the love first started. It seems it has always been this way.

Ratna Jennifer Sturz

Listen, You Fire Flingers

Listen, you fire flingers and earth shakers!
Listen to me!
Let me talk for a while.

I am a woman.
I am the earth
And I am the sea.
I walk upon myself
And swim in myself.
I am not afraid of myself nor anyone else
Because I am too busy creating things.
I am not afraid of myself
Nor any of the manifold creatures
That roll within me
Or walk upon me.

I am the earth,
And I am the pear tree
Growing out of my own belly.
I am the pear tree,
And I am the oriole singing in my own branches.
I am the oriole,
And I am the young in my own nest,
And the worms in their beaks.
I am the fair freckled eggs
And the twigs they rest upon.
I am the twigs,
And I am the saliva binding them together.

I am the earth,
And I am the sea on my own breast.
I am the sea,
And I am the whale rocking in me.
I am the whale
And the whale's teeth
Straining sea change through my mouth,

Engaging myself and savoring myself,
And enjoying all my invisible parts.
I am the whale's teeth,
And the sea anemone,
Created with the flower throat
Hungry and wide open
To engorge the marvels of the sea.
I am the sea,
Starfish and stone flower,
I am the dolphin rolling in my own belly.

I am the sea
And I am the earth.
I am a woman, yes.
Fire healer and earth maker,
Author of the world.
Not of skyscrapers
But of stones.
Not of poems
But of the flesh of poems.
All cathedrals were copied from me,
And all humble little churches.
I live off myself
And dine on the mysteries and fomentations of my own life.
And from this food I create life anew,
And every extension of life
Feeds me anew,
Until I am rolling with dolphins,
And blowing with pears,
And flowering with songs and seasons.

So listen, you masters of ten minutes of my ten billion years,
Possessors of small parts of my flesh,
Generals and commandants
And politicians:
Listen to me!
I ask you not to use your fire flinger.
I ask you not to singe the hair from my head,

Not to scar my face,
Not to scorch my flesh,
Not char my bones.
I speak to you as the mother of many children
And beseech you:
Do not put us to the torch.
And I warn you:
We shall not die without fighting.

For the moment I want to speak to you persuasively and seductively
As my birds and blossoms and trees have done,
Dropping the petaled chaplets of their songs
And the ripened bird-notes of their pears
Into your hands.
Bright and sorrowful,
I want to love you!

But if the time should come,
Fire flingers and earth shakers,
When you are no more,
And I lie cooling myself another million years,
I feel sure that my seasons and my birds
Will come again.
The spears of ice will come again.
And delicate April will lay his long green fingers on my arms
And blow his green breath into my hair.
Aching June,
Throbbing July,
And bursting August will know me,
And September the hoary midwife...
The season of flowers,
The season of leaves,
And the season of fruit
Will come again,
And again will come the spears of ice.
But I shall not fear them,
Nor the mouths feeding upon me,
Nor the young beak

Returned to share my flesh.
Tomorrow I shall be green again,
Tomorrow I shall roll the dolphins in my belly,
And launch my songs
And my billion colored wings
Against eternity.

Elizabeth L. Sturz

Prayer to the Future

You live inside us, beings of the future.
In the spiral ribbons of our cells, you are here. In our rage
for the burning forests, the poisoned fields, the oil-drowned
seals, you are here. You beat in our hearts through late-
night meetings. You accompany us to clearcuts and toxic
dumps and the halls of the lawmakers. It is you who drive
our dogged labors to save what is left.

O you who will walk this Earth when we are gone, stir us
awake. Behold through our eyes the beauty of this world.
Let us feel your breath in our lungs, your cry in our throat.
Let us see you in the poor, the homeless, the sick.
Haunt us with your hunger, hound us with your claims,
that we may honor the life that links us.

You have as yet no faces we can see, no names we can say.
But we need only hold you in our mind, and you teach us
patience. You attune us to measures of time where healing
can happen, where soil and souls can mend.
You reveal courage within us we had not suspected,
love we had not owned.

O you who come after, help us remember:
we are your ancestors. Fill us with gladness for the
work that must be done.

Joanna Macy

Prayer of Thanksgiving

We give thanks to the source of life, to the miracle of breath.
To the seen and unseen, the senses and intuitions.
To the tastes and smells, the touches and caresses.

We give thanks to the rising sun for another chance in another day.
To the work that awaits, and the tasks completed.
To creativity yearning to express, break free,
And to that which has blossomed and flowered.
To the difficult transits and narrow passages,
And for the gliding through with ease.
To the joys and pains of self discovery, and to all that is yet unknown.

Thanks and gratitude for the circles in which we sit
And the heart songs that we share.
For the drum to beat and the rattle to shake.
For the dance we dance and the music we make.
And to the Muse, when she visits,
We feel blessed by her presence.

Eternal thanks to the beauty of the Mother,
And to her limitless grace.
To her plants and trees, her fruits and herbs.
To the creatures who fly, swim and run, wild and free.
To her sacred springs and her vast deep oceans.
To the rain that soaks her thirsty earth
And the warming sun that follows with rainbows.

Mere thanks are not enough for her rising moon,
Her ebbs and flows, her waxing and waning.
For enveloping darkness and jeweled night sky.
For the resting time, reflecting time; for sleep, dream, renewal.

Great source of miracle and wonder,
Great Goddess of life-death-life, of alchemical magic,
Make for us another day.
Fill it with sun and rain, with waters of life, fires of passion,

With prayers of the heart and yearnings of the soul.
Fill us with dreams and visions, with truth and wisdom,
With wildness and remembrance, with love and compassion.
Make for us another day, Great Goddess,
Until our days run out, your mystery revealed.

Marigold Fine

Village Mother

Gouache Painting

Durga Bernhard

A Prayer for Peace

(April 2004)

Our prayer goes up to the heavens
And surrounds our blue-green earth
As a cradle to rock a troubled world to peace.

Our love is stronger than violence
Our passion is greater than anger
Our truth is bolder than lies
We are one heart, one mind, one spirit,
Rocking our weeping planet to peace.

We are strong for the grieving
We are soothing for the anxious
We are help for the weary
As our energy is released.
Arms outstretched and our world embraced
Rocking them all to peace.

Blessed be.
Blessed be.
Blessed be.

Alicia Knight

The Peacemaker's Gift

A Dream

Sunrise. The Peacemaker and I stand together: me, a mixed blood Native American woman in a white buckskin dress with white leggings and moccasins, and he, a tall black man wrapped in lion skin. We gaze out over lush grassland dotted with occasional trees and clusters of low shrubs. A landscape of fertility. The Peacemaker sweeps his arm across the view.

"See this great earth," he urges strongly. "Hold her lovingly in your heart, for truly she is your mother." I nod my head in affirmation and the scene shifts.

Noon. Now we stroll slowly, arm in arm, through a vast forest along a narrow path of soft earth. The tree-filtered sun warms us. A soft wind rustles the varied leaves and birds call out as we pass. We walk a long time, slowly and steadily to where the trees end and a high sand dune rises up before us. We trudge slowly over the sliding land and descend to the edge of a green sea. The ocean heaves and rolls before us, a wild and living thing.

"Here is the great water," he proclaims rapturously. "The water cleanses everything. Tell them to go into the water." I bow my head again, yes. The Peacemaker bends low and scoops a handful of ocean into his hand, pours it over my lowered head. I gratefully receive this silent blessing.

Sunset. We stand now on a red stone cliff overlooking a sea of people of all colors, all tribes, all nations. The red glow of the sinking sun highlights the gathering. People walk around quietly or sit expectantly, clearly watching and waiting for something.

"A great change is coming," the Peacemaker announces firmly. "Watch for the white birds. When you see them, you will know it is beginning." I nod again and then look up into his loving eyes. He places his hand on my chest.

"Do not grieve so much in your heart," he admonishes me gently and kindly. The sorrow rises up, my eyes water. "All will be well," he promises, "all will be well."

I feel the depth and strength of this promise and my suffering is eased. He takes both of my hands in his and raises them, palms up, to his mouth. He kisses the center of each palm tenderly and I am startled momentarily by the great lovingness that flows from him. He speaks once more: "Tell them all—that from this day onward their hands do not belong to them anymore. Tell them to use these hands well, for now their hands belong to the Peacemaker."

He looks into my eyes and his eyes are fierce, his voice imperative. "*Your* hands are *my* hands, these hands belong to *me.*"

Low thunder, a streak of lightning pierces the dusky sky. The Peacemaker is gone, or rather, transformed. A great white eagle wings its way up into the dark tapestry of the night.

My hands hum and burn, and I stare at them, stunned. These open hands are large, the hands of a tall man, clearly not my hands. Suddenly in the center of each palm a dark circle opens and the night sky appears there, a swirl of stars, an unfolding galaxy. Only a brief mesmerizing moment—and then the starry circle fades, and I see my own smaller, woman's hands once again. Then I remember the Peacemaker's words. These are not my hands and I must use them well. These are the hands of the Peacemaker.

Valerie Wolf
Grandmother White Bear

We Must Insist

We must insist
   that we sit
   in circles
At nighttime
   when the sun goes down

Capture fire
   in wood or wax
Let the yellow flame
   pull the circles
   inward
   while our souls pulse

It is not enough
   to have captured
   fast energy
   in thin brown wires

It is not enough
   to be able to turn on
   moving pictures
   of one another
   in our own homes
People moving
   People talking
   People making love
   on flat screens

The time has come to
Return

Let us surround ourselves
We must surround ourselves
   with each other

Then we can relax
   and let our smooth arms caress
Arm over arm
Let his face rest on
   your shoulder there
Allow her feet to
   be intertwined
   with your toes

Chants will come
   from underneath
   where your heart beats

Sway
   sway
   back and forth
   to and fro
Conjure up
   the ancient witches
   who long to be there
See the angel
   standing by your side

It's all there for us
   all there not far
   from the surface

Take these steps
   little ones

Throw away your
   remote control
And in a couple of months
   give away the TV

You may yearn to fill the
silence
    so much so
    that you
    learn to look
    inside yourself
    in that deep place
    where all the hubbub
    of your first cry began

Breathe there
    from inside you
In that place
    of your first voice

Breathe
    Breathe in
    Breathe out
    1000 times
    but do not count
Only be
    the breath

Tend to your heart
    spend time
    in its alleyways
See where you've
    become lonely

Let yourself
    be lonely
Hear the wolf
    howling there
Look into
    his lime-green eyes

Get your feet to
    take you walking
Find others
    Invite them over

Light a fire of
    wood or wax

Join hands

It is
    most
    necessary

Jean Mahoney

Afterword

Safe Houses: A Vision

They are in cities, towns, villages, on mountains, and near rivers. They are small townhouses and large lodges, modest apartments with prayer rooms, holy rugs and sacred paintings, or condominiums with swimming pools and hot tubs. They are log cabins in the woods, rustic cottages on the beach, urban Victorian buildings. They exist in suburban homes with welcoming rooms and at warm kitchen tables in ordinary neighborhoods all over the world.

Together, they form an underground pathway—a system of safe houses where women and men offer sanctuary, spirit, hope and healing. Each place exists within the mind of Spirit. Each place channels the divine. Each place feeds prayer, serves the sacred, honors the earth. Lives are mended there, and hearts given peace. People of all religious traditions are treasured, and all forms of prayer are honored. Here, women with kind eyes and strong hearts midwife souls. Men of gentle being and wise spirit gather others in sacred community. When we visit these places we feel we have entered the web of existence. We have mended our part of the whole.

This underground pathway has woven itself together into a worldwide wisdom body, though each part has no full knowledge of the whole. The pathway exists in every town, city, and community all over the world. There is no village without one; though these places are generally not apparent. Safe houses have no signs, are not churches or temples, print few brochures, do not proselytize. Some publish their work of spirit, study, prayer and joyous laughter, but most do not. Yet pilgrims find their way to these houses. We will continue to do so. When we find these places, we are transformed, our brittle skin falls away; we emerge as new people.

There is one safe house where over many years I have been taught and healed. Inevitably I arrive in need of clarity, in the swirl of daily work and activity; here the sacred reasserts itself and I am quieted and opened. At this safe house lives a medicine woman of wise mind and heart who midwives souls. She has been birthing me for years. Regularly I come to her when it is time for a new push, and she moves me through some essence of life attempting to emerge into the light. And into the light truth is born; I stand, more whole, more able to walk the world. I am once again pilgrim and soul seeker, full with the love of spirit and the world. Then I return to my home on an ordinary street with lovely neighbors and a hidden creek, and I become the woman with the kind eyes and wild heart who welcomes others. My home, now too, has become a safe house, part of the web.

There are many safe houses in the town where I live, and in the town where you live too. This morning the vision revealed itself. I saw myself and countless others, likely millions, within an invisible web that encases the entire world. In my little town, in my simple home, my partner and I join with the other women and men of kind eyes and strong hearts all over the earth. Some of these people we know, a few more we will someday meet, the vast majority we will never know. But we all exist within the underground pathway of safe houses, and within the mind of Spirit.

Some of you reading this text may recognize yourselves. Perhaps there is a safe house where you go for healing and sanctuary. Perhaps you have your own safe house, or are on your way to creating one. You are a part of this web. Your safe house does not have to write a grant, establish a foundation, build a building or launch a website, though some may do any or all of these things. It simply needs to offer itself to healing and Spirit, and to provide sanctuary to others—women, men, children, animals, forests, trees, rivers, seeds, plants. Together, we are part of this underground pathway. We carry this sanctuary wherever we go. We offer it where we are. These safe houses exist through us. We are the container. As Deena Metzger counsels, so too is the path of the safe house: *Be and provide sanctuary.*

The network of safe houses will continue when the larger culture can no longer sustain itself. In times of collapse or upheaval, we will know how to live without that culture, for we have created our own. We know how to heal, how to tell the stories, how to hold and honor grief, how to carry beauty. And we will midwife a new world.

There is before us a future that is tenable, a web that is whole. We will be there, all over the world, a hidden future that lies underneath. We are creating the new culture, preparing ourselves. The future awaits. We are building it now. It lies in our hands, a shimmering web, gossamer, light, tenable and whole. We are each that fine thread of the web, the mist of dew, the light filtering the crevices. We are each spun within the mind of Spirit—old Grandmother in the center, weaving us into a whole, re-weaving us each night in dream, spinning us out into the world, alive, whole, real.

Yes, you've come to a safe house. Welcome.

Carolyn Brigit Flynn

Acknowledgements

Thousands of individual acts of sacred creation are at the core of this book.

I am deeply grateful to the poets, writers, artists, photographers, and composers in *Sisters Singing*. Their devotion to creative work and their living connections with the sacred have inspired and changed me. Working with each of these writers and artists has truly been a joy.

Cindy Morley, Linda Holiday and Steve Scholl all read early copies of the manuscript and provided detailed, intelligent and heartfelt feedback. I referred to their notes repeatedly during the last year of finalizing the book, and I am deeply grateful. I want to offer thanks to John Barisone, who provided legal review for our *Sisters Singing* team. Gratitude to Cara Lamb for copyediting the final manuscript with her steady eye. Thanks also to Kate Munger, founder of Threshold Choir, who completed notation for a number of songs in the book, and whose community of singers is an inspiration.

Jerome Paul transcribed twelve original songs from audio recording with consummate skill. He also transcribed all the remaining songs from sheet music, and supplied some chording. We are grateful for his dedication over and above the call of duty, which brought forth the truly beautiful music section that graces this book.

Steve Scholl came along at just the right moment and became a member of our *Sisters Singing* team. He brought his profound commitment to the sacred and to women's voices, as well as his expertise in publishing and marketing. It feels right that a joyous man of spirit is helping to bring *Sisters Singing* to the world.

I want to thank the women of my writing groups, who are the seed of inspiration for this work. The spring after September 11, 2001 we devoted ourselves to writing about prayer. I sensed something raw, astonishing and powerful had broken open, and ultimately came to see that contemporary women's sacred writing during these times should be gathered into a new volume.

For almost twenty years my beloved friend Deena Metzger has provided a beacon for me, and countless others, as I have found my sacred work in this world. My gratitude flows to her boundlessly—enough, I hope, to last well beyond both of our lifetimes.

Three women held this book with me, day to day, from the beginning. Melody Culver, as the book's primary copyeditor, is woven in and around every word in *Sisters Singing* many times over. She is my second eye, my early morning consultation, my true sister. Melody's assistance was the key to making the complex process of working with more than one hundred writers possible. She has, indeed, *sistered* this book in a thousand invisible ways. A woman of boundless heart and wise insight, she has a true gift and love for tending language. As a writer and editor, she has made this book shine.

Jane Nyberg is the ground upon which *Sisters Singing* stands. As founder of Wild Girl Publishing, she devoted herself to this anthology, and was the force behind including original music and art—which made the complexities of publishing a major new anthology infinitely more demanding. Because of her, *Sisters Singing* is the elegant and handsome volume it has become. I am profoundly grateful for her painstaking care and devotion, deep wisdom, and good judgment. I know that her abundant gifts and the joy of her wild heart will come to her many times over.

Of course, in the end it is the one sleeping in the next room who makes all the difference. My spouse, Jean Mahoney, held faith at times when the mountain of editing details felt unclimbable. Over several years when it was needed, she provided her fresh and unbiased writer's eye to editing and page layout at all hours of day and night. Her insight, faith and boundless love provide a wellspring which every day teaches me what is truly sacred.

Finally, I want to acknowledge the spirits of *Sisters Singing*, who are strong indeed. These ancient great-great-grandmothers reached down their arms a few years ago and claimed my life as their own. I have attempted to faithfully act as their servant, which in the end entailed many things I could not have foreseen, blessings and abundance beyond my imaginings, and endless days and nights of work. It has been one of the deepest privileges of my life to be in their company, and it is sweet to know that with this volume they travel even more deeply into the world. All gratitude and blessings upon you, my Grandmothers. All blessings upon you.

ABOUT THE
CONTRIBUTORS

Contributors

Rae Abileah is an imaginative writer, an artivist (blending art and activism), and a national organizer with CODEPINK Women for Peace, a creative women-initiated movement working to end the U.S. occupation of Iraq and to prevent future wars. Rae grew up in Half Moon Bay, California and graduated from Barnard College. She is a contributing author to *10 Excellent Reasons Not to Join the Military* and her poetry has been published in several journals and zines. When not on the road for PINK protests, she tends to the heart fire that compels her to work for justice by surfing, eating leafy greens, hiking in the redwoods, calling the Congressional switchboard on speed dial, and remembering to breathe deeply. Rae is humbled and inspired to be included in the goddess group of contributing women authors.

Marcy Alancraig first began hearing the sacred voices of the natural world when she was a child. At first dismissing those messages as pure imagination, she now takes them seriously and crafts her fiction from them. Her work concerns the interaction between humans, the ancestors, and plants and animals. She lives amid the trees in Santa Cruz, California, where she writes and teaches. Her first novel, *The Ghosts Between Us*, is forthcoming from RockWay Press.

Terese Armstrong makes her home in Asheville, North Carolina. Expressing her love of nature through photography and videography, Terese hopes that the beauty of the Earth will inspire us all to walk tenderly upon her.

Kate Aver Avraham is a published children's author (*Joey's Way*, Margaret McElderry Books/MacMillan, and upcoming in 2009 from Charlesbridge Publishing, *What Will You Be, Sara Mee?*), a poet, teacher and artist. Her poetry has appeared in *Calyx, A Journal of Art and Literature for Women, Nimrod International Journal* (where she was a finalist for the Pablo Neruda Poetry Prize), and many other journals and anthologies. She is the founder of Blue Moon Creations, a nonprofit artistic endeavor that aids charities both locally and internationally. She volunteers as an art therapist with senior citizens as part of the Family Service Agency's I/You Ageless Art program. Kate lives with her husband, English bulldog, and tabby cat in the house where she grew up, by the sea she loves in Santa Cruz, California.

Ruth Barrett is a Dianic high priestess, ritualist, and award-winning recording artist of original Goddess songs. Her numerous recordings have been among the pioneering musical works in the Goddess Spirituality Movement. She is author of *Women's Rites, Women's Mysteries: Intuitive Ritual Creation* (Llewellyn, 2007). Ruth served the Los Angeles women's community as cofounder and religious director of Circle of Aradia (CoA) for two decades, and is currently director of Temple of Diana, Inc., a national Dianic religious and educational organization. Ruth has taught magical and ritual arts in the Dianic tradition at festivals and conferences across the U.S., in Canada, and in Great Britain. www.templeofdiana.org and www.dancingtreemusic.com.

Linda Barton   Poetry was not what I planned on. It dropped in my lap like a screaming, huge oak tree and has stayed with me for the last fourteen years. I am grateful for its vast, lusty and at times tricky ways. Poetry allows me the spaciousness to be rooted in the world. I am wildly curious to see where it leads me next. I can be reached at lindabarton@mindspring.com.

Connie Batten lives on a ridgetop in the Santa Cruz mountains, where she draws vitality from the changes of light through the seasons. She has published articles on feminist parenting, survivors of suicide, Buddhism and menopause.

Lisa Beaulieu   I live in the San Francisco Bay area with my husband and two cats. I take as many writing workshops as will fit into a week, and read a poem every day.

Sandia Belgrade   I have been fortunate to have my writing informed both by spirit and the natural world, and to be able to share my work with others by having poems appear in anthologies and magazines. I was one of the winners of the 1998 Anna Davis Rosenberg Poetry Award. Two poetry books have been published: a translation of Renée Vivien and a book of my own poetry, *Children of the Second Birth*. It is an honor to have a poem from my new collection, *The Running Shape of Wisdom*, included in this inspiring anthology.

Alison Bermond 1953–2008, lived close to the Pacific Ocean and was in love with language and story for as long as she could remember. As an artist, storyteller, healer and writer, she trusted the power of the imagination and of art to inspire us and show us peaceful ways that we can participate in "Tikkun Olam", the mending of the world. She gave thanks for the amazing, visionary and passionate women who walked this road with her; their open-hearted ears and fearless voices gave her courage. Alison was honored to be included here and dedicated her words to her wild and wonderful daughter and to all the children.

Durga Bernhard grew up in the Hudson Valley of NY and has been a freelance illustrator and fine artist for more than 25 years. She is the illustrator of 22 children's books and the author of 5, including fiction and nonfiction, natural science titles and multicultural folktales. Durga's work encompasses several different styles and has been published on everything from book, magazine, and CD covers to business logos, brochures, websites, and publicity for religious and ecological causes. Her creative activities also extend to West African dance and drum, which she has studied and taught for almost twenty years. She is the mother of three, and lives with her family in the Catskill Mountains of New York.

Mary Blaettler is a writer who fell in love with words at an early age, entranced by the flow of them around the family dinner table. She is also a producer, teacher and artist in *kirigami*, the art of free-cut paper. She has been a student of African drumming for many years and appreciates the influences of this heartbeat within her writing. She composes songs and drumpoetry as well as prose, performing and leading circles in her community. She is a devotee of the goddess Brigid (she who gave us poetry, midwifery and smithcraft), and with a group of magical women keeps Brigid's flame alive in these troubled times. Mary can be reached at marydrummer@cruzio.com.

June BlueSpruce   I began writing and reading poetry in the Pacific Northwest in the 1970s. My work has been published in two chapbooks, *clear cut* and *I Am Ready to Speak*; the anthology *My Lover is a Woman: Contemporary Lesbian Love Poems*; in *What Will Take Root? A Raven Chronicles Open Forum* on 9/11 and its aftermath; several journals; and on the Poets Against War and Voices in Wartime websites. I work as a shamanic dreamer and healer, coach and consultant. Deep thanks to herons, trees, oceans, people, spirits and all beings for their gifts of poems; to my partner, Martha Read, and our sons, Jeremy and Mikaelin; my teachers, Deena Metzger and Grandmother White Bear (Valerie Wolf); and the writing and healing communities that offer so many blessings.

Martha Boesing has written more than 40 produced plays, led workshops, and directed plays for theaters throughout the country. She was the Founder and Artistic Director of At the Foot of the Mountain Theater in Minneapolis (the longest running professional women's theater in the country) from 1974-84. She has won several national awards, including an NEA, a Bush fellowship, and the Kennedy Center's Fund for New American playwrights. In the Sixties, she was a company member of the Firehouse Theater (iconoclastic, experimental theater), and her work remains true to the ideological concerns of that time. She now lives in Oakland, close to her four grandchildren, and creates theater pieces for The Faithful Fools, a street ministry in the Tenderloin district of San Francisco.

Gaza Bowen, 1944 – 2005, was an internationally known wearable artist, sculptor, book artist, and printmaker whose work spanned many genres and media. She received an NEA individual fellowship in 1995. Gaza was also a shoe historian, lecturer, educator and generous teacher of the art of custom shoemaking. Perhaps best known for her wearable shoes and shoe sculptures, her work was always remarkable for its fine craftsmanship, dry wit, and social commentary. Gaza was fascinated by the way in which the history of use/abuse becomes indelibly etched into the very fiber of matter and how those traces of incorporated memory can evoke meaning in the viewer. She viewed her art as a continual inquiry into the nonverbal communication between people and objects.

Gail Brenner   My home is Santa Cruz, California, where life under the great redwoods is a daily dance with the spirit. The rich, rugged beauty of the Central Coast inspires reverence…and writing, as do the barefoot memories of a Carolina childhood, and the extraordinary gifts of family and friendships. From such good sources, words take shape and become a small tribute, a celebration, a prayer. I teach English as a Second Language at the University of California, Santa Cruz, and do freelance editing. Previous publications include *English for Dummies* (Wiley, 2002); *Webster's New World American Idioms Handbook* (Wiley 2003); and (co-author) *ARCO Master the TOEFL* (Peterson, 2004, 2005, 2006). "Mystery's Shoes" is my first poetry submission.

Deborah Edler Brown is a poet, performer, journalist and author. She was born in Brazil and raised in Pittsburgh, where the magic of words captured her at an early age. Her poetry has appeared in several anthologies and in various journals, including *Kalliope*, where she was the 2005 winner of the Sue Saniel Elkind Poetry Prize. Brown was also the 1997 National Head-to-Head Haiku Champion and a member of the 1998 Los Angeles National Slam Team. She is the co-author of *Grandparents as Parents: A Survival Guide to Raising a Second Family* (Guilford Press, 1995). Brown consults and teaches privately in Los Angeles.

Louisa Calio is a poet, artist, writer, performer and traveler, current Director of the Poet's Piazza for Hofstra University, published internationally, and winner of several awards: 1978 Connecticut Commission of the Arts Award, 1987 Women in Leadership Award, and the Barbara Jones and Talisan prizes for Poetry (Trinidad). She was recently honored, along with Alice Walker and other feminists who changed America (1963-76) at Barnard/Columbia University. Cofounder and Director of City Spirit Artists, a nonprofit arts organization in Connecticut, she has written, taught and dedicated her life to the arts for more than 30 years. In 2007, she organized and exhibited in "A Passion for Africa," a photography and poetry exhibit that opened in Montego Bay, Jamaica, where she lives part of the year. See www.italianamericanwriters.com/Calio.html for more.

Debbie Carlson is a writer, gardener, teacher and global nomad. Although she currently resides in the Pacific Northwest of the United States, she has been privileged to live in Japan, England, Germany and Scotland. She is the busy mother of two energetic toddlers, Gabriel and Daniel, and joyful partner of David Blatner.

Shawna Carol is an internationally recognized sound healer, author, singer, composer, and recording artist. She is author of *The Way of Song: A Guide to Freeing the Voice and Sounding the Spirit*, published by St. Martin's/Griffin. She is the top-selling artist on Ladyslipper Records with her CD *Goddess Chant*. Ms. Carol has been a featured guest on Wisdom Television, and served as the core music faculty at the Omega Institute for five years. She has taught SpiritSong at the Goddess Conference in Glastonbury England, The New York Open Center, the Women of Wisdom Festival in Seattle WA, Julia Cameron's Creativity Camp, and Paul Winter's Living Music Village.

Libby Chaney is an artist. She was born and raised in Ohio and has lived in California since 1966. She has a B.F.A. from Ohio Wesleyan University and has made, studied and taught art most of her life. Wanting to bring more figurative images into her abstractions, she has recently shifted her focus toward writing and storytelling. Libby lives in Mill Valley with her husband and has two grown children, two cats, an elderly dog and a view of Mount Tamalpais.

Miriam Chaya, writer, actor, director, producer, educator and documentary filmmaker, has written solo performance pieces about her spiritual journey and performed them throughout the country. *Odyssey of a Jewish Woman*, her critically acclaimed one-woman show, was seen on PBS. She is a graduate of the Jewish Spiritual Leadership Training Program at Chochmat HaLev in Berkeley. She wrote, directed and produced *Timbrels and Torahs: A Celebration of Wisdom*, a documentary film showing the importance of creating ceremony to honor the wisdom of our elders. She is the author of two feminist children's books, *The Forest Princess* and *Return of the Forest Princess*. Visit www.timbrelsandtorahs.com or write to her directly at mirchaya@aol.com.

Kimberly Childs lives in the beautiful mountains of Asheville, North Carolina with her husband Carl and 2 shi-tzus. Kimberly has received many gifts through visits to The Laurels Nursing Home with her dogs, bringing pet therapy to the residents. She has meditated for the past 35 years and finds this practice a constant rudder against the vicissitudes of life. In 1996 she developed neurological problems which make blinking and speech difficult. These have become her greatest teachers.

Catherine Holmes Clark   At 62, I'm just getting started writing the words that want to be passed on. Earlier I raised two daughters, painted faces on the mall in Washington, D.C., sewed mythic clothing and soft sculpture, taught witches to fly, helped create a tiny church, and built online communities. A subversive dedication to play—improvisation, moving from deep sources, opening the imagination—tells me to "keep dancing" when I'm stuck, and makes me relish feeling my mind stretched. I'm a cyborg—feel like a limb is missing without my computer—and a hermit, due to chemical sensitivities. I wear not only purple, but also a garden hat covered with aluminum foil to shield me from UV. Gaian feminist Buddhism keeps me sane. www.loudzen.com/catherine.

I'm **V. Diane Corbin**, age 75, married at 19, divorced at 42. Parent of four girls, one boy, grandparent of three granddaughters, two grandsons. After five universities in three states, a B.A. in English. Back in California, one child with me, I worked in Social Work, attended Fresno State University and received an M.S.W. Retired now, I'm active in areas of civil liberties and rights, peace, social justice, women's rights, the environment, racism, etc. I grew up Southern Baptist in Oklahoma but now I'm Unitarian Universalist, Humanist, Wiccan, Pagan. It works for me. I've wanted to write ever since I figured out words, a first poem at age six, then off and on as my life unfolded and I'm not done yet.

Johanna Courtleigh is a licensed therapist, writer, singer and performance artist living near Portland, Oregon. She is the founder of One Planet One Peace. Her goal is to help people come to deeper self-love, awareness, personal empowerment, ease and integrity, both internally and in their relationships with others. To awaken that which longs to know itself out beyond the confines of the small perceptions of the mind, and in so doing, help change and heal the world. She can be contacted via www.johannacourtleigh.com or www.oneplanetonepeace.com.

Beth Coyote: Published in *synapse*, *When It Rains From The Ground Up*, *Snow Monkey*, *Chrysanthemum*, *Gumball Press*, *Mindfulness Bell*, *Mute Note Earthward*, and *Tattoos on Cedar*. Two chapbooks, *Reclaiming Mercy* and *I Am Ready to Speak*.

Kathleen Crocetti is a local costume designer, performance and installation artist who moved to Santa Cruz in 1996. *Counting Lives Lost: Making Tangible an Abstract Measurement of Grief* is a community installation that could not have come to fruition without the assistance of more than 150 volunteers. From inception to first installation was three years of labor intensive emotional work. The piece was initially installed at Sierra Azul Nurseries in Watsonville on Memorial Day 2006, and continued to grow in size until its removal in September of 2006. Every weekend you can find Kathleen forming more 4-inch clay figures, making one small memorial for every person who has died in the Iraq War conflict. A new installation date and site have not been set. www.carmelart.org/artists_pages/crocetti/crocetti.html

Melody Culver received the elusive Chameleon Award in 1990 and continues to explore evolutionary traits of adaptability and versatility. In her present persona as freelance copyeditor, she peruses texts and manuscripts with enthusiasm and joy. She loves the sun and ocean climate of Santa Cruz, California and enjoys her grown son, camping, swimming, and spending an unreasonable amount of time reading.

Riva Danzig was born in the Bronx in 1948 to a family of Jewish working class intellectuals who believed Spirit (or God as She was called then) was a concept for the weak and uneducated. Riva's path to Spirit, though circuitous, has taken her exactly where she's needed to go in order to get there. More often than not, she finds herself happy to be alive, thrilled with her beautiful children and her dear friends. She has been and remains the grateful recipient and bestower of love, passion, friendship, and caring, and is embarking on the next phase her life with curiosity and abandon.

Pavita Decorah   "Lily and the Deer" is almost a true story. Once I lived in the village of Blue Wing and spent hours walking in those enchanting and mysterious woods. Now I am seventy and back home in the Colorado Rockies, as the director of a retreat center. Here in the San Luis Valley, our struggle is to save Mother Earth from oil, gas and water exploitation. My partner lives in Taos. Just driving to see her, past ancient and sacred Mt. Blanca, is a beautiful experience.

Ahraiyanna Della Tone was born into an Italian family in 1955 in Manhattan and raised in the Bronx. She acquired a Doctor of Veterinary Medicine degree from Cornell in 1982. She is mother to an angel named Timothy, a Reiki Master, an animal communicator, a dancer, a Lover, a heart resonance healer, a White Buffalo Woman and a teacher of One Heart Medicine. To Ahraiyanna, all life is the Beloved and all relationships are sacred. It is her most passionate desire to live this truth moment to moment. She resides in Santa Cruz between the redwoods and the Pacific Ocean, deep in the heart of the Great Spirit.

Coleen Douglas lives in Santa Cruz, California on the northern tip of Monterey Bay. Being outside in nature has always provided her a strong connection to the Oneness, Divine Spirit. Coleen is a singer and percussionist, from blues and soul to calypso and samba. She ministers in music with the Inner Light gospel choir, where the message honors all paths that lead to Truth (www.innerlightministries.com). Coleen lives with her partner Ellen, opening to life's changes now that the kids are grown. Life is full. Love is here.

Michelle Doyka, M.F.A. "Prayer in the Andes" is one of a series of line drawings about life in ancient times. I have often wanted to go back and live in the past, and these drawings allow me to do so in my imagination. Most of my art reflects antiquity through symbol or image and expresses the desire to connect with ancestral roots, mine or anyone else's, for that matter. It is said that until you know your past, you will not know where you are headed. That made it easy for me to then understand: we come from Art and are heading into Art.

Lora Dziemiela is a Reclaiming-influenced Witch currently living in Pittsburgh, Pennsylvania. She can often be found experiencing the passions of life through poetry, song, dance, and ecstatic ritual.

Joyce Eakins, M.F.A., who has exhibited internationally, teaches art at the university level. At present she is immersed in painting Hands and Hearts for healing. She creates personalized meditation icons with unique symbols for each individual. The process begins with a "laying on of hands" which opens the door to universal healing energies. Line, form, space, color, light, and texture begin to flow like a river onto the paper. The healing imagery emerges and the healing process begins. Start your healing process by reaching your hands and hearts out to Joyce Eakins at cojoycevt@aol.com.

Pamela Eakins lives atop a high cliff at the westernmost edge of the North American continent. In this place of monumental erosion, she communes with ocean waves enfolding one into the next, magical dark-eyed silkies, and iridescent ravens. Through the years, Pamela has donned the cloaks of professor, author, counselor, and peacemaker. She has given birth to babies, attended the dying, lived and loved in several cultures, and spoken multiple tongues. Her poetry grows like stalks of wild yarrow out of the untamed earth that spawned her; it is the mystery of the cosmos that sets her heart aflame. You can reach Pamela Eakins at www.pamelaeakins.net or by writing to Pacific Center, Box 3191, Half Moon Bay, CA 94019.

Lisa Espenmiller lives in Oakland, CA with her husband where they nurture a magical California Native and Mediterranean garden. Her poems appear in numerous literary journals including *DMQ Review, Black Bear Review, Home Planet News* and *Women's Studies Quarterly*. Lisa works as a technical writer and editor.

Maria Fama is the author of three books of poetry. Her work appears in numerous publications and anthologies. In 1998, she was a finalist in the Allen Ginsberg Poetry Awards. Fama has read her poetry in many cities across the country, read one of her stories on National Public Radio, cofounded a video production company, and recorded her poetry for CD compilations of music and poetry. Maria did her undergraduate and graduate work in history at Temple University. Fama's poems were awarded the 2002 Aniello Lauri Award in Creative Writing and the 2006 Amy Tritsch Needle Award for Poetry. She lives and works in Philadelphia.

Acclaimed Canadian singer/songwriter **Ferron** began writing songs at age 10, bought her first guitar in her late teens, and sang her way from coffee shops and benefits to paid gigs. Her first LPs were picked up by Ladyslipper Music, and in the next decade she produced *Testimony, Shadows On a Dime, Phantom Center, Resting with the Question, Driver,* and *Still Riot.* Ferron has played the largest venues in the U.S., including Carnegie Hall and Boston's Opera House. She is one of Canada's foremost folk musicians and one of the most influential writers and performers of women's music. Her recent release, *Turning Into Beautiful,* was recorded in an old farmhouse on an island in British Columbia.

Marigold Fine has been a video producer/documentary filmmaker since 1984 and is the creator of Full Circle Productions. Her award-winning documentaries have been seen internationally. Marigold is a SPECTRA Artist in the Schools through the Cultural Council of Santa Cruz County. She teaches video camera and editing, and video performance art. She is a freelance writer, editor, and scriptwriter, with a screenplay in progress. She received a degree in Journalism and Communications from the University of Illinois, and was an advertising copywriter in a previous incarnation in Chicago. Marigold enjoys integrating her love of storytelling and her creative, intuitive wild woman. Her passion is positive, life-affirming media, and empowering images of women. www.fullcirclevideo.com

Carolyn Brigit Flynn is a writer and teacher dedicated to language as a pathway to soul and spirit. Her poems and essays have appeared in literary journals and anthologies nationwide, including *Calyx, A Journal of Art and Literature by Women, The Pedestal Magazine, Porter Gulch Review, Black Buzzard Review, Intimate Kisses: The Poetry of Sexual Pleasure, Inside Grief: Death, Loss and Bereavement,* and *New to North America: Writings by U.S. Immigrants, Their Children and Grandchildren.* She is the editor of *The New Story: Creation Myths for Our Times,* and teaches writing groups and spiritual retreats called Writing to Feed the Soul. She lives near the ocean in Santa Cruz, California. www.carolynbrigitflynn.com

Sara Friedlander has been working in the Santa Cruz community as a psychotherapist, a writer, and an artist for thirty years. Her photography, however, goes back to her first trip abroad at the age of nineteen. Whether printing single unaltered photographs or combining and extending multiple images with oil paint, her intention is always to honor her subject, be it an individual, a culture, or the natural terrain.

Carol Gaab: Crone in training, lover of nature and the animals that inhabit it, architect of visionary spaces, Jungian therapist, cancer survivor, artist, wife, grandmother/auntie to a beautiful little girl, avid gardener, lifelong student, adventurer in life, world traveler, discovering my poetic voice, wanting to be part of helping to change the world, dedicated to navigating the deep caverns and waters within me, nourished by being in real relationship with others, curious, grateful.

Cooper Gallegos: The silence and beauty and chance for reflection at Pema Osel Ling had a profound effect on me and my writing, and in many ways marked my spiritual awakening. I have been writing since I was a small child watching my father struggle with the Great American Novel. I have an affinity for the marginal among us and see the miracle in small flowered weeds that make their way up through cracked concrete. I have previously published in *Writing for Our Lives*, *Looking Back*, *I'm Home*, and *What It's Like To Love a Woman*, and have read my work on Central Coast Public Radio. I am currently writing a novel set in the 1970s in the Mojave Desert. I can be reached at coopersleuth@aol.com.

Bakol Ruben Gellar has lived in Canada, Israel, Senegal and the United States. Although she was born in Canada, Israel is her true home. She has worked as a high school teacher, researcher, radio broadcaster, actress, advertising representative for a newspaper, and practitioner of acupressure. She presently lives in Bloomington, Indiana, where she is involved with the Jewish Renewal Community and has acted on stage, radio and in film. Recently she has become the co-artistic director of the Jewish Theatre of Bloomington. She looks forward to the day when she will return to Israel.

Pesha Joyce Gertler is Seattle's Poet Populist Emerita 2005-2006. She teaches Creative Writing at N. Seattle Community College, the University of Washington's Women's Center, city parks, living rooms, and numerous venues. She cofounded and coordinates a reading series sponsored by the college. Her poetry has appeared in numerous journals and anthologies and has received many awards. Both her poetry and teaching are grounded in her belief in the ongoing need for women's voices, the healing power of writing, and the magic of sitting in a circle of women and writing together. Further details may be found at www.PeshaJoyceGertler.com.

Cheryl Gettleman, the prolific writer of boxes of unpublished short stories,stacks of poems, two screenplays and one novel, lives in Santa Cruz, California, with her husband and Airedale. Tennis, travel, books, and film balance the life of this busy writer. Contact beachcg@sbcglobal.net for info on her blog.

Elenna Rubin Goodman is devoted to the creation of healing, peacemaking, and compassionate understanding on our beautiful and beleaguered planet. She works with individuals and communities desiring to navigate our times as sacred journeys. Spirit and the ancestors guide her. The wisdom of our bodies, of the earth, story, dreams, ceremony, silence and Council are among her medicine allies. In her medicine pouch, bearing the tail of the "ancestor squirrel," is this prayer: *Holy One, Hinuynee. Here I am. Please use me well.* The continuing generosity of Spirit, the earth, of the ancestors and many of her fellow beings who share these times sustains her. To elder and teacher Deena Metzger, and to her beloved partner Garner, she offers her unending and imperfect gratitude.

Deborah Gorman, M.A., M.F.A., is a visual artist, poet and teacher. At the height of the AIDS pandemic, her extensive experience in group process, mediation and grief and loss counseling facilitated her work with terminally ill patients and their families. As an intern at Coming Home Hospice and Shanti Project in San Francisco, Deborah's use of art and poetry with her patients was a valuable tool for healing and self expression. A practitioner of Zen Buddhism and a graduate of Being with Dying, Deborah currently facilitates "The Year to Live Project" and teaches art and poetry classes in her studio. For more information about upcoming classes and published works, please go to www.deborahangyogorman.com and click "contact."

Nancy Grace was born and has lived in the Santa Cruz area her whole life and is the mother of two beautiful grown daughters. Early in childhood, she found music to be a way of expressing her deepest feelings. She has finally realized a lifelong desire to support herself through music, delighting in being a "Music Together" teacher, offering musical encouragement and opportunities for young families, and voice coaching and guitar accompaniment lessons for adults. Nancy's search for meaning has led to a life devoted to building a deep connection to spirit and following the call of this voice. The song "Godfather" was written out of a healing experience she had in a guided meditation to remember a positive memory of her father.

Marci Graham weaves her love of Continuum Movement, participation and leadership in Love, Intimacy and Sexuality Workshops, her sculpting, painting, and creative writing into a vibrant exploration of her inner landscape that is reflected in her storytelling and poetry in this volume. "Writing turns my life experiences into tools for sharing with others how I navigate from one place in my heart and body to another, which just may awaken more possibilities for love and peace." Since 2000 she has interned Love, Intimacy and Sexuality Workshops by the Human Awareness Institute (HAI). Starting in 2006, Marci is co-leading Nature Moving Women retreats with her sister, Jade Sherer. Marci is the mother of three loving, grown children and lives in Aptos, California with her partner, Jason Weston.

Vivian Gratton was born in New Mexico and spent her childhood in Dallas. She has worked for oil companies, taught people about earthquakes, written science curriculum, trained tribal leaders in renewable energy, written grant proposals, birth-assisted, led ceremonies, and worked with children with learning differences. She is currently a counseling psychology graduate student. She lives with her partner and two children in Santa Cruz, California.

Bayla Greenspoon is a transplanted Canadian now living contentedly in magical Mt. Shasta, California with her dear partner Raven, dog Wyatt and cat Mylo. Bayla had the good fortune of growing up with a father who had music in his soul and with a family who constantly sang Broadway tunes, good old folk songs and Yiddish melodies. Bayla uses songs and chants to teach children, comfort the dying, celebrate life passages, and to inspire and express all manner of emotions. She believes that everyone can sing, and that one of the greatest travesties of North American culture is the lack of community singing. She would like to help change that…one voice at a time!

Lara Gularte is the editor of *Convergence* (www.convergence-journal.com), a literary and art online journal. She has served as poetry and art editor for *Reed Magazine*, San Jose State University's literary journal. Gularte received the 2005 Anne Lillis Award for Creative Writing and Phelan Awards for several of her poems. Her poetry has appeared in numerous journals, including the *Santa Clara Review*, *The Montserrat Review*, *Kaleidoscope* and *Art/Life*. Her chapbook, *Days Between Dancing*, was published by Poet's Corner Press in 2002. Gularte's poems have been translated into Portuguese by the University of the Azores. Her work was presented at an international conference on storytelling and cultural identity in June 2005, at Angra do Heroismo on the island of Terceira.

Reem Hammad is an Arab-American woman living in Los Angeles, California. She was born in Syria and grew up in Lebanon before immigrating to California. For the past 25 years, Reem settled in with her husband, worked, raised her two boys, went to college and received her Bachelor of Fine Arts from UCLA. Reem is now a ceramic artist who has recently chosen writing as another outlet for self-expression. Her childhood memories and the world she has left behind inspire her creative work.

Lea Haratani lives in Davenport, California with her son Holden, daughter Kamila, husband Colin, twelve chickens and a dog named Miyotis. She works as a communication specialist for the Santa Cruz County Resource Conservation District. She enjoys traveling to faraway places, trail running, and reading in her spare time.

Lawrie Hartt trained as a musician and served as a university chaplain, congregational minister, consultant and retreat leader for many years prior to being called by dreams and the natural world into the old ways of shamanic practice. She works as a spiritual counselor and healer in Southern California.

Jody Healy, whose mission is to heal hearts through song, has been singing since childhood and writing songs most of her adult life. Currently her songs appear on: Barbara McAfee's *Coming from the Heart* (2006), Debbie Nargi-Brown's *Into the Rhythm* (2004), The Threshold Choir's *Listening on the Threshold* (2004), Cider Jazz *Mug Shots* (2003), and her own upcoming CD. She is an executive coach for MBAs at Stanford Graduate School of Business and concurrently runs her own business, Creative Change Consulting and Training. As a life coach, she considers herself a "Joy Detective." She is gifted at recognizing and supporting individuals and groups to awaken to the joy of fulfilling their life purpose. Her interests include human and organizational transformation and world travel. She resides in Santa Cruz, CA.

Linda Holiday lives in Santa Cruz, California. Her life path took her to Japan in 1973, where she trained intensively in Aikido, a modern martial art dedicated to the cultivation of peace. Linda is the head instructor of Aikido of Santa Cruz, a nonprofit school (www.aikidosantacruz.org). She has a sixth-degree black belt and an M.A. in East Asian Studies from Stanford University. She is writing a book on the spiritual practice of Aikido, with her teacher in Japan. Linda finds greatest joy in writing, in the practice of Aikido, in the sacred places of Japan, and in Nature, especially the high mountains of California.

Nora Jamieson lives in Canton, Connecticut where she works with women individually and in groups. She has been bringing women together with a spiritual focus for 15 years and currently holds a monthly Women's Council and Into the Deeps dream groups. She is cofounder of Women's Temple In Her Name. For more information, see her website www.norajamieson.com.

Jonell Esme Jel'enedra is the author of *Stilt Walking at Midnight* (Hummingbird Press 2004). "It was in the midst of my own incredibly painful divorce that I encountered the beautiful, but terribly wounded man for whom I wrote "Prayer". And it was the moment when I began to hold his heart in my prayers that I felt my own broken heart begin to heal." She lives and works in Santa Cruz, California.

Sarah Jones stumbled upon her passion for literature and writing poetry during high school. It has been a loyal companion throughout her journey. Her notebooks have traveled with her through many adventures, heartbreak, and joyous moments. Currently she resides in San Francisco and teaches a peer leadership class in a middle school.

Alicia Knight grew up all over the world, including many formative years in Southern California, specifically "The OC" before it became pop-culture cool. Now Alicia lives in Virginia, below what she calls the "sweet tea line," the geographic point at which the waitstaff in restaurants begin asking if you prefer your iced tea "sweet or unsweet." The psychological sweet tea line demarks the state of the Southern mind: full of angst, still defensive, and too proud for its own good. This is the place of Alicia's ancestors, who whisper to her of their triumphant joys and painful sorrows. In between writing for politicians who borrow her words to speak their minds, Alicia writes poetry and prose whenever the spirits or events inspire her.

Deep-rooted daughter, sister, wife, stepmom, friend, peacemaker, and elder-in-training, **Sarah Knorr** works, dreams, and votes for a place at the table for all. Her recent work has appeared in *Tough Times Companion, Moondance, Ashé*

Journal and the *Women Artists Calendar.* Honored to keep company with the women whose works fill *Sisters Singing,* she gives thanks to Wild Girl Publishing for dreaming and birthing this book into being.

Caroline Koch (Stronck), a native of the San Francisco Bay Area, has always possessed an affinity for the literary arts. Influenced both by contemporary literature and by an innate sense of Spirit, Caroline, a recent Silicon Valley retiree, now devotes herself to a fledgling career as a fiction writer; she is currently working on a novel and several short stories. She lives with her husband and son in the hills of northern California.

Karen Koshgarian retired as an art educator in 1999, after inspiring teenagers in Silicon Valley for 32 years. She now carries a digital camera 24/7 in hopes of documenting an alien visit from infinity and beyond. In the meantime, she creates artists' books, botanical illustrations, studies calligraphy, writes a thought-provoking blog, and creates collaborative murals with her life partner of 20 years, a corporate worker bee who keeps her in the lifestyle to which she is accustomed. She passionately loves Pixar animation and dramatic film, collects world music, is a Macintosh addict, and is never without something to read, be it a book, magazine, an interesting pamphlet, or a cereal box. More of her work can be seen at www.twokandoux.com.

By the time **Robin Rector Krupp** was 2, if her mother didn't give her paper, she pulled up her dress and drew on her thighs! Robin encourages a wide range of art in herself and others. She is grateful to have presented art to more than 300,000 people from Y'upik Eskimo villages, to the Venetian Hotel in Las Vegas, and to schools in South Africa. Her advanced art degrees are from Pomona College and CSUN. She has taught in five colleges and universities. She writes and illustrates children's books, including the award-winning *Let's Go Traveling.* Her most recently illustrated book, written by E. C. Krupp, is *The Rainbow and You.* Robin received lifetime achievement awards from the Children's Literature Council and Women's International Center.

Cara Lamb has been writing ever since she learned how. She has worked as a street vendor, a hot tub installer, a nude model, a nonfiction book editor, a COBOL programmer, a kitchen designer, a mover, a graphic designer, an event planner, and the Playboy Advisor. She has an M.A. in spirituality. She has written, and tossed, a fantasy novel, and is now at work on a fairy tale. She produces prayer books in Hebrew and unlikely quilts. She studies tarot, Torah, dreams and mythology, mixing them in her mind into a strange and wonderful soup. She never wears shoes unless she has to, and flosses almost every day.

Emily Lardner   I have had many wonderful spiritual teachers, including Quakers, Catholics, Presbyterians and Buddhists, as well as bees, raspberries, goats and children...always inviting a kind of presence and awareness, and an opportunity to participate in the sacred part of life. I teach academic writing and co-direct a center for professional development to improve the quality of undergraduate education. I love walking.

Sonya Lea is a sixth-generation Kentuckian who lives in Seattle, Washington. She has written for *The Southern Review, the Seattle Post-Intelligencer, Tricycle*, and *nthPosition*, and has received three screenwriting awards. Sonya is at work on a collection of essays based on her family's transformation during her beloved's cancer treatment, and the link between personal and collective memory. Contact her at sonyalea@gmail.com.

Lori Levy's poems have appeared in *Lullwater Review, Portland Review, Rattle, MacGuffin, International Poetry Review, The Comstock Review, Jewish Women's Literary Annual, Hawaii Review*, and others. Born in New Jersey, she grew up in Vermont, lived in Israel for 16 years, and now lives in Los Angeles with her husband and three children. Lori may be reached at avilori@yahoo.com.

Heather Lewis enjoys photography in the natural world.

Rose Lobel is a novelist, poet, mother, gardener, and radio programmer. Some of her poems and playlists can be found at www.redplumpoetry.com.

Joanna Macy, Ph.D., is a scholar of Buddhism, Systems Theory and Deep Ecology, known widely for her workshops and trainings for activists. Her many books include *Coming Back to Life, Widening Circles,* and *World as Lover, World as Self.* For information about her work and calendar, see www.joannamacy.net.

Jean Mahoney is a writer who roams and wanders in and out of the fog in Santa Cruz, California. She has been writing for forever, at least since 1958 when she published two editions of the "Mahoney Family News" in her own handwriting. Since then she has enjoyed writing poetry, essays and short stories and hopes to continue this practice until at least 2048.

Maía   I live and write in Southern California. My first word, "bird" (imitating a blackbird) and, 12 years later, first sonnet, "To A Sunflower" (imitating Shakespeare), previewed a lifelong devotion to both natural history and nature mysticism. Later, I experimented with essays and short fiction about homeless people, eccentrics and artists. For ten years, I read my work in planetariums, sea life museums, libraries and cafes. I've published in more than 60 journals and anthologies, including *Intimate Nature* (Ballantine) and *Shared Sightings* (John Daniel & Co.) I am gathering a collection of poems written in response to the death, in 2005, of my partner and muse, Charlie, called *The Spirit-Life of Birds*—also finishing a near-future novella called *See You in My Dreams*.

Susan Manchester lived on Santa Cruz Island off the coast of California from 1992-1997. While managing Scorpion Ranch and working as a guide and naturalist, she was in daily interaction with the elements. Susan assembled a body of poetry and photographs. "On This Day" was Susan's first attempt to recall in glimpses her life on the island.

Christine McQuiston, M.L.A., has been writing poetry since she was eight years old. She is in love with the limitless music of creation. Poetry is her path for finding the essence of the sacred in all and everyday things. Some of her work appears in the *We'Moon Datebook*, 2005 and 2007 editions. Contact christine_mcquiston@yahoo.com for a sample of her self-published poetry reader, *3-Fold Quarterly*. She lives and works in San Francisco, California.

Carmen Rita Menéndez Núñez was born, raised, and educated in Puerto Rico. She also holds an M.A. in Spanish Literature from UCLA. Ms. Menéndez spent twenty years teaching the literature and language of her soul, subsequently moving into the field of leadership in the public affairs arena. The transition into addressing issues of social justice in education happened in a wink. For the next thirteen years, as part of a school reform initiative in Los Angeles, Ms. Menéndez was instrumental in creating trusting environments across cultural differences. The great gift of these various endeavors, and their common denominator, was the discovery of her untold stories, and the inevitability of telling them. Ms. Menéndez is also a certified Iyengar Yoga teacher in Los Angeles.

Holly Metz lives and photographs in the Gila River Indian Community in Arizona.

Deena Metzger is a poet, novelist, essayist, healer-medicine woman. Her most recent books include *From Grief into Vision: A Council*; *Doors: A Fiction for Jazz Horn*; *Entering the Ghost River: Meditations on the Theory and Practice of Healing*; *The Other Hand*; *Writing for your Life: A Guide and Companion to the Inner Worlds*; *Tree: Essays and Pieces* (including *The Woman Who Slept with Men to Take the War Out of Them*); *Intimate Nature: Women's Bond with Animals (coeditor)*; *A Sabbath Among the Ruins*; *Looking for the Faces of God and What Deena Thought*. She is working on a new novel, *La Negra y Blanca. Ruin and Beauty: New and Selected Poems,* from Red Hen Press, will be published in 2008. She lives at the end of the road with the wolves Tschee Wa'Yah, Shoonaq' and Cherokee. www.deenametzger.com

Peggy Tabor Millin lives and writes in Asheville, North Carolina. Through her business ClarityWorks, she facilitates women in writing process so they can move past fears, find inspiration, and discover their writing voice. Her book, *Mary's Way,* was published in the U.S. and Mexico. She has published short fiction and nonfiction in various magazines and literary journals, including *Thema* and *Native Peoples*. Peggy lived a year in the Mediterranean and worked eight years with the Eastern Band of Cherokee Indians. A student of Zen Buddhism, her study of eastern religions, metaphysics, and dreams shapes her worldview and authenticates her voice. She is currently working on a book on writing process and the feminine. Learn more at www.clairtyworksonline.com.

Anne Mize's passion for the outdoors led her to the Arctic Wildlife Refuge, the Tongass Forests of Southeast Alaska, and mountains throughout the United States. Her fascination with African cultures and wildlife has drawn her back to Africa for nearly 25 years, where she has worked with women's cooperatives, village banks, and conservation-related development projects. She adopted her

13-year-old daughter from Ethiopia. With poems and stories published in *Scent of Cedars*, *Cup of Comfort for Sisters*, *Sun Magazine*, and *Christian Science Monitor*, Anne presently teaches creative writing to middle school children.

San Francisco native **Marcia Moonstar** began writing poetry as a teenager. She has performed in coffeehouses, bookstores, and at many women's events throughout the Northwest with her unique style of performance poetry, which has grown over the years to include music, dance and masks. In March of 2001 Marcia released her first CD of poetry with new age and world music, entitled *Moon Magic*. She self-published three poetry books and designs greeting cards and posters with her poetry. Marcia looks forward to traveling with her poetry performance and Moon Wise astrological workshop. She currently lives in Seattle. For more information about Marcia's creative endeavors, see her website www.marcymoonstar.com.

Cathy Moore   I am a certified nurse midwife and a belly dancer. I attend births at a hospital in Boston, MA. My work "catching babies" has been a deep well of inspiration for my dances. I am a co-owner of The Goddess Dancing belly dance company. We teach and perform belly dance as a tool of personal empowerment for women. Our dances tell stories, enact myths, and depict goddesses and mortal women. "A Midwife's Invocation" began as a prayer that I wrote for myself while in midwifery school. I later adapted and fleshed it out with the intention of creating a performance art piece comprised of spoken word, music and dance. Learn more about me and my company at www.thegoddessdancing.com.

Maggie Milazzo Muir lives in Santa Cruz, California, nestled between the redwoods and the ocean, with her husband Andrew and daughters Chelsea and Katelyn. Her greatest joy comes from mothering, and she has the good fortune and privilege of supporting other families in her work as a lactation consultant and family counselor. For many years she worked as a doula, providing in-home care to mothers and babies in the precious first weeks and months postpartum. As a girl, her family provided foster care for infants, and she credits her parents for nurturing her deep love of babies.

Kate Munger is a singer and songwriter who lives with her family, sings, works and swims along the shores of Tomales Bay, and has led community singing for more than 30 years. In 2000 Kate founded the first Threshold Choir for women who are called to sing at the bedsides of people who are dying, ill, or in a coma, and with women who are incarcerated. Today there are 45 Threshold Choirs and 800 singers in the U.S. These choirs bring together a magnificent community of huge-hearted, collaborating, creative women who know that true service heals everyone. The choirs have released two CDs: *Listening at the Threshold* and *Tenderly Rain: Songs of Gratitude, Remembrance & Keeping Watch*. www.thresholdchoir.org.

Art historian, editor, and Master Gardener, **Katherine Metcalf Nelson** has taught at Westminster College, Mississippi State College, California College of

Arts and Crafts, and the University of California. She has written numerous articles and is the author of *Apricot Eggs*, an autobiographical fish tale, and *Night Fishing*, an illustrated dream journal. Katherine has been an editor for *Utah Holiday* and *ARTNews*. She now lives in Seattle, Washington. After two decades of teaching and writing about art, a Felco #8 pruner replaced my pen. Clearing a tangle of Himalayan blackberries and morning glory vines in our garden, I saw the light. Since then, the language of plants has led me from artwork to earthwork.

Jane Nyberg is the founder of Wild Girl Publishing. At a writing retreat in the Santa Cruz mountains, Jane reconnected to the wild girl who ran free chasing the wind, the one who climbed into treetops and made trails through empty lots, who boldly spoke her mind and knew she belonged on earth. This wild girl's joy is to publish books that encourage each of us to find and recognize our wild souls. www.wildgirlpublishing.com.

Maria Papacostaki is the great-granddaughter of a priest, the granddaughter of a gambler, and the daughter of a cook. Therefore, she is endowed with a perfect, if at times slightly imbalanced, mixture of reverence, instability, and sensuality. She is a lover of many things, including: her two children, swimming through the myriad blues of the sea, the moon, food, the musky smell of Greek churches and the candles that light them, and finally, mornings with a book and a good cup of leafy tea. This bio was written by her daughter.

Laura Wine Paster, a writer and licensed clinical social worker, leads writing and healing groups that support the creative, emotional, and spiritual growth of women. A certified group leader in the Amherst Writers & Artists Method, she coauthored *The Jewish Women's Awareness Guide*. She is the proud grandmother of Naomi, Eleanor, and Judah. She lives in Walnut Creek, California, with her husband and their two dogs.

Sandra Pastorius   I have practiced astrology for 25 years, offering private consultations, workshops and public talks. For ten years, I authored "The Lunar Monthly Muse by Laughing Giraffe" using the Moon cycle as a teaching wheel. While living in Santa Cruz, California, I worked at Gateways Books and Gifts as Event Coordinator, hosting many visiting authors. I produced several Astrological Forums during this time. In the 1990s I was part of a circle of women known as the "The Holy Hemp Sisters", which brought together the spirit of circle and the power of intention into our political voice. I now live in Ashland, OR, and offer readings and workshops with an emphasis on "The Zodiac As Medicine". E-mail DancesWithPlanets@opendoor.com

Sylvia Bortin Patience is a mother, grandmother, and home birth midwife in Santa Cruz County, California. She writes about birth and death, and what comes in between. Many of her poems are inspired by the ocean and mountains near her home. Sylvia has had poems published in *Calyx, A Journal of Art and Literature by Women, Porter Gulch Review, La Gazette*, and *The Anthology of Monterey Bay Poets*.

Hannah Peabody, 16, attends San Lorenzo Valley High. One afternoon when she was 14, Hannah sat down with some blue and white paint and began to doodle. Two hours later she knew the piece was finished, but has never figured out who this woman is, or why she appeared that day. Along with being open to her creative process, Hannah enjoys an eclectic group of friends, singing, dancing, playing piano and guitar, soccer, swimming, water polo, and reading books that move her.

Judy Schatan Phillips is honored to be included in *Sisters Singing*, her second publication with Wild Girl Publishing. Judy, a native Californian, lives and loves in Santa Cruz, California with husband Dan, family and friends. She is engaged in writing, painting, yoga, food, movies, swimming, walking, talking, reading, sleeping, planting and tending her succulents, traveling and being a grandma.

Deborah Phoenix   The desert poem "One Precious Moment" came to me when I was trying to cheer up my best friend. We have been going to Joshua Tree together annually for over a decade. Together, yet individually, we've shared sacred time in the desert ever since our first vision quest. This poem was inspired by an opening in my heart to bring the desert back to him when he could not return "home" to Joshua Tree one spring. No matter how harsh the desert is, its sacred beauty and teachings help us bring back "medicine" to our people. This poem was my way of bringing that "medicine" back to an Elder of my Clan, my best friend.

Moved by the spectrum of life's journey, **Kathleen Pouls** taps deeply into her creative resources. Joining elemental and subtle energies, her works are expressions of her inner and outward experience. "From the primordial essence in the clay of the earth, through the hands of the artist, present feelings and ancient echoes resound, inviting the creative to come forth." Kathy teaches Creative Process Art & Clay classes. She is also an acupuncturist, working with traditional Chinese medicine, energy and MicroRelease bodywork, reflexology, and injury and trauma resolution. www.kpoulshealingarts.com

Lynx Quicksilver was born in Edinburgh, Scotland. "Music is my life and kindness my religion." She has always sung, as far back as she can remember. Her father taught her saxophone and how to read music when she was eight. In high school, she took up guitar to accompany her singing, and during her college years at Sarah Lawrence evolved into an accomplished singer-songwriter and performer of classical and folk music. In the last ten years, Lynx has played bass guitar in various bands, and now is a master of styles, from opera to country and Portuguese-American fadista. Lynx presently lives in Huntsville, Alabama. She has just released a CD of original songs, *The Wound Heals*.

Becky Reardon is a singer and composer whose rounds and songs celebrating the earth and stars, the seasons and the sacred diversity of life are sung by song circles and choirs all over the United States and the British Isles. She lives and works and takes lots of walks near Taos, New Mexico. Her two CDs, *Follow the Motion* and *Songs for a Walk*, can be ordered by e-mailing breardon@taosnet.com.

Ziggy Rendler-Bregman is one of nine children and mother of three. While a student at UC Santa Cruz, she cofounded the children's literary and art magazine *Stone Soup* and later worked as a printmaker, art teacher, administrator and community organizer. Her advocacy provided increased funding for arts education for schools both locally and throughout California. An active member of Holy Cross Catholic Church, she practices a monastic way of study, art and daily meditation. She recently made a pilgrimage to the Saccidananda Ashram in southern India and will return to Ireland to explore its literature, spirit, history and art with her daughter, sister and mother. Ziggy and her husband Jesse live in Santa Cruz California, where she is compiling a book of poems and drawings.

Coleen Rhalena Renee lives as a Healer, musician and writer in the beautiful Pacific Northwest. She teaches SpiritSong, archetypal transformation and BodyListening. Coleen loves working with clients in transition, those initiating change in their lives and those learning to navigate the challenges of change that life brings. Coleen cofounded BodySong Healing and Arts Center in Seattle, and travels and teaches in her ancestral lands in the Ohio Valley. Coleen is a member of the Sacred Fire Choir and performs internationally. Visit Coleen at www.ColeenRenee.com.

Jane E. Reyes, M.A.   I have been creating art since I could pick up a pencil. My art is about transformation and history and life and color and joy and politics and healing. A rich African-Latina heritage influences my simple palette of red, blue and yellow. I am an artist, educator, gardener, herbalist, mother, grandmother, activist and lover of life. I was born and grew up in Oakland, CA and have lived in Santa Cruz County for the past thirty-six years. I can hear the surf at night while I fall asleep in my beautiful place two blocks from the beach. This little paradise allows me to reflect and contemplate in a certain atmosphere of calmness. Enjoy!

Rhiannon is a vibrant, gifted singer, composer, performance artist and master teacher who has brought her unique and potent blend of jazz, world music, improvisation and storytelling to audiences for more than three decades. In 1976 Rhiannon cofounded the groundbreaking all-female jazz quintet Alive! She is a founding member of innovative a cappella ensembles Voicestra (with Bobby McFerrin) and SoVoSo. She continues to tour with Bobby internationally, in addition to pursuing her own solo and ensemble performances. Teaching has been a strong and continual theme in Rhiannon's professional life. In clinics and workshops around the world she teaches her own unique body- and spirit-based vocal improvisation process. Rhiannon regards music as a vehicle for healing, community building, transformation, and social change.

Award-winning author and documentary filmmaker **Nancy J. Rigg** has campaigned tirelessly worldwide to ensure that rescue personnel have the equipment and training needed to handle dangerous swiftwater and flood rescue operations. In addition to articles published in fire-rescue journals, magazines, and newspapers, Rigg has produced and appeared in documentary programs for the Discovery Channel, Public Television, BBC, and other news and information outlets. She facilitates an online memoir writing group for the Story Circle Network; moderates information and support websites for swiftwater rescue personnel, the SwiftH20-News, and for families who have lost loved ones to drowning, the Drowning Support Network; and serves on the Board of Directors of the Higgins and Langley Memorial Awards in Swiftwater Rescue.

In 1968, **Diane Roberts Ritch** received a B.A. in Art from California State University at Los Angeles with a study emphasis in weaving, surface design and art history. After graduating, she exchanged the loom for the more portable needle and thread. She traveled abroad and studied the world's embroidered textiles for many years. Diane taught needle arts locally and nationally until the mid-1980s, when she was introduced to handmade Japanese paper. Seduced by its strength and versatility, she began to embroider, dye, sew and weave it. Moving from textiles to paper seemed a natural progression. Not surprisingly, paper invited the traditional treatments of drawing and painting; recent work reflects little of Diane's textile training and more of her fine art foundations.

Sarojani Rohan Motherhood has graced me with curiosity and trust in holiness everywhere, and in the magic and miracle of surprise. Teaching for 26 years, I continue to find joyous inspiration in children's innate communion with delight and wonder. Poetry is my way in to make sense of the Mystery—and my way out of dark corners and closets full of tigers and monsters and other things that go bump in the night. As I grow older I find I am opening and deepening and have a sincere willingness to be dazzled.

Kim Rosen, MFA, is a poet and spoken word artist as well a teacher and facilitator of inner work. Through her practice of learning and speaking poems by heart, she has become a voice for poetry's power to awaken, inspire and heal. She offers "Poetry Concerts" and workshops in collaboration with many gifted musicians, where the alchemy of music and poetry becomes a force of transformation. Her latest CD, *Only Breath*, is an interweaving of spoken poems of ancient and modern poets with the music of cellist/composer Jami Sieber. Currently she is writing a book about the art of learning, living and speaking poetry by heart. www.kimrosen.net

Since 1965 **Susan Rothenberg** has been sculpting earthy women in clay, concrete and bronze. Some of this art is full human scale. Of her work, Susan says, "Women are powerful, joyful, loving and sassy. We are deeply connected to each other, nature and spirit. This is what I want my sculpture to express." Her elemental art has been exhibited frequently in the United States and Europe. She can be reached at susan@coincidence.net.

Gaël Roziére My mother was a poet. I love words. I am a mother and a grandmother. I want to pass my pulse on in words. I write for the pure joy of it. I write to remember, to record, to bear witness. I write to heal, to open passageways, to reground. I'm a CranioSacral therapist. My favorite writing is in the company of others, particularly Carolyn Brigit Flynn's writing group, where time after time she leads us to the depths of the earth, the stars and the patterns that dance us. For this I am eternally grateful.

For **Carolyn Davis Rudolph** it began with a journal, then another and another. Though she squirms when introduced as a writer or poet, a small *yes* dances. Her writings are a spiritual dialogue placed on the altar of life to unearth why she has been sent here, a meditation on the mysterious partnership between the unreasonable suffering and the dazzling beauty a human heart is expected to hold. Carolyn began channeling the performance piece "The Shaman Housewife" while stranded in suburbia with her husband Rudy and two sons. Leopard-skin spandex and a feather boa are involved. She swims with sea creatures and doesn't enter the water. Any time now she plans to settle down.

By the light of the moon **Karen Sallovitz** writes poetry and science fiction. She has just completed her first sci-fi novel, *The Unwinding*. By the light of day she is a Certified Advanced Rolfer and a muckraker in Santa Cruz, California.

Electric cellist and vocalist **Jami Sieber** reaches inside the soul with compositions that are contemporary, timeless, lush, and powerfully evocative. She has worked in a variety of musical settings that have taken her as far as China, Korea, the Balkans, Italy, France, Russia, and recently to Thailand, where she had the most enriching experience of improvising and recording with the Thai Elephant Orchestra outside of Lampang. She has toured nationally and internationally with her band, Rumors of the Big Wave (1984-1995) with Rhiannon, Ferron, Jennifer Berezan, and as a soloist. Jami has released four independently produced recordings, each a sonic journey exploring the breadth and magic of acoustic and electric cellos, with compositions that will open the heart, defy the mind, and, at times, set the body dancing. www.jamisieber.com

Gretchen Sentry I am, on occasion, a writer, grandmother, dieter, dollmaker, seer and collagist, but hardly ever in that order. I'm thinking of adding curmudgeon to the list. And possibly mathematician, but that would be a total fabrication.

Linda Serrato I have been writing for several years. I have a B.A. in Liberal Studies from Chico State University and an M.A. in Creative Writing from San Francisco State University. Being a Latina, a native Californian, a mother, a teacher—and just a woman in general—has informed my writing. The interaction between the inner and the outer landscape has had a great influence on my work, as has my relationship with the Virgin Mary, and of course my ongoing love affair with the moon. I currently teach elementary school in Chico, California.

Sharon Rodgers Simone is a poet, writer and public educator who has devoted her life to healing the wounds of violence and moving toward a more peaceful world. She is the mother of six children and has three grandchildren. Sharon lives in Redlands, California with her husband, Pat, and granddaughter, Jessica Ann.

Marcia Singer, M.S.W., directs the Foundation for Intimacy in the Los Angeles/SFV area. A shamanic artist-healer and hypnotherapist with a Masters in Clinical Social Work from UC Berkeley, this former nightclub entertainer is a consultant on Conscious Aging. Marcia teaches improv to seniors, sings to the terminally ill, and runs wisdom circles for older women. She self-published a national songwriter's tipsheet for 16 years, wrote three children's awareness primers (P.L.A.Y.House Press), edited Marshall Rosenberg's first nonviolent communication booklet, and freelances for SoCal publications. "Lillian" is excerpted from a manuscript entitled *Iron Jane: Tales of Awakening A Wild Heart*. Marcia anticipates publication of *The Tao of Play: Joy, Originality, Vitality and Connection for Life*.

Patti Sirens is an ex-New York poet and punk rock musician turned surfer/kayaker. She comes from a family of mermaids, fishwives, net menders, and bootleggers. Her poetry has won prizes in the Artists' Embassy International Dancing Poetry Contest, National Writer's Union Poetry Contest, and the Virginia Poetry Society Contest. Her first book of poetry, *Antarctica*, was published by Burning Bush Publications in 2000. She lives in Santa Cruz, California.

Judith Tamar Stone is a psychotherapist, consciousness teacher and writer. Through a process she has created called Body Dialogue, Judith gives voice to the body. In honor of her body and the loss of not having had a child in this lifetime, her prose is often dedicated to the spiritual birth of her creative process and mission. She lives in Boulder, Colorado with her husband and life partner, Michael.

Elizabeth Lyttleton Sturz was born in the Texas hill country midway between Lone Man and Lone Woman Mountains, lived in Marshall, Beaumont and Dallas, and attended the University of Texas and George Washington University Graduate School. She wrote about U.S. life and literature for the U.S. State Department and the BBC, lived four years abroad and published four books, one with Herb Sturz, her husband. Her poetry was published in the *Saturday Review* and elsewhere. She worked four years for an antipoverty agency and is founder and president of Argus Community in the South Bronx, which provides personal development, skills training and jobs for people left behind. Her book about Argus, *Widening Circles*, was published by Harper & Row.

Ratna Jennifer Sturz Something about the process of writing draws me into more mythical and symbolic realms of being. Writing widens access to imagination and thoughts, exposing awareness and subtlety that might otherwise remain abstract or hidden. This process of self-unfolding also helps define my life path. I am a longtime practitioner of yoga meditation, an educator and a coach towards mind/body/soul wisdom. I have an M.A. in Counseling from Santa Clara University, California and a B.A. in political science from Washington University, Missouri. Originally from New Jersey, I have lived in the Santa Cruz, CA area since 1975. www.coaching-essence.com

Michelle Sumares   Taking a leap of faith and leaving the certainties of home, career and community, Michelle recently moved from the familiarity of the San Francisco Bay area of California for the Blue Ridge Mountains of western North Carolina. She is currently working in clay, exploring the aesthetics and social issues associated with the female form. Michelle enjoys painting watercolor portraits, using art as a tool for healing and transformation, and producing graphic design work for individuals and organizations. Capturing nature using digital photography is an enjoyable pastime. The image of the single lotus flower entitled "Contemplation" was taken at the Atlanta Botanical Garden.

Marie Summerwood is an author, wailing woman and composer of women's sacred chants. Included here are selections from her highly acclaimed first CD, *She Walks With Snakes. Step Into The River*, her second CD, is recently released. Marie teaches workshops for women to write their own sacred chants. The first CD from this work is *Memories From The Lost Pines—A Labyrinth of Chants*, from PineCrone Labyrinth Retreat in Texas. Marie is a playwright, author of *In Praise of She, The Muse*. Her work can also be experienced through workshops on the sacredness of grief and wailing, and through her performance art piece on the spiritual reframing of torch music.

Barbara Thomas's artistry flows through her life, her paintings, writing, clothing and relationships. She has lived at the edge of a mountain all of her adult life. For the past 17 years she has lived in the heart of a redwood forest. She has a clear awareness of the presence and influence of the nonphysical world interpenetrating the physical world. This close connection with the spirits in nature has influenced her painting, her writing, and every part of her life. Relating with nature in such an intimate way has been a nurturing support and wise teacher as she has moved through her husband's death and opened to an exploration of life as an individual, no longer as part of a couple.

Mary Camille Thomas is a rare native resident of Santa Cruz, California who considers herself lucky to have returned after living in Davis, Germany, Los Angeles, Holland, and on the road in a motor home. A cradle Catholic, she dips her cup into the sweet water of the spiritual life wherever she finds it, whether in a Benedictine monastery on top of a mountain or in an Ohlone sweat lodge, whether reading St. Theresa of Avila or Rumi. Although Mary is a librarian by profession, she wanted to be a writer almost from the time she learned how to read, and has written two novels.

Elizabeth Tozier grew up in a military family, stationed all over Europe and the U.S. Watsonville, a small agricultural town on the Central Coast of California, was the only permanent home she knew. In 1972, she graduated from Stanford

University. For more than twenty years, she has taught English and history in a continuation high school. She and her husband of many years divide their time between Santa Cruz County and northeastern California. Their two children are young adults. Elizabeth's lifelong dream of being a writer has come to fruition in her women's writing circle.

When **Alysia Tromblay** started singing into a hairbrush at the age of three, her parents decided that perhaps she might want to learn to play the piano as well. A graduate of Ithaca College School of Music, Alysia is a gifted healer, teacher, singer and songwriter now living in Washington state. "All of what I do, really, has to do with a quality of prayer, a way of acknowledging my passion for the Sacred and its ability to transform humanity." "Mother Mercy" was written as a direct response to September 11th. Alysia formed the Bon Future Fund, a nonprofit trust to provide higher education for indigenous children of Tibet living as refugees in India and Nepal. Please visit www.alysiatromblay.com.

Jodine Turner   While living in Glastonbury, England, the ancient Isle of Avalon, Jodine began writing the "Goddess of the Stars and the Sea" trilogy. These visionary novels tell the story of spiritual evolution, culminating in the present-day "Shift of the Ages". The novels carry keys to embodying the Sacred Feminine and are an initiatory journey into the Mysteries of the Goddess. First in the trilogy is the highly acclaimed *The Awakening: Rebirth of Atlantis*, followed by the award-winning *The Keys to Remember. Carry on the Flame* is soon to be released. Jodine presently lives in Oregon with her husband, Christopher. She is a therapist and a consecrated priestess.   www.jodineturner.com

Andrea van de Loo   Sixty-four years old, I am at this turning point in time. The desire to spearhead, together with brother and sister warriors, a new way of life, a new way of being and relating for peace on our planet, is burning in my heart. I have spent decades in an intensive inner exploration, digging up, reclaiming, rejecting, winnowing out the dross from my personality, thinning the veils between my mind and the living truth. I have learned that trust arises as I practice transparent truth, kindly. In that spirit I share myself with you. Wherever I go, I look into your eyes and behold the Beloved.

Leslie Claire Walker hails from the lush bayous, beaches, and concrete jungles of the Texas Gulf Coast. She can often be found indoors with her laptop and an extra large cup of tea—or outside, listening to the voice of the land. Her stories have appeared in *L. Ron Hubbard Presents Writers of the Future, Volume XVI, Andromeda Spaceways Inflight Magazine, City Slab*, and *Fantasy Magazine*. She is passionately dedicated to the transformation and healing of all the worlds through the magic of story.

Carmella Weintraub   My work is about color, light and evocative images. I design silk scarves and fashion accessories. The color palette is rich and intense, reflective of years living on the water in Hawaii and California, where color is a way of life. The movement and light-reflective qualities of silk push color to its utmost brilliance and beauty, and the flora and fauna of the natural world are a constant source of design inspiration. Like most artists, I am motivated by the intrinsic pleasure of capturing the light and color of the world. The cultivation of beauty through light and color is a healing force, one which will help transform our world.

Danelia Wild is a writer, singer and healer living in Los Angeles. She worked for many years as a reporter specializing in covering crime and the courts for a variety of newspapers, wire services and radio. She has also worked in literary publishing and as a consultant to nonprofit organizations. Her poetry has appeared in various anthologies and magazines and she has published three chapbooks of her work. She was born in Los Angeles to an Irish mother and an American father.

Cathy Williams has been teaching her ART & SOUL Workshops since 1989. She has taught extensively throughout the United States and in Indonesia and Italy. To be honest about it, Cathy is a remarkable teacher. Her workshops open the way for deep creative principles to be felt and experienced. She delights in seeing her students discover and then ride their own unique expressions. Cathy sings, she writes, she paints and she dreams herself into constant joy. To find out more, visit her website www.artandsoulworks.com.

Elizabeth Williams is an untamed EcoFeminist artist living in Santa Cruz, California, surrounded by talented artists, poets, musicians, political activists, dancers, actors, and lovers of life. Her paintings and found-object sculptures can be described as neo-folk. Her work is narrative, with themes of heroic women, the circus, nature, animals, history, mystery, spirituality, animism, the feminine divine, and ecology. Elizabeth was born in 1955 and raised on a dairy farm in rural Massachusetts during the consciousness-raising Sixties. She graduated from the school of the Worcester Art Museum in 1976, and settled in Santa Cruz after a few years of exploring the U.S. She earned a B.F.A. at UCSC in 1995. She is a full-time artist.

Valerie Wolf / Grandmother White Bear is a shamanic healer, dreamer, teacher and writer in an eclectic Medicine Ways tradition. Her lineage includes Nimipu, Cherokee, Blackfoot, Tupi, and Celtic ancestors. She is committed to restoring the ancient shamanic traditions of working with dreams to learn to be in right relationship to our Earth Mother and all Beings who dwell here. She teaches Medicine Dreaming and is currently writing a book on a shamanic paradigm for dream understanding. She founded Dream Weavers, a nonprofit foundation that explores and supports indigenous dreaming wisdom throughout the world. She also trains shamanic healers, and leads medicine walks and vision quests. Valerie lives in Topanga, CA with her husband Glen; son, Nick; two wolf/dogs Tara and Bear, and cat Fiona.

Diane Wolverton is a woman in love with the lusciousness of life, beauty and the pleasure of inhabiting a human body. Her love informs her work as a teacher and advocate of sustainable business as well as her play as gardener, writer, mystic and celebrant. She holds a Doctor of Ministry degree in Spirituality from Wisdom University. She is the author of the book, *Return of the Yin: A Tale of Peace and Hope for a Troubled World* and the play, *Bring Back My Body to Me.* www.dianewolverton.com

Sara Wright I am a naturalist, a writer, ritual artist, dreamer, and teacher who lives in the western mountains of Maine. I teach Women's Studies, Psychology and English at the University of Maine and Central Maine Community College, and hold an M.A. from Goddard College. I share my small log cabin with an assortment of animal friends both inside and out, and am presently being initiated by Nature into my crone years.

Credits

Grateful acknowledgment is made for permission to use the following previously published material. Unless otherwise noted, copyright is held by the individual writer or artist.

Marcy Alancraig, "Song at Sand Hill Bluff," in *Porter Gulch Review*, Spring 2002. "Last Moments," under a different title, in *Porter Gulch Review*, Spring 2005.

Ruth Barrett, "Kadistu," from the CD *Parthogenesis*, Ladyslipper Records, Tidal Time, BMI, copyright ©1990. "Laughing Maiden," from the CD *The Year is a Dancing Woman-Vol I*, Dancing Tree Music, Tidal Time, BMI, copyright ©2003.

Durga Bernhard, "Jazz Spirit," "Black Madonna," and "Village Mother," copyright ©Durga Bernhard, durgabernhard.com.

June BlueSpruce, "Heart Wood," in the chapbook *I Am Ready to Speak*, Garlic Gulch Poets, Seattle WA, 2000.

Maria Fama, "Canyon de Chelly," in *Liberty Hill Poetry Review*, Issue 3, Fall/Winter 1995. "The Roses" in *Philadelphia Poets*, Vol. 9, No. 2, October 2003.

Ferron, "Testimony," from the album *Testimony*, Lucy Records, Nemesis Publishing, copyright ©1980. "Light of My Light," from the album *Not a Still Life*, Nemesis Publishing, copyright ©1978.

Marigold Fine, "Prayer of Thanksgiving," in *Celebrating Women's Spirituality Calendar*, Crossing Press, 1994.

Bayla Greenspoon, "Somehow or Other," from the tape *Diversity*, Bashaert Productions, copyright ©1994.

Nora Jamieson, "Holy Longing," under the title "Drifting" in *Women's Story Circle Journal*, Vol. 4 No. 4, November 2000.

Lori Levy, "The Blue Embrace," in *Voices Israel*, Vol. 25, 1997-98.

Joanna Macy, "Prayer to the Future," in *Prayers for 1000 Years*, edited by Elizabeth Roberts and Elias Amidon, Harpercollins, 1999.

Christine McQuiston, "Cosmosis," in *3-Fold Monthly*, Vol.III, No. 20, Three Spirals Productions, 1998.

Carmen Rita Menendez, "Beets of Life," in *Yoga Vidya Journal*, Spring 2006.

Deena Metzger, "Oh Great Spirit," in *Animals as Teachers and Healers*, by Susan Chernak McElroy, originally from New Sage Press, 1995, reprinted Ballantine, 1997. "Walking the Creek," in *From Grief Into Vision: A Council*, by Deena Metzger, Hand to Hand Press, 2006.

Peggy Tabor Millin, "Sliding Down the Great Mother's Breast," in *WNC Woman*, July 2003.

Ann Mize, "Arctic Wolf" and "Sunrise at Dark Canyon," in *Scent of Cedars: Promising Writers of the Northwest*, edited by Anne Schroeder, Russell Dean & Company, 2002.

Marcia Moonstar, "Earthia," in the poetry collection *Dancing the Dance of Self*, 2001, and from the CD *Moon Magic*, Virago Records, copyright ©2001.

Kate Munger, "Earth is Woven Through My Body" and "Guide Me," from the CD *Listening at the Threshold*, copyright ©2004.

Becky Reardon, "The Turtle Remembers," from the CD *Listening at the Threshold*, copyright ©2004.

Coleen Rhalena Renee, "Spirit Love," in *Fire Dance*, Songbook of Sacred Fire Choir, 2006.

Rhiannon, "The Arms of the Mother," from the CD *Out of the Blue*, RhiannonMusic, copyright ©2003. "Somos Tejedoras," from the CD *Coming Into Our Voice* by MUSE Cincinnati's Women's Choir, copyright ©1992.

Kim Rosen, "In Impossible Darkness," from the CD *Naked Waters*, by Kim Rosen and Cathie Malach, Earthsea Records, copyright ©1998.

Jami Sieber, "The Arms of the Mother," from the CD *Hidden Sky*, Out Front Music, copyright ©2004.

Sharon Rodgers Simone, "My Own Strange Song," under the title "A Penetrating Light" in *Psychological Perspectives: A Semiannual Journal of Jungian Thought*, Issue 46, Autumn 2003.

Marcia Singer, "Lillian," in *Whole Life Times*, August 2005.

Marie Summerwood, "She Walks with Snakes," "The Beauty of the Woman," and "Let It In, Let It Go," from the CD *She Walks with Snakes: Women's Sacred Chants*, copyright ©1998.

Alysia Tromblay, "Mother Mercy," from the CD *As It Rains*, Dreamtime 9 BMI, copyright ©2003.

Contributor Index

About Wild Girl Publishing

Wild Girl Publishing offers literary and artistic works of beauty and spirit that speak to the soul and help bring forth a new way of living on behalf of the earth and all beings.

We are a small independent press formed by a group of writers in Santa Cruz, California. We have particular interest in publishing the work of new voices and of women writers.

The name of our publishing house emerged during a writing retreat in the redwood forest of the Ben Lomond mountains. In that beautiful place, Jane Nyberg, founder of the press, reconnected to the wild girl within herself—the one who used to run free, chasing the wind, climbing into treetops, making trails through empty lots, the one who boldly spoke her mind and knew she belonged on the earth. That wild girl was jubilantly happy to be recognized once again. From this joy was born the intention to publish books to encourage each of us to know our own wild souls

Wild Girl Publishing
PO Box 1301
Santa Cruz, California 95061
www.wildgirlpublishing.com

About the Editor

Carolyn Brigit Flynn is a writer dedicated to language as a pathway to soul and spirit. As an artist, writer and educator, she infuses her work with the intention to serve the spirits of healing for humanity and for the earth. As a teacher, she provides a powerful container for writers to generate new work from the depth of their souls.

Her poems and essays have appeared in literary journals and anthologies nationwide, including *Calyx, A Journal of Art and Literature by Women, The Pedestal Magazine, Porter Gulch Review, Black Buzzard Review, Intimate Kisses: The Poetry of Sexual Pleasure, Inside Grief: Death, Loss and Bereavement* and *New to North America.* She is the editor of *The New Story: Creation Myths for Our Times,* an anthology of prose and poetry.

Karen Koshgarian

Carolyn lives near the ocean in California with her spouse, three cats, redwood trees, spirits and ancestors. She teaches writing groups and facilitates writing retreats in the Santa Cruz Mountains and in Ireland. For more information see www.carolynbrigitflynn.com.